SOCIAL ISSUES IN CC
NATIVE AMERICA

MW00782427

Social Issues in Contemporary Native America

Reflections from Turtle Island

Edited by

HILARY N. WEAVER
University at Buffalo, SUNY, USA

ASHGATE

Published by
Ashgate Publishing Limited
Wey Court East
Union Road
Farnham
Surrey, GU9 7PT
England

Ashgate Publishing Company
110 Cherry Street
Suite 3-1
Burlington, VT 05401-3818
USA

www.ashgate.com

British Library Cataloguing in Publication Data
A catalogue record for this book is available from the British Library

The Library of Congress has cataloged the printed edition as follows:
Weaver, Hilary N.
  Social issues in contemporary native America : reflections from Turtle Island / by Hilary N. Weaver.
    pages cm
  Includes bibliographical references and index.
  ISBN 978-1-4094-5206-5 (hardback) -- ISBN 978-1-4094-5207-2 (pbk.) -- ISBN 978-1-4094-5208-9 (ebook) -- ISBN 978-1-4724-0678-1 (epub) 1. Indians of North America--Services for. 2. Indians of North America--Social conditions. 3. Social work with Indians--North America. I. Title.
  E98.S46W43 2013
  970.004'97--dc23
                                                                        2013026754

ISBN 9781409452065 (hbk)
ISBN 9781409452072 (pbk)
ISBN 9781409452089 (ebk – PDF)
ISBN 9781472406781 (ebk – ePUB)

MIX
Paper from
responsible sources
FSC
www.fsc.org   FSC® C013985

Printed in the United Kingdom by Henry Ling Limited, at the Dorset Press, Dorchester, DT1 1HD

Contents

List of Figures

Notes on Contributors

Jessica Black is Gwich'in Athabascan from the village of Fort Yukon, Alaska. She is currently a doctoral candidate at Washington University in St Louis and also works as a consultant for the Council of Athabascan Tribal Governments in Fort Yukon, Alaska. Jessica's dissertation focuses on the intersection between tribal members' participation in governance and its relationship to well-being, both at the individual and community level.

Cindy Blackstock, PhD, is a member of the Gitksan First Nation. She serves as the Executive Director of the First Nations Child and Family Caring Society of Canada and as an Associate Professor for the University of Alberta. She has worked in the field of child and family services as a front-line child protection worker, instructor, researcher, and policy maker for over 25 years. As author of over 50 publications, her key interests include exploring and addressing the causes of disadvantage for Aboriginal children and families through public education and engagement promoting equitable, culturally based interventions. Current professional interests include holding fellowships with the Ashoka Foundation and the J.W. McConnell Family Foundation, and being a mentor for the Trudeau Foundation.

Roe Bubar, JD, is a Native Studies Scholar and Associate Professor jointly appointed in the Department of Ethnic Studies and School of Social Work. Roe also serves as Affiliate Faculty in Women's Studies at Colorado State University. She teaches Indigenous courses. Her current research agenda considers intersectionality and sexual violence, health disparities, child maltreatment in tribal communities, and Native youth and STD/STI messaging. Roe has over 20 years of experience in the field and continues to work with tribes, states, federal agencies, and NGOs in tribal communities on a variety of research issues, including child sexual abuse and related projects.

Marian Bussey is an Associate Professor at the University of Denver's Graduate School of Social Work, with experience teaching in the areas of mental health, trauma, research, and social work history. Her practice background in working within community mental health and drug treatment centers led to an exploration of the role of trauma in clients' lives, and the social work approaches, both social justice and clinical, that can help clients transform the trauma. Her academic work as a program evaluator introduced her to a decade-long partnership with the Denver Indian Family Resource Center, and her co-author, Dr Lucero.

Priscilla A. Day, MSW, EdD, is Department Head and a tenured full professor at the Department of Social Work at the University of Minnesota Duluth. She is also the Director for the Center for Regional and Tribal Child Welfare Studies. Dr Day's areas of research are American Indian families. She is the author of many published scholarly articles and book chapters. Dr Day is an Anishinaabe and an enrolled tribal member of the Leech Lake Reservation. She is a pipe carrier and Ogichidaakwe on a traditional Big Drum for her tribal community. She is the mother of three wonderful adults and grandmother to four beautiful children.

Thalia González is an Assistant Professor at Occidental College. In her teaching and scholarship she has developed an interdisciplinary, multicultural, and community-focused approach to understanding increasingly complex and interdependent relationships between law, race, and society. She has authored articles on juvenile justice, collaborative models of community problem-solving, racial inequity in education, environmental justice, and economic development. She maintains a deep commitment to activism and works closely with community organizations in Los Angeles to advance social and political justice.

Edwin González-Santin, MSW, is the Director of the Office of American Indian Projects, Senior Academic Professional at Arizona State University, and School of Social Work since 1984. He serves on Inter Tribal Council of Arizona Inc., Social Services Working Group; provides ICWA training to tribal and state child welfare workers; and is a trainer for ITCA's Child Protection Academy. He is a member of the Board of Directors for Native Connection; the Arizona Courts Improvements Project Indian Child Welfare Liaison Committee; National Child Welfare Workforce Institute; Tribal VisTA tribal technical center. He is a recipient of the Points of Light Foundation Presidential Lifetime Of Service Award: Kent C. Ware Lifetime Achievement Award for Service to the Phoenix-Metro Native Community, as well as other Community and University awards.

Michael Anthony Hart is a citizen of the Fisher River Cree Nation residing in Winnipeg, Manitoba, Canada. He is currently the Canada Research Chair in Indigenous Knowledges and Social Work and Associate Professor at the University of Manitoba. His current work is focused on how different Indigenous nations' helping practices can inform social work, cultural continuity, and the social concerns of older Indigenous people.

Amy Locklear Hertel is Director of the American Indian Center at the University of North Carolina at Chapel Hill. She is an enrolled member of the Lumbee Tribe of North Carolina and a descendant of the Coharie Indian Tribe. She earned a BA in Communications from UNC Chapel Hill (1997) and an MSW and JD from Washington University in St Louis, where she is presently a doctoral candidate. Amy has experience around asset building, community development, and grassroots giving as means toward tribal self-determination. She lives in Chapel Hill with her husband, Johann, and their daughter, Ava, and son, Ahren.

Nancy M. Lucero (Mississippi Choctaw) is an Assistant Professor of Social Work at Colorado State University–Pueblo where she enjoys teaching research, social policy, and courses in American Indian history, policy, and practice. Nancy is passionate about giving voice to the urban Native experience, and she focuses especially on understanding the ways in which urban Natives maintain their cultural identities and connectedness while fully participating in contemporary urban life. Nancy has served the Denver Indian Family Resource Center in various capacities since 1998, and recently assisted the agency to formalize its specialized practice model for urban Indian child welfare.

Diane McEachern, PhD, LCSW, is of Scotch-Irish ancestry and an Assistant Professor of Rural Human Services at the University of Alaska, Kuskokwim campus in Bethel, Alaska. She has lived and worked in the Yup'ik/Cup'ik region of Alaska for over 15 years, first as an itinerant social worker and currently with the University. Her research interests include the intersection of adult learning, Indigenous populations, and social work education. Ongoing personal and social reflection/action on issues of racism, social justice, and cross-cultural communication inform her work and scholarship.

Barbara Mainguy, MA, MFA, is a creative arts psychotherapist and is the Education Director for the Coyote Institute. She began her career as an artist, and through becoming an artist in residence in the mental health system in Toronto became aware both of Indigenous culture and of alternatives to conventional psychiatry. She has studied ways to quantify spiritual transformation using mixed methods approaches and has published a paper on how the level of spiritual transformation relates to medical outcome among people diagnosed with illness who work with traditional Indigenous healers. She practices at Otter Creek Associates in Brattleboro, Vermont, where her special interests are psychosis and chronic pain.

Dr **Lewis Mehl-Madrona** (Cherokee on mother's side, Lakota on father's side) has, since 2008, been developing a Center for Narrative and Indigenous Studies affiliated with the Coyote Institute for the Study of Change and Transformation in Vermont. He is a graduate of Stanford University School of Medicine and is certified in family medicine, geriatrics, and psychiatry. He also holds a PhD in clinical psychology. His research involves elaborating the way traditional healers and elders view themselves and their work, and investigating outcomes of client interaction with healers. He is also involved in looking at the ways in which traditional culture and healers interact with mental illness, presented in papers and in his most recent book, *Healing the Mind through the Power of Story* (Bear and Company, Rochester, VT).

Bob Prue is an Assistant Professor in the School of Social Work at the University of Missouri–Kansas City. Bob has a professional social work background in mental health, substance abuse, domestic violence, and community organizing in American Indian communities. His research interest is on the interface of traditional Native American and Western systems of mental health and substance abuse treatment and prevention, with an emphasis on the role of the Native American Church as a protective factor against substance abuse. Bob is a member of the Sičháŋǧu Lakȟóta Oyáte.

Gladys Rowe is a member of Fox Lake Cree Nation in Northern Manitoba and a graduate student in the Faculty of Social Work at the University of Manitoba. Her current research focus is in the area of Cree identity development, Indigenous research methodologies and personal and ancestral stories towards healing.

Andrea Tamburro, EdD, MSW is a member of the Shawnee Tribe. She is also the Bachelor of Social Work Program Director at Indiana University on the Northwest campus. She earned her Education Doctorate from Simon Fraser University in British Columbia, Canada. The Master of Social Work degree was earned through the University of Iowa. Her main research area is Indigenous social work curriculum, publishing in the area of decolonization of social work education and practice. Practice areas include Indigenous social services, child welfare, mental health, domestic violence, and criminal justice. She teaches policy, research, and practice.

Paul-René Tamburro "Môjassadop Spiwi Pakholigan" ("Began with a Drum" in Abenaki) is enrolled with the Nulhegan Abenaki (Vermont). He has been a social work educator in both Canada and the USA, including Heritage University and the Reservation-Based Program at TESC, both in Washington, IUPUI and Indiana State University in Indiana, and Thompson Rivers University in BC. His MSW focused on Aboriginal child welfare and his PhD focused on Indigenous cultural revival. He is currently in private practice as a consultant on Indigenous healing and is a Licenced Clinical Social Worker.

Kristen Wagner is Assistant Professor of Social Work at the University of Missouri–St Louis. She holds a PhD from Washington University–St Louis (2011), an MSW from Washington University–St Louis (2005), and a BA in Psychology from the University of North Dakota (1997). Her research and teaching interests center on social inclusion as part of program and policy interventions in both domestic and international contexts around three key areas: asset development interventions, culturally relevant community development strategies, and community-based participatory research methods. Kristen lives in St Louis with her husband, Jason, her son, Andrew, and her twin daughters, Amanda and Jadee.

Hilary N. Weaver (Lakota) currently serves as Associate Dean for Academic Affairs in the School of Social Work, University at Buffalo, State University of New York. She has published extensively on Indigenous populations and cultural issues in the helping process. She serves as President of the American Indian Alaska Native Social Work Educators' Association and regularly presents her work nationally and internationally, including at the United Nations Permanent Forum for Indigenous Peoples. Her most important role is raising two strong, culturally grounded, Indigenous youth, Iris and Wanblee.

Introduction

Haudenosaunee teachings tell us that as Sky Woman fell through a hole in the sky she was caught on the wings of geese and prevented from falling into the endless water below. Small animals repeatedly dove under the water until one successfully came back with mud. This mud was then placed on the back of a turtle to provide firm earth on which Sky Woman could survive. This is the origin of Turtle Island (aka North America), home to Indigenous Peoples, the descendants of Sky Woman, since time immemorial.

Indigenous Peoples persist within settler societies, often invisible, depicted in stereotypical ways when noticed at all, and typically marginal in terms of social, health, and economic indicators of well-being. There is, however, interest in developing a better understanding of these populations. Recent reports by National Public Radio on the significant numbers of Native American children removed from their families and placed in non-Native foster homes and by Amnesty International on violence against Native American women have garnered public interest. In addition to a variety of social problems, Indigenous Peoples also display considerable strengths and resilience. This, too, is part of the complex portrait of contemporary Native America. This book gives readers a glimpse into some facets of contemporary Native American life.

Indigenous Peoples are people of the land whose cultures, societies, and livelihoods have traditionally been intimately intertwined with their surroundings. Far from being generic, being Indigenous is linked to a particular place. As time moves forward, many Indigenous people find themselves separated from the territories traditionally occupied by their ancestors and living in multicultural settings, thus bringing new ingredients to a contemporary Indigenous identity.

Being Native American has political as well as ethnic and cultural elements. Native Americans are citizens of their own nations that preceded the existence of the United States and Canada. Records of tribal membership are kept on tribal rolls, with descendants of members typically also being eligible to have their names placed on the rolls (enrollment). In contemporary times, however, there are some tribes who only enroll based on matrilineal descent; others only enroll based on patrilineal descent. Many also require documentation of a particular amount of biological heritage or blood quantum (e.g., one-quarter, one-eighth). Some tribes have had their rolls closed for decades, making it impossible to list descendants as tribal members. Such issues around enrollment complicate clear definitions of who is and is not Native American. Indigenous identity is a multifaceted, complex, and sometimes controversial issue.

Terminology can also be a contentious issue as no clear consensus, but many strong preferences and regional differences, exist on the labels used for and by Indigenous Peoples. Native American and American Indian are the terms most commonly used in the United States, although some Indigenous people resist any label that includes the term "American," associating this term with colonization. Aboriginal and First Nations are terms commonly used in Canada. Indigenous is a term used around the world to recognize the first inhabitants of a land. The power to self-identify and have the name that you use for yourself recognized is something that has often fallen victim to the powerful forces of colonization; thus Haudenosaunee, Lakota, Cree, and Niimipu all found themselves lumped under the label "Indian." The authors in this volume use labels that are considered the most acceptable and respectful in their particular settings.

According to the US Census, there are 5.2 million Native Americans in the United States, or 1.7 percent of the population. This represents a 39 percent increase over the 2000 census (Norris et al. 2012). "According to OMB [the US Office of Management and Budget], 'American Indian or Alaska Native' refers to a person having origins in any of the original peoples of North and South America (including Central America) and who maintains tribal affiliation or community attachment" (Norris et al. 2012, 2).

The 2006 Canadian Census identified 1,172,790 Indigenous Peoples consisting of 50,485 Inuit, 389,785 Métis, and 698,025 First Nations people, or 3.8 percent of the Canadian population. This represents a 45 percent increase over 1996 data (Statistics Canada 2012). Both the United States and Canada have more than half of their Indigenous populations living in urban areas rather than on land still under tribal control.

As Indigenous Peoples, Native Americans retain some rights of self-governance and some control over land, known as reservations in the United States and reserves in Canada. Treaties, or legal agreements made between Indigenous and European nations (and subsequently the US and Canada), serve as the basis for many contemporary reservations as well as social and health programs. The legal status of Indigenous Peoples, treaties, and sovereignty are discussed in the first part of this book, thus providing a foundation for understanding other issues.

The Indigenous population in the United States is growing, comparatively young, and disproportionately affected by social, health, and economic problems (Indian Health Service 2011, Ogunwole 2006). Both historically and in contemporary times, social workers have been concerned with many of the issues facing Indigenous Peoples. At times, social workers have approached their work with Indigenous Peoples in paternalistic ways that reflected the values of the larger colonial society. At other times social workers have been at the forefront of advocating for social change on behalf of Indigenous Peoples. The second part of this book examines how social work and social work education have (or have not) been responsive and respectful in their interactions with Indigenous Peoples.

The next part of the book examines Indigenous Peoples across the life cycle, including an exploration of issues pertinent to youth, families, and elders. This section also reflects on family disruption and efforts to keep Native youth within an Indigenous context, thus promoting cultural continuity. Social issues, health, and overall wellness of Native Peoples and communities are discussed in the final part.

The authors of these chapters provide thoughtful examinations of many of the key aspects of contemporary Native American lives. The beginning of this book gives a brief description of the authors' backgrounds. In keeping with Indigenous traditions, introducing the authors helps to provide a context for understanding the chapter content. While it is not possible to cover all topics related to social issues and Native Americans, this volume seeks to provide a broad spectrum of information so as to give the reader a representative picture of contemporary issues. All contributors to this volume stand on the shoulders of those who came before us. Indigenous scholars, activists, healers, and community members, as well as their non-Indigenous allies, have fought for the well-being of Indigenous Peoples from the beginning.

As many Indigenous traditions tell us, we exist within the context of Seven Generations. The resources, cultures, languages, and ways of helping that persist, do so because generations ago our ancestors planned for the well-being of the current generation. Likewise, we have a responsibility to the generations that follow. The authors of this volume have come together with a good mind to share our knowledge of social issues and contemporary Native people and to pass this along to both our contemporaries and those who follow. These efforts reflect current thinking and actions that strive for a better future. We offer these words to all who will listen. *Mitakuye Oyasin*. All my relations.

References

Indian Health Service 2001. IHS Fact Sheets: Indian Health Disparities. http://www.ihs.gov/newsroom/factsheets/disparities/. Accessed September 11, 2013.

Norris, T. Vines, P.L., and Hoeffel, E.M. 2012. *The American Indian and Alaska Native Population: 2010*. United States Census Bureau.

Ogunwole, S. 2006. We the People: American Indians and Alaska Natives in the United States. *Census 2000 Special Reports*. US Census Bureau.

Statistics Canada 2012. 2006 Census: Aboriginal Peoples. http://www12.statcan.ca/census-recensement/2006/rt-td/ap-pa-eng.cfm. Accessed September 11, 2013.

PART I
Policy Foundations

Social policies both reflect and serve as the foundation for how Indigenous and non-Indigenous Peoples relate to each other. A firm understanding of the social, economic, and political status of contemporary Native Americans requires an examination of the evolution of social policies from historic times through the present. Policies undergird services, as well as the whole relationship between Indigenous Peoples and settler societies.

Indigenous Peoples are legally distinct from other ethnic groups that make up settler societies. This has led to the development of separate and unique policies. While both the US and Canada are settler societies of British origin, their social policies have evolved independently. The chapters by Weaver and Hart and Rowe provide readers with overviews of social policies in the US and Canada, respectively. In particular, Hart and Rowe's chapter firmly grounds our understanding of social policies within the context of colonization. These chapters provide a foundation for understanding subsequent content on social, health, and economic issues.

Chapter 1

Sovereignty, Dependency, and the Spaces in Between: An Examination of United States Social Policy and Native Americans

Hilary N. Weaver

Social policies both reflect and set the stage for understanding the realities of Indigenous Peoples in the United States. Policies mirror the values, norms, and beliefs of the eras in which they were developed, as well as the priorities of the policy makers. "US Indian policy has followed a schizophrenic pattern with policies that are contradictory and mystify the relationship among the tribes, the US government, and the individual states of the union" (Wall 2010, 5).

Policies have shifted considerably over time, and continue to shift to reflect the values and priorities of those in power in the United States. Over time, it is possible to see dramatic policy changes as similar to pendulum swings, rather than a steady progression in a consistent direction. While initially it may be difficult to see the logic behind changes in policies, on closer inspection it is possible to understand shifts as a reflection of long-standing tension between federalism and states' rights (Wall 2010). Additionally, with the benefit of hindsight, it is apparent that federal policy shifts often occur in response to an economic crisis and the need to stimulate the national economy using Native American capital (Wall 2010).

Ongoing themes emerge throughout the examination of social polices related to Native Americans, with the overarching theme being contrasting opinions about the amount of sovereignty retained by Native people. Additional sub-themes emerge, such as the tension between federal paternalism and Indigenous self-determination and the interplay between assimilation and maintenance of distinctiveness.

This chapter begins with a discussion of sovereignty as the foundation for relations between the United States and Native Americans. Value stances that guide policy makers such as assimilation, paternalism, and self-determination are also examined within this platform. Major policy shifts are reviewed according to the era in which they occurred. Variations in policies across regions are briefly described followed by concluding remarks about the trajectory of social policies in the US.

The subject of US social policies and Native Americans is an expansive one. This topic has been addressed in multi-volume books and even this requires only briefly addressing significant issues. The goal of this chapter is to set the stage; to provide readers with a basic understanding that will enable them to thoughtfully process the content of subsequent chapters. In no way does this chapter presume to cover policy issues in depth, but rather to introduce ideas.

Understanding Sovereignty, its Erosion, and Federal Paternalism

The United States Constitution recognizes Native American tribes as sovereign nations. Article 1 gives Congress the power to regulate commerce with Indian tribes, as they do with other foreign nations. This understanding of sovereignty was affirmed by the US Supreme Court in 1832 *Worcester v. Georgia*, which held that states are excluded from regulating or taxing Indian country as this is an infringement on Indigenous sovereignty (Ford 2010). In other words, at that time, states had no authority over tribes.

While recognition of sovereignty has been articulated in the Constitution and by the Supreme Court, viewpoints that contradict this stance have always existed. For example, at the time of Columbus's voyage, the Vatican pronounced that a Christian prince has the right to invade land occupied by infidels (Bragaw 2006, Ford 2010). This position suggests that Indigenous Peoples had few if any rights, and certainly the Vatican did not recognize Native Americans as sovereign nations.

Within a generation of the Vatican proclamation, however, contrasting voices were raised by Christian leaders. In 1532, Dominican theologian Francisco de Vittoria stated that "Natives of the Americas possessed natural legal rights as both sovereign nations and children of God and must be treated accordingly" (Bragaw 2006, 161). These divergent viewpoints articulated almost 500 years ago still echo today and undergird inconsistencies in social policies.

Even when Indigenous sovereignty was acknowledged, this did not mean that Europeans considered Indigenous Peoples to be their equals. While Native American tribes might be recognized as self-governing nations, they were typically viewed as inferior (Ford 2010). Originally the popes, then the presidents beginning with Washington, used the term "Great Father" to describe their relationships with the tribes (Bragaw 2006), thus suggesting a paternalistic rather than an equal relationship from early on.

President Jefferson provides a good illustration of the complex and mixed perspectives held on Indigenous sovereignty by early Americans. While espousing ideas of progress, civilization, and ultimately assimilation as a goal for Native Americans, he was also a strong advocate of sovereignty and treaty rights (Bragaw 2006). Rather than using military might to promote American policies, he preferred to encourage compliance (i.e., voluntary removal with federal support rather than forced removal; Bragaw 2006).

Policies adopted during Jefferson's presidency created the political and legal environment for the Indian Removal Act of 1830.

Jefferson's administration undertook what would become an irreversible shift in the federal government's Indian policy. The administration moved away from the policies pursued by the British Empire, the Confederation, and the federalist administrations, which had sought to limit frontier conflict by controlling the pace and direction of frontier settlement and closely regulating trade. It moved to a policy that aggressively used land acquisition, settlement, and trade as tools to force assimilation or removal across the Mississippi. Jefferson's administration negotiated and assumed an obligation on the part of the federal government to Georgia to extinguish the sovereignty of the Cherokee and Creek nations, an obligation that was irreconcilable with federal treaties pledging federal respect and protection for those nations' sovereignty. (Bragaw 2006, 160)

Other presidents would not even give the pretense of recognizing Indigenous sovereignty. Andrew Jackson saw treaties as absurd and blatantly denied sovereignty, claiming Native Americans were subjects of the United States (Bragaw 2006).

The federal government has regularly infringed upon Indigenous sovereignty and prohibited Native people from enacting and enforcing certain laws. For example, with the passage of the Major Crimes Act, tribes no longer had the authority to prosecute offenders of major crimes on Native American land. Forced land successions and removal also indicate limits on sovereignty (Ford 2010). Rather than wholly sovereign entities, Native American tribes were treated as domestic dependent nations, making true sovereignty an illusion (Boxer 2009).

In spite of significant infringements on sovereignty, in some respects Native American tribes continue to carry out functions of independent nations. For example, the Haudenosaunee, Lakota, and Ojibwe separately declared war on Germany in 1941 rather than being bound under the United States declaration (*The Economist* 2012). One particularly notable example of continuing sovereignty is that many tribes run gaming operations on tribal land, even when states prohibit gambling. In another example, continued control of tribal membership decisions is a central tenet of sovereignty and self-determination. In 1978, the US Supreme Court affirmed tribes have exclusive purview in making membership decisions as a central part of tribal self-governance (Riley 2007). Additionally, tribes can issue their own passports, as the Haudenosaunee continue to do. Sovereignty, however, must be recognized by others to have practical application. In an infamous incident in 2010, British authorities refused to recognize the Haudenosaunee passports of a lacrosse team, denying their ability to travel and forcing them to forfeit an international tournament they were favored to win (*The Economist* 2012).

In the 1831 US Supreme Court case *Cherokee Nation v. Georgia*, Chief Justice Marshall wrote for the majority:

Indian tribes were merely 'domestic dependent nations' existing 'in a state of pupilage.' He said that their relation to the United States 'resembles that of a ward to his guardian.' Justice Marshall's characterization of the tribes as 'dependent nations' evolved into the trust doctrine and basically says that the relationship between the United States and the native peoples is that the United States is their caretaker. (Ford 2010, 407)

This 1831 decision sets the model of guardianship. Typically, guardianship is a temporary relationship in which a guardian prepares a ward for independence. This implies that US policy should temporarily take a protective and guiding stance toward Native Americans while ultimately preparing them for integration into mainstream US culture. As a result of these divergent goals of protection and integration, federal policy "has lurched back and forth, sometimes aiming for assimilation and at other times, recognizing its responsibility for assisting Indian development" (Boxer 2009, 8). Once established, only Congress can determine when the guardianship role will end (Ford 2010).

The Pendulum Swings: Assimilation versus Distinctiveness; Paternalism versus Self-determination

As noted above, Indigenous sovereignty has eroded, but vestiges remain. The question is how much sovereignty has been retained and how this is expressed. The 1800s through 1934 was a time when Native people lost significant amounts of land, and assimilation threatened the continued existence of Indigenous Peoples as distinct entities. Subsequently, the Indian Reorganization Act of 1934 provided a direct reversal of previous policies and promoted the retention of land and cultural distinctiveness. By the 1950s, policies shifted again and relocation and termination sought to put an end to Native Americans and tribes as distinct within the fabric of American society. Recognition of the severe, unintended negative consequences of these policies shifted the tide once again as activism in the 1960s and 1970s saw the advent of policies promoting self-determination in a variety of venues such as health, child welfare, and self-governance.

1800s–1933: The Erosion of Sovereignty

After the establishment of the United States, the young nation's growing population sought to expand its hold over land and other resources. These resources seemed within easy reach as Native Americans decreased in military might and population. This era saw a decreasing recognition of Indigenous sovereignty. Native people were removed from traditional territories to Indian Country beyond US boundaries, and to reservations within the US. Efforts at assimilation sought to eliminate Native Americans and their tribes as distinct entities, thus integrating them into US society and freeing up their land and other resources for American use. Significant policies of this era included removal, placement on reservations, boarding schools, restrictions on religious freedom, allotment, and the bestowal of US citizenship.

In 1786, the United States established the first reservation for Native Americans. This was initially done under the precept that separation preserved sovereignty. In creating this reservation the United States

claimed that its intent and future approach was to treat each tribe as an independent nation. In theory, while the notion of tribal sovereignty sounded like a move in the right direction, especially considering the fact that Europeans had disenfranchised countless Native American tribes, the tribes were already sovereign and what the United States was really trying to do was to obtain more land. For instance, in a letter from President Jefferson to William Henry Harrison, in 1803, Jefferson expressed his goal of 'draw[ing] [Native Americans] to agriculture [because it would] cause them to [withdraw themselves to the culture of a small piece of land.' He also stated his desire to 'see the good and influential individuals among them in debt [because it would make them] willing to lop [off the debt] by a cessation of lands.' (Ford 2010, 401).

Once the United States became militarily strong enough, removal became official policy (Wall 2010). By moving the Eastern tribes to land west of the Mississippi river, their lands could be opened for American settlement. Small pockets of Indigenous Peoples remained in their territories, thus illustrating the incompleteness of the removal policy, but overall removal was generally seen as successful by the United States as vast tracts of lands were now devoid of Indigenous Peoples.

After the Civil War, rather than large-scale removal, tribes were confined to reservations, generally on small portions of their traditional territories. It was more cost effective and politically expedient to keep them in remnants of their territory than forcefully remove them to Indian Territory (Wall 2010).

During the nineteenth century, the US government officially embraced policies aimed at forced assimilation and the break-up of Native families (Graham 2008). In 1867, the Commissioner for Indian Affairs advocated for the forced removal of Native children as the only solution to the Indian problem, beginning 100 years of US policies of separating Native children from their families and nations (Graham 2008).

The residential schools were a primary example of a policy promoting assimilation. Pratt, the first director of Carlisle Indian School, is often credited with the slogan "Kill the Indian: Save the Man," which reflected the change in strategy from physical genocide to cultural genocide. Thousands of Native youth were taken, often forcibly, to boarding schools far from their families and communities. At these schools they were educated in Christian virtues and vocational trades so they could subsequently find their place in American society and no longer exist as culturally, linguistically, or religiously distinct. Indeed, Native languages and religious expression were forbidden and harshly punished at the boarding schools. From the opening of Carlisle in 1879 until the mid 1960s, thousands of Native children were removed from their families and educated in the boarding schools, thus setting in motion generations of Native children raised in institutions with limited knowledge of what it means to be a family member, community member, or how to raise children traditionally.

The suppression of Indigenous spirituality received systematic codification in 1883 with passage of the Indian Religious Crimes Code which banned Indigenous spiritual practices such as the Sun Dance (Forbes-Boyte 1999, O'Brien 1991, Smith 2006, Venables 2004). Religious prohibitions were part and parcel of efforts at "civilizing savages" and assimilating Indigenous Peoples into the American mainstream. The ban on all Indigenous spirituality officially continued until the 1930s (O'Brien 1991), but in reality impediments still exist to free exercise of many traditional Indigenous spiritual practices (Weaver 2011).

Communal ownership of lands (i.e., reservations) was seen as a barrier to assimilating Native people into individualistic, mainstream American culture. If Native people could be reformed into nuclear families with individual land holdings, this would both facilitate cultural assimilation and free up coveted reservation lands for American settlement. Division of land (or allotment) became a primary tool of assimilation policy (Wall 2010). In 1887, Congress passed the Dawes Act. Under this policy, reservation land was divided and allocated in individual plots. Once land was divided and allotted, the remaining land was opened for sale to outsiders. Under this policy, land in Native American hands shrank from 134 million acres in 1887 to 48 million half a century later (Boxer 2009).

In the late 1800s and early 1900s, US social policy emphasized assimilation through various means such as removing children from their families and communities, education focused on Christianity and vocational skills, prohibition of Indigenous spirituality, and ending communal ownership of lands. In a logical culmination of these multipronged assimilationist strategies, in 1924, Congress passed legislation granting citizenship to Native people who had not already acquired it (Boxer 2009). This Congressional Act was done unilaterally without consultation with the tribes or consideration for the fact that many Native people still considered themselves citizens of their own nations.

1934: A Brief Respite and Re-affirmation of Distinctiveness

The 1930s saw a remarkable shift in federal policy toward Native Americans. While previous policies emphasized assimilation and undermined sovereignty, in 1934 the Indian Reorganization Act, nicknamed the Indian New Deal, had virtually diametrically opposed intentions.

The primary momentum behind this dramatic change was a former settlement house worker named John Collier, who became Commissioner of Indian Affairs in 1933. Collier had a life-changing experience when visiting the Pueblos of the Southwest. He believed in preserving Indigenous ways of life and respect for the environment as antidotes to American materialism (Boxer 2009).

Another catalyst for change was the 1928 Meriam Report, which documented great disparities in health, education, nutrition, and economic opportunities for Native Americans (Wall 2010). Between the Meriam Report and John Collier, the time was ripe for change. The Indian Reorganization Act put an immediate end to allotment (Boxer 2009). Collier set up commissions to visit reservations and assist tribes in writing their own constitutions and modifying their governance structures accordingly (Wall 2010).

During the 1930s the allotment policy ended, the right to sovereignty and self-governance was affirmed, and prohibitions of Indigenous spirituality were relaxed. In many ways this was a remarkable era in Native American policy. This era, however, had dark undercurrents as well. Many Native youth continued to be removed from their families and communities to be educated in residential schools. The push for reorganization of tribal governments was largely led by the frenetic energies of one driven man who had his own ideas about what tribal governments should look like, rather than a grassroots movement where Indigenous Peoples had a significant voice in tribal reform. Still, the remarkable shift from policies promoting assimilation to the end of allotment and a federal recognition that tribal self-governance has value is virtually unprecedented.

The 1950s and Early 1960s: Relocation and Termination

The 1950s saw a return to values promoting the assimilation of Native people into the American mainstream. In particular, two policy efforts embodied these intentions: relocation and termination. Both these policies were designed to end the relationship between the tribes and United States (Wall 2010).

Relocation was a federal program designed to move Native people from reservations to cities. This program was a means of taking them from reservation poverty and isolation and promoting assimilation (Boxer 2009). Relocation workers stationed on reservations were pressured to recruit as many Native people as possible for the program (Burt 1986). Through this federal initiative, the Bureau of Indian Affairs provided limited assistance finding housing and jobs. Because support was minimal, many Native Americans ended up in slum areas. Most had few skills and could only find low-wage, insecure jobs. Racism and cultural dislocation were major problems for newly relocated Native Americans (Burt 1986).

While relocation was ostensibly promoted as a way to reduce poverty for Native Americans, it was also a cost-saving measure for the federal government. Relocation involved a smaller federal role than other poverty reduction measures such as reservation-based economic development. After relocation, Native Americans were no longer eligible for federal services, thus further curtailing federal spending and responsibility (Burt 1986). In 1940, 8 percent of Native Americans lived in cities. By 1960 this had changed to 30 percent (Boxer 2009).

The relocation policy designed to move people off reservations went hand in hand with the termination policy designed to end the existence of reservations

(Wall 2010). Termination was the legal abolition of the tribes and their reservations. Under this policy, Native Americans would be legally, socially, and economically integrated into mainstream America. Individual Native people would receive monetary compensation for liquidation of tribal assets. Termination disbanded federally recognized tribes, removed their tax-exempt status, ended federal assistance, and ended hunting and fishing rights. Its proponents spoke euphemistically of termination as a mechanism to free Native Americans from federal supervision and paternalism, create equality, and facilitate self-reliance (Kelly 2010, Puisto 2009).

In 1953, Congress passed House Concurrent Resolution 108, the first of the termination bills (Boxer 2009). In addition to ending Native Americans' status as federal wards, this would open former reservation land for outsiders. The Menominee of Wisconsin and Klamath of Oregon were among the first tribes selected for termination. Both these tribes had large land holdings and timber resources (Boxer 2009). Three other large nations were also terminated in 1953: the Flathead, Pottawatomie, and Turtle Mountain Chippewa (Kelly 2010). Between 1953 and 1960, the federal government terminated sovereign recognition for 109 Native nations (Kelly 2010). The termination policy was abandoned in the 1960s when it became apparent that it led to dramatic increases in poverty.

The 1960s and Beyond: Indian Activism and the Era of Self-determination

The 1960s was a time of dramatic social changes in the United States. The nation-wide emphasis on civil rights translated into energized activism and a renewed push for self-determination for Native Peoples. In 1970, President Nixon returned land to Taos Pueblo and articulated a policy of self-determination for tribes that has been followed by subsequent administrations (Wall 2010). Promotion of self-determination policies can be seen as attempts to address past wrongdoings and erroneous policies (Graham 2008). As was evident with the termination policy, erosion of tribal authority hurts economic development. Conversely, support of self-determination has led to significant economic benefits (Keohane 2006).

International discourse has also emphasized self-determination for Indigenous Peoples. Self-determination is a principle enshrined in international law and emphasized in the United Nations charter (Graham 2008). International definitions of self-determination include ideas of cultural survival, non-discrimination, economic development, political freedom, and other basic human rights (Graham 2008).

In 1975, the Indian Self-determination and Education Assistance Act allowed tribes and tribal consortia to take over administration of federal programs (Keohane 2006). Under this act, tribes can assume management of health-care programs from the Indian Health Service (IHS). Currently, tribes manage more than half the IHS budget (Warne 2011). Likewise, the Tribal Self-governance Act of 1994 offers tribes the option of administering other federal programs.

In 1978 the American Indian Religious Freedom Act (AIRFA) was passed. This Act was originally comprehensive and acknowledged past federal government infringement on the religious freedom of Native Americans, but Forest Service lobbyists succeeded in undermining AIRFA's protection of sacred sites (Harjo 2003). Ultimately, AIRFA was an important statement of principles of religious freedom for Native people, but these principles were largely unenforceable (Weaver 2011). While AIRFA contained significant limitations, it did lay the groundwork for repatriation of human remains and sacred objects housed in federal museums. Ceremonial use of peyote was recognized in a 1993 amendment to AIRFA (Harjo 2003, Smith 2006).

During the current era, two social policies stand out as being enigmatic and divergent from general US social welfare policy: the Indian Child Welfare Act (ICWA) and the Indian Health Service (IHS). While at a casual glance it may seem that these policies and services contradict American principles of treating people equally without regard to race, in fact these Native-specific policies are grounded in the Indigenous status of Native people, treaty rights, and addressing historical injustices. The ICWA is a landmark affirmation that tribes have authority over matters that threaten to alienate their members from the group. IHS, on the other hand, emerges from federal responsibilities taken on through treaties and, while offering increasing opportunities for self-determination, is more grounded in federal paternalism.

The Indian Child Welfare Act
The ICWA was conceptualized as partial reparation for human rights violations committed against Native people (Graham 2008). Congress reviewed the massive displacement of Native children into non-Native adoptive homes, foster care, and educational institutions in the 1970s, and called for sweeping reform (Graham 2008). Congress worked directly with Native nations in developing the ICWA, resulting in the Act giving considerable jurisdiction and control to tribes (Waszak 2010). The intent of the policy is to promote stability and security of Native family life. ICWA shifts the balance of power away from states so tribal communities can regulate their own child welfare issues.

ICWA governs cases where Indian children face removal from their homes, such as the termination of parental rights, foster care, or adoption. An "Indian child" is defined as an unmarried minor who is either a tribal member or is eligible for membership and a biological child of a member (Basic 2007). Tribal courts have exclusive jurisdiction over children residing on reservations, and concurrent jurisdiction over those living elsewhere. When a state court does have jurisdiction and orders foster care or termination of parental rights, they must follow a set of placement preferences designed to preserve the child's cultural context.

The ICWA has met challenges to its constitutionality because it is not based on ethnicity but rather Indigenous status, the government-to-government relationship between the federal government and tribes, and the federal trust responsibility (Fort 2006). However, since 1982 the Indian Family Exception Doctrine has been circumventing the ICWA (Cross 2006). Courts render decisions on what constitutes an Indian family or Indian culture, and if those are not deemed to be present in a particular case, then the ICWA need not be followed. For example, a child whose Indian father was incarcerated could not invoke the ICWA as he was already away from the child and child welfare proceedings would not interfere with an existing Indian family. This nuclear model is inconsistent with tribal conceptualizations of family (Cross 2006).

The Indian Health Service
In 1955, the federal government transferred responsibility for Native American health from the Bureau of Indian Affairs to the US Public Health Service, thereby creating the IHS. The IHS now serves 1.5 million Native people in 35 states. The IHS mission is to provide services and improve the health of Native Americans (*The Nation's Health* 2005).

Multiple treaties promised physicians and medical supplies to tribes in exchange for land cessions. In other words, "American Indians and Alaska Natives purchased the first prepaid health plan in history" (Westmoreland and Watson 2006, 601). The federal trust responsibility for health care was affirmed and codified in the Snyder Act of 1921, as amended, and the Indian Health Care Improvement Act of 1976, as amended (Westmoreland and Watson 2006).

The legal and moral foundation of provision of health services to Native people is the federal trust responsibility, yet the reliance on discretionary funding to support health care for Native people compounds health disparities (Schneider 2005, Westmoreland and Watson 2006). The federal government spends half as much per IHS beneficiary than those receiving Medicaid or federal prisoners (Keohane 2006). Reforming financing by re-classifying spending on Native American health from voluntary to mandatory is a necessary but not sufficient condition of decreasing health disparities. Adequate federal funding for Native American health programs is both a moral obligation and a legal duty (Westmoreland and Watson 2006).

There are also significant questions about the quality of care provided by the IHS. Investigations in the 1970s revealed that IHS health-care service providers, as well as others under contract with the IHS, performed coerced abortions and sterilizations on as many as 25 to 50 percent of Native women between 1970 and 1976. These procedures are tantamount to eugenics policies and fall within the UN definitions of genocidal practices (Rutecki 2011).

Differential Application of Social Policies across Settings

While federal policies have generally been intended to apply to all Native Americans, many policies were implemented incrementally or by region and the policy was amended or abandoned before complete implementation. For example, allotment was implemented on some reservations, but the policy ended before being implemented on others, thus leaving some reservations with checkerboard patterns of alienated land where other reservations were left intact.

Likewise, the Indian Reorganization Act went from reservation to reservation promoting the adoption of tribal governments modeled on constitutions much like state governments, but IRA commissions reached some reservations and not others before this policy ended. Today, some tribes have "IRA governments" while others do not.

Termination, at one time intended as a federal goal for all tribes, required specific legislation naming each tribe to be terminated. This policy was implemented with some tribes, and, while others were slated for termination, the policy was discontinued before being fully implemented. Additionally, some tribes like the Menominee successfully petitioned Congress to have their termination overturned.

Another notable way in which policies have been differentially applied is discrepancies based on urban versus reservation residence. For example, while ICWA and IHS programs ostensibly serve the needs of Native people in general, funding streams often target reservation areas even though the majority of Native people no longer live on reservations.

While many different Indigenous groups exist within the boundaries of the United States, they are not all treated equally from a policy stance. Notably, Indigenous Peoples in Alaska and Hawaii are not covered by many of the same policies affecting other Native Americans.

The US has always treated Alaska Natives differently than other Indigenous Peoples within its boundaries. This disparate treatment is largely a result of Alaska's isolation and its late acquisition by the United States. Only with statehood in 1959 did serious questions arise about land rights. Major oil discoveries in the 1960s added urgency to settling land claims prior to the development of the significant infrastructure needed for profitable oil production. Congress stipulated that the matter must be resolved quickly, with Native input, without establishing a reservation system, and without creating a lengthy trusteeship. In other words, the principles are dramatically different from how Congress has treated Native Americans in the lower 48 states (Chaffee 2008).

In 1971, the Alaska Native Claims Settlement Act (ANSCA) was passed as a way to resolve land claims and clarify rights to land and natural resources within the state. In exchange for relinquishing claim to over 360 million acres of land, Native Alaskans received clear title to 45.5 million acres and payments totaling $962.5 million. At this time, all reservations except one were revoked and for-profit corporations with Native Alaskans as stockholders were developed to manage the money and the land (Chaffee 2008).

Native Hawaiians, also Indigenous Peoples within the boundaries of the US, are typically not covered by most social policies aimed at Native Americans. Hawaii existed as a monarchy before its government was overthrown, and it subsequently had its territory absorbed as a state. No treaties exist between the US government and Hawaiians. Likewise, Hawaiians are not considered a "tribe," or to have retained vestiges of self-governance. Hawaiians do not have reservations akin to those on the mainland US; however, the Hawaiian Homes Commission Act of 1920 established 62 Hawaiian homeland areas held in trust for Native Hawaiians by the state of Hawaii (Grieco 2002). Additionally, some specialized policies and programs have been developed to address the needs of Native Hawaiians, such as the Native Hawaiian Health Care System created by federal legislation in the 1980s (Braun and Browne 1998). By and large, however, far fewer social policies directly target Native Hawaiians than their Indigenous counterparts on the mainland.

Comparisons with International Indigenous Groups

There are many similarities between Native Americans and other Indigenous groups around the world. "Virtually all indigenous nations exist within the borders of larger nation-states who owe them duties. All too often, the relationship between indigenous groups and the nations in which they reside is marked by a denial or complete abrogation of the responsibilities owed to indigenous peoples" (Riley 2007, 963). In recent decades, Indigenous Peoples have started using international human rights instruments to assert their rights.

In the 1960s, a decolonization movement swept the world. In the US, legislation was developed that promoted self-determination and court decisions affirmed tribal autonomy. "Tribes had the opportunity to develop their resources and economies in a manner that created the illusion of tribal control, but within a set of limitations set by American business and industry" (Wall 2010, 13).

As part of the worldwide movement for decolonization and self-determination for Indigenous Peoples, the United Nations recently adopted the Declaration on the Rights of Indigenous Peoples, in spite of opposition from the US, Canada, and Australia (Graham 2008). As part of this manifesto there is recognition that Indigenous populations typically suffer from poverty, health problems, a lack of education, and a variety of social problems in disproportionate numbers. This international statement of principles gives various Indigenous populations support in their push for sustainability with their host governments.

Like the US, Canada and Australia are dealing with the legacies of their policies of forced removal of Indigenous children (Graham 2008). Residential schools were a primary tool of forced assimilation in all these countries, as were suppression of culture, alienation of lands, and bureaucratic control of Native governments.

As part of promoting socialization and assimilation into the dominant society, both Canada and the United States had "gendered" aspects to their policies. Indigenous populations across North America often espoused egalitarian gender roles, and some Native societies were matrilineal. In order to undermine the status of women in Native American societies, most treaty commissions would not allow women to sign as leaders, boarding schools taught gender-based vocational roles that reflected the divisions of US society, and the allotment policy favored giving land to male heads of households (Weaver 2009). Canada took its gender-based policies considerably further with the Indian Act, which disenfranchised Native women who married non-Native men. Subsequent policies restored the band status of these women (Champagne 2006).

As part of a broad, international self-determination movement, Native people have begun to assert more control over their own education. In the US, some tribes have taken more control of education for youth in grades k-12, as well as developing a system of higher education through tribal colleges. Likewise, Canadian Natives are beginning to seek more control of education (Champagne 2006). In some instances the push for self-determination manifests as a striving for more political independence. The Canadian recognition of Nunavut as a separate, Indigenous territory takes self-determination and self-governance much farther than in the US. Likewise, Native Hawaiians continue to advocate for more self-determination (*The Economist* 2005, Heffner 2002), yet they find themselves with far fewer rights in this regard than their mainland counterparts.

Conclusion

From historical times to contemporary days, social policies for Native Americans have been shaped by the ongoing tension around recognition of sovereignty and its implications. In eras when sovereignty is recognized to continue (albeit in a limited form), policies reinforcing self-determination abound. In eras when sovereignty is denied, policies focus on assimilation into American society and minimization of distinctiveness. An unfortunate middle ground between the extremes of sovereignty and assimilation are paternalistic policies that recognize Native Americans as distinct, yet less competent and in need of federal protection.

In contemporary society it is politically unlikely, and perhaps virtually impossible, that true sovereignty for Native Americans will ever be promoted. Given awareness of the heavy-handed assimilationist policies of the past, it is also highly unlikely that the American public would find a return to such policies to be palatable. This leaves us in the uncomfortable position of attempting to promulgate social policies that fulfill federal obligations to Native Americans in ways that minimize paternalism and reinforce a level of self-determination that will always fall short of true sovereignty.

International pressures for decolonization and self-determination are likely to continue and may play a role in shaping US social policy toward Native Americans. On the other hand, as a small population within US boundaries, the needs of Native people rarely receive priority when other social concerns, both domestic and international, hold the attention of policy makers.

In the larger scheme of US social policies, policies related to Native Americans hold a marginal place. Major policies such as the ICWA and IHS are anomalies compared with other child welfare and health policies, just as Indigenous Peoples are somewhat of an anomaly in the larger US society. We remain somewhat distinct from the larger scheme of things. As we move forward after centuries of colonization it is apparent that policies are not likely to end our cultural distinctiveness completely. Tribes still exist as distinct entities in spite of the diligent efforts of policy makers to undermine and ultimately end their existence. For the foreseeable future, it is likely that we will stay the course of federal policies that promote limited self-determination for Native Americans with an uncomfortable but ever-present undercurrent of paternalism.

References

Basic, C. 2007. An overview of the Indian Child Welfare Act of 1978. *Journal of Contemporary Legal Issues*, 16, 345–9.

Boxer, A. 2009. Native Americans and the federal government. *History Review*, September, 7–12.

Bragaw, S.G. 2006. Thomas Jefferson and the American Indian nations: Native American sovereignty and the Marshall court. *Journal of Supreme Court History*, 31(2), 155–80.

Braun, K.L. and Browne, C.V. 1998. Perceptions of dementia, caregiving, and help seeking among Asian and Pacific Islander Americans. *Health and Social Work*, 23(4), 262–74.

Burt, L.W. 1986. Roots of the Native American urban experience: Relocation policy in the 1950s. *American Indian Quarterly*, 10(2), 85–99.

Chaffee, E.C. 2008. Business organizations and tribal self-determination: A critical reexamination of the Alaska Native Claims Settlement Act. *Alaska Law Review*, 25(1), 107–41.

Champagne, D. 2006. Native-directed social change in Canada and the United States. *American Behavioral Scientist*, 50, 428–49.

Cross, S.L. 2006. Indian family exception doctrine: Still losing children despite the Indian Child Welfare Act. *Child Welfare*, 84(4), 671–90.

Forbes-Boyte, K. 1999. Fools Crow versus Gullett: A critical analysis of the American Indian Religious Freedom Act. *Antipode*, 31(3), 304–23.

Ford, A.R. 2010. The myth of tribal sovereignty: An analysis of the Native American tribal status in the United States. *International Community Law Review*, 12, 397–411.

Fort, K.E. 2006. Beyond minimum standards: Federal requirements and state interpretations of the Indian Child Welfare Act. *Court Review*, 45, 26–31.

Graham, L.M. 2008. Reparations, self-determination, and the seventh generation. *Harvard Human Rights Journal*, 21, 47–103.

Grieco, E. 2002. *The Native Hawaiian and Other Pacific Islander Population: 2000*. US Census Bureau.

Harjo, S.S. 2003. American Indian Religious Freedom Act at 25. *Indian Country Today*, August 1, 1.

Heffner, J. 2002. Between assimilation and revolt: A third option for Hawaii as a model for minorities world-wide. *Texas International Law Journal*, 37(3), 591–622.

Kelly, C.R. 2010. Orwellian language and the politics of tribal termination (1953–1960). *Western Journal of Communication*, 74(4), 351–71.

Keohane, J.R. 2006. The rise of tribal self-determination and economic development. *Human Rights*, 33(2), 9–11.

O'Brien, S. 1991. A legal analysis of the American Indian Religious Freedom Act. In C. Vecsey (ed.), *Handbook of American Indian Religious Freedom*. New York: Crossroad, 27–43.

Puisto, J. 2009. "We were very afraid": The Confederated Salish and Kootnai politics, identity, and the perception of termination, 1971–2003. *American Indian Culture and Research Journal*, 33(2), 45–66.

Riley, A.R. 2007. Tribal sovereignty in a post-9/11 world. *North Dakota Law Review*, 82, 953–65.

Rutecki, G.W. 2011. Forced sterilization of Native Americans: Later twentieth century physician cooperation with national eugenics policies? *Ethics and Medicine*, 27(1), 33–42.

Schneider, A. 2005. Reforming American Indian/Alaska Native health care financing: The role of Medicaid. *American Journal of Public Health*, 95(5), 766–8.

Smith, H. 2006. *A Seat at the Table*. Berkeley, CA: University of California Press.

The Economist 2005. Sun, surf, and succession. *The Economist*, 376(8442), September 3, 2005.

The Economist 2012. Gambling on nation-building. *The Economist*, 402(8779), April 7, 2012.

The Nation's Health 2005. Indian Health Service marks 50th anniversary. *The Nation's Health*, 35(8), 10.

Venables, R.W. 2004. *American Indian History: Five Centuries of Conflict and Coexistence*. Santa Fe, NM: Clear Light Publishing.

Wall, S. 2010. Federalism, Indian policy, and the patterns of history. *Wicazo Sa Review*, 25(1), 5–16.

Warne, D. 2011. Policy issues in American Indian health governance. *Journal of Law, Medicine, and Ethics*, Spring, 42–5.

Waszak, S. 2010. Contemporary hurdles in the application of the Indian Child Welfare Act. *American Indian Culture and Research Journal*, 34(1), 121–35.

Weaver, H.N. 2009. The colonial context of violence: Reflections on violence in the lives of Native American women. *Journal of Interpersonal Violence*, 24(9), 1552–63.

Weaver, H.N. 2011. A cruel and surreal result: Restrictions on Indigenous spirituality in the land of the free. In J. Schiele (ed.), *Social Welfare Policy: Regulation and Resistance among People of Color*. Los Angeles: Sage.

Westmoreland, T.M. and Watson, K.R. 2006. Redeeming hollow promises: The case for mandatory spending on health care for American Indians and Alaska Natives. *Government, Politics, and Law*, 96(4), 600–605.

Chapter 2

Legally Entrenched Oppressions: The Undercurrent of First Nations Peoples' Experiences with Canada's Social Welfare Policies

Michael Anthony Hart and Gladys Rowe

Canada is a colonial society, although Canada's Prime Minister believes otherwise. During an interview at the G20 conference in 2009 he stated, "We have no history of colonialism" (*Canada Newswire* 2009). Such denial serves to perpetuate colonial oppression. This theme of oppression runs entrenched throughout Canada's historical and contemporary social policies related to First Nations Peoples. Similarities and differences exist between experiences of First Nations,[1] Métis,[2] and Inuit[3] Peoples regarding the Government of Canada's exertions of power. This chapter seeks to present this theme primarily in relation to the First Nations Peoples of the northern part of Ininiwi-Ministik (North America). It begins with a historical overview, then moves to early policies established by the British colonies that became part of Canada. The early laws and policies of Canada are then briefly reviewed. Several contemporary events are addressed, including First Nations women's fight for their rights, the efforts of First Nations to be included in the constitution, and the Royal Commission on Aboriginal Peoples. A closer review of child welfare as a policy area exemplifies Canada's continuing colonialism. The chapter closes with a discussion on dismantling these colonial processes.

---

1   A Canadian term developed as a result of historical and political events. First used by the National Indian Brotherhood in 1981 to address the Canadian rhetoric around "two founding nations" (Frideres and Gadacz 2008).

2   Defined by Métis National Council (1983) as: "An Aboriginal peoples distinct from Indian and Inuit, descendants of historic Métis who evolved into what is now Western Canada, as a political people, with a common political will; and descendants of those Aboriginal peoples who have been absorbed by the historic Métis."

3   In Inuktitut, the word Inuit means "the people," whose origins go back nearly four millenia. There are many recognized Inuit communities, language groups, and delineated cultural areas (Frideres and Gadacz 2008).

Historical Context

It is important to recall Patterson's point (1972, cited in Frideres and Gadacz 2008) that history is written from a national point of view and that differing perspectives are pulled out and discredited. Accepted history is written from the point of view of the colonizers (Memmi 1991). Indeed, Frideres and Gadacz (2008) stated, "it is essential to realize that the history of Canada … has been written mainly by English-speaking Euro-Canadians, specifically of British/French ancestry" (12). First Nations understandings of history have been largely excluded.

When European explorers first set foot in the northern part of Ininiwi-Ministik, now referred to as Canada, First Nations Peoples spanned the entire territory. There were established economic, social, and political systems evidenced through economic processes that redistributed wealth throughout societies, social structures ranging from small groups interconnected through clan systems to large permanent settlements, and a democratic political system that brought distinct nations together under a great law of peace (DeMeo 2006, Dickason 2002, Mann 2005). Many initial interactions were beneficial to both First Nations Peoples and European settlers. Settlement of territories by Europeans was successful, due in part to the support of various First Nations Peoples, and they were initially in control of a shared economic system and militarily stronger than the settlers (Dickason 2002, Frideres and Gadacz 2008, Trigger 1985). Over time this relationship between First Nations and European settlers changed. Mutuality was soon dismissed for inequity that greatly improved the positions of newcomers while oppressing First Nations Peoples.

An important example of this shift in power is when King George III of England issued the Royal Proclamation of 1763 that, amongst other things, recognized First Nations entitlement to the land, identified the Crown as the only legitimate force to enter treaty negotiations with First Nations for access to their land, and unilaterally placed First Nations Peoples and their lands under the dominion and protection of the British Crown. Evident in the wording of the Proclamation, First Nations Peoples were deemed inferior to the British and in need of protection. Designation of First Nations Peoples as inferior also reflected changes in the economic relationship between First Nations and European settlers (Frideres and Gadacz 2011, Miller 2000). During the late seventeenth and eighteenth centuries, many First Nations were drawn into the European fur trade to such a degree that previously independent economies became significantly dependent upon the settlers' economy. The amalgamation of the Northwest and Hudson Bay Companies entrenched dependency through removal of competition for purchasing furs and greatly reduced First Nations' economic position, which was further devastated through collapse of the fur trade in the early 1800s. The balance of power had shifted to favor settlers.

Establishing Colonial Policies: Oppression in the Guise of Civilization

Colonial attitudes based on paternalistic oppression fully emerged in propaganda campaigns in the middle of the nineteenth century. Campaigns initiated in the British colonies focused on the "need" to develop, civilize, and protect First Nations Peoples (Tobias 1999). Amongst the experimental ways to civilize and protect the "savages" was the establishment of the reserve system where First Nations Peoples were taught to farm and receive religious and educational instruction. Further reflecting this paternalism, development of legislation and policies imposed greater control over First Nations Peoples and their territories. This control extended from birth to death and covered the peoples' social, cultural, economic, and political systems.

In the 1867 Canadian Constitution, "Indians and the land reserved for Indians" were to fall under federal jurisdiction; paternalism was ingrained in the very definition of the country. The immediate goal of Canada's first Prime Minister, John A. MacDonald, was unification of the British colonies from coast to coast, through development of a national railroad. This required the Crown to initiate treaties with First Nations so their lands could be accessed.

Treaties were and are held in a sacred manner by First Nations and remain as enforceable agreements between the First Nations and the Crown (Frideres and Gadacz 2011). They included commitments to provide education and medicine, assurance against famine, and annuities, all in perpetuity. They also included access to, and a say in, the use of Crown land, including recognition that land would be "reserved" for use by, and continued self-determination, of First Nations. However, it is suggested the Crown representative participated in bad faith and imposed, rather than negotiated, agreements (Frideres and Gadacz 2011). Further, many First Nations found their identity being redefined and the treaties ignored (Frideres and Gadacz 2011).

Concurrently, the Government increased efforts to control First Nations through establishing new laws and policies which cumulated in 1876 under the "Act to Amend and Consolidate the Laws Respecting Indians," commonly referred to as the Indian Act. Under this, "Indians would lose control of every aspect of their corporate existence" (Milloy 1991, 152). Paternalistic laws, amendments, and policies continued into the mid twentieth century. The "Indian Advancement Act," for example, appointed the Indian Agent, a non-First Nations person and representative of the Minister of Indian Affairs, in each band[4] as the chairman of the band's council. Further, the Government of Canada passed a law making it illegal to receive any payment to support First Nations Peoples to settle legal claims, effectively removing the possibility of First Nations Peoples having fair representation in the court system.

---

4   Band is the term identified in the Indian Act to refer to a group of First Nations peoples. First Nations peoples use the term "First Nation" in place of band. At present there are more than 600 First Nations, or bands, in Canada.

Establishment of political, economic, and cultural control over First Nations Peoples ensured that power remained within the Government's confines. After witnessing, for example, the success of First Nations in adapting to farming and ranching, a law was passed making it illegal for First Nations Peoples to sell grains or produce beyond that needed for sustenance (Venne 1997). The Government of Canada sought control over First Nations' cultures by outlawing activities central to First Nations such as the potlatch held by many First Nations of the west coast, and giveaway ceremonies conducted by First Nations in prairies (Miller 2000). Introduction of the pass system controlled movement of any First Nations person on and off reserve, pending an Indian agent's approval.

In addition to efforts to control First Nations Peoples politically, economically, and culturally, the Government of Canada heavily oppressed First Nations people socially. Efforts included an educational system established by the Government of Canada with support of several Christian denominations. This system sought to assimilate First Nations children to produce "a generation of English speaking Indians, accustomed to the way of civilized life" (Frideres and Gadacz 2011, 59). Towards assimilation, the residential school system operated for over 100 years beginning in the 1880s, based upon the previously established industrial school system. By 1920, attendance was made compulsory, children were forbidden to speak their Indigenous languages, cultural practices were harshly oppressed, and most often spent more than half the day in manual labour (Miller 2000). Former students of several generations have shared their experiences of being physically, sexually, emotionally, and mentally abused while in these schools (Dieter 1999, Fontaine 2010, Fournier and Crey 1997, Miller 2000). Negative intergenerational impacts continue, as issues around parenting, neglect, and patterns of abuse are passed on to children and grandchildren of those who attended the schools (Chansonneuve 2005, Dieter 1999, Fournier and Crey 1997).

Reconsidering the Policies? Assimilation in a New Era

After the Second World War, a shift towards a more benevolent society pushed the Canadian government to examine its treatment of First Nations Peoples. Between 1946 and 1948, a special joint committee of the Senate and House of Commons was established for the purpose of reviewing the Indian Act. The joint committee found that the minister overseeing Indian Affairs had too many discretionary powers and recommended allowing First Nations movement towards self-governance (Leslie 2002). The committee recommended the federal government establish a claims commission to address many long-standing grievances forwarded by First Nations Peoples. The overall message was that there should be a move from forced assimilation to supporting First Nations Peoples to integrate into Canadian society (Leslie 2002). It is worthwhile to note that the Canadian Welfare Council and the Canadian Association of Social Workers (CASW) submitted a joint brief that strongly recommended the extension of provincial social services, including child welfare, to Aboriginal Peoples on reserves (Johnson 1983), and that they favored "full assimilation of Canada's Aboriginal population" (Jennissen and Lundy 2011, 97). Clearly, the committee was suggesting a different line of action, but the response from the Canadian government was to ignore most of the recommendations and to primarily tinker with the Indian Act by removing a few provisions such as the outlawing of First Nations dances and ceremonies and reducing the number of penalty clauses against First Nations. As a result, the 1951 Indian Act returned to the assimilation philosophy of the original Indian Act of 1876 (Miller 2000).

In 1960, a significant change to the Indian Act ensured First Nations individuals received the Federal vote without the requirement that they forfeit recognized status as Indians (Leslie 2002). Previously, in order to vote in a federal election Indians had to give up their legal rights or status as Indian. Another key event, publication of the two-volume Hawthorn Report, occurred in 1966 and 1967 (Hawthorn 1966, 1967). This report identified First Nations Peoples as "citizens-plus"; meaning they were citizens of Canada with full recognition of all that citizenship entails, plus held certain rights as Indians. The report, developed in consultation with First Nations Peoples, called for, amongst other things, protection of treaty rights, recognition of the principle of self-government, funding for economic and social development, and the settlement of land claims (Leslie 2002).

In 1969, the Liberal government of Pierre Elliot Trudeau and the Minister of Indian Affairs, Jean Chrétien, ignored the Hawthorn Report. Instead, they distributed the "Statement of the Government of Canada on Indian Policy" (Government of Canada 1969) which became known as "the white paper." This outlined the intent to achieve equity between First Nations Peoples and other Canadians by repealing the Indian Act, rejecting all land claims, terminating all treaties between the Crown and First Nations, and fully assimilating First Nations people into the Canadian population. This policy was no different than when Duncan Campbell Scott, Deputy Superintendent General of Indian Affairs, set out 50 years earlier to get rid of the Indian problem by assimilating Indians into the Canadian body politic and closing the Department of Indians Affairs (Titley 1992).

First Nations people were outraged and reacted with counter documents. Such documents included, *Citizens Plus*, or "The Red Paper" (Indian Chiefs of Alberta 1970); *A Declaration of Indian Rights: The BC Indian Position Paper* (Union of BC Indian Chiefs 1970); and *Wahbung* (Manitoba Indian Brotherhood 1971). One of the most pointed reprisals was Harold Cardinal's (1969) book, *The Unjust Society*, in which he stated,

> In spite of all government attempts to convince Indians to accept the white paper, their efforts will fail, because Indians understand that the path outlined by the Department of Indian Affairs through its mouthpiece, the Honourable Mr. Chrétien, leads directly to cultural genocide. We will not walk this path. (139)

Under pressure, the federal government distanced itself from this policy, particularly after the Supreme Court's *Calder* decision recognized that First Nations Peoples were living in organized societies and occupying the land at the time of contact, and thus title to the land is retained because of occupation regardless of the recognition of successive governments (Dupuis 2002, Frideres and Gadacz 2008).

First Nations Women Fight their Oppression

This effort by the Federal government to squash First Nations rights through the white paper was not the only point of assault at the time. In 1971, Jeannette Corbière Lavell of the Wikwemikong Band had married a non-First Nations male and subsequently had her status as an "Indian" removed. She initiated a court case to challenge subsection 12(1)(b) of the Indian Act which outlined that Indian women who married non-Indian men would lose their status, while Indian men would maintain their status regardless of who they married. Concurrently, Yvonne Bedard was challenging the Council of the Six Nations Indians who, in following the Indian Act, refused to allow her to live in a house bestowed to her by her mother since she was married to, but separated from, a non-First Nations man.

The Government of Canada and 13 Aboriginal organizations opposed these women's challenges of the subsection (Native Women's Association of Canada, nd). Their case, *Canada (AG) v. Levall [1974] S.C.R. 1349*, was heard in the Supreme Court in 1974 and the Court ruled against the women. It was decided by the Court that the Canadian Bill of Rights was not intended to suppress federal legislation over Indians. Three years later, Sandra Lovelace filed a complaint with the United Nations Committee on Human Rights after she was forbidden to live in her community, the Tobique Reserve, for the same rationale used against Lavell and Bedard. While the Committee determined they were not able to consider whether Ms Lovelace was denied equity before the law and the equal protection of the law as outlined under article 26 of the International covenant on civil and political rights, since she was married prior to the enactment of the covenant, they did state that she was "denied the right guaranteed by article 27 to persons belonging to minorities, to enjoy their own culture and to use their own language in community with other members of their group" (United Nations Human Rights Committee 1981, 9).

Embarrassed on an international stage, the Government of Canada was pushed to address discrimination in subsection 12(1)(b) of the Indian Act. Further, Canada's recently adopted Charter of Rights and Freedoms of 1982, which included gender equality, meant that the Government of Canada had to address the issue. Their response was the development of Bill C-31 that revised the Indian Act. Under this Bill, passed in 1985, a person with two parents who are recognized by the Federal government as status Indians would be identified as an Indian under 6.1 of the revised Indian Act. A person with only one parent who is recognized by the Federal government as a status Indian would be identified as an Indian under 6.2 of the revised Indian Act. A person with 6.1 status would be able pass on her or his status as Indians to her or his children regardless of the status of the other parent, while a person with 6.2 status could not pass on her or his status to her or his children unless that person married another Indian with status.

Bill C-31 has resulted in what has been commonly referred to as the "second generation cut-off" where great concern arose due to the fact that unless status Indians marry other status Indians, the second generation will be cut off as status Indians. This action has been interpreted as a continued effort by the Federal government to assimilate First Nations people into Canada's body politic and remove the government's legal obligations and responsibilities to First Nations people.

Constitutional Changes and the Recognition of First Nations Rights

The repatriation of the Canadian Constitution from Britain and its inclusion of the new Canadian Charter of Rights and Freedoms also demanded attention by First Nations Peoples, and served as a mechanism to draw national and international attention to the systematic exclusion of their perspectives and concerns in these processes. Increased lobbying efforts produced pressure to ensure a focus on Aboriginal Peoples, meaning Indian, Inuit, and Métis Peoples, was included in the Constitution. The repatriated Constitution was proclaimed on April 17, 1982 by Queen Elizabeth II, with all governments except Quebec signing on.

Sections 25, 35, and 37 of the constitution directly addressed Aboriginal Peoples. Section 25 of the Charter of Rights and Freedoms, stated:

> The guarantee in this Charter of certain rights and freedoms shall not be construed so as to abrogate or derogate from any aboriginal, treaty or other rights or freedoms that pertain to the aboriginal peoples of Canada including (a) any rights or freedoms that have been recognized by the Royal Proclamation of October 7, 1763; and (b) any rights or freedoms that may be acquired by the aboriginal peoples of Canada by way of land claims settlement.

Section 35 stated, "existing aboriginal and treaty of the aboriginal people are hereby recognized and affirmed," defined Aboriginal people of Canada as the Indian, Inuit, and Métis Peoples of Canada, noted that treaty rights included existing and those acquired through land claims agreements, and confirmed that treaty rights are guaranteed to male and female persons. Section 37 required the holding of a First Ministers Conference on matters affecting Aboriginal Peoples of Canada, including identification and definition of Aboriginal rights to be included in the constitution. It stipulated that representatives of the Aboriginal Peoples of Canada were to participate in the discussions. This was considered by the First Nations as a step towards recognition of their right to self-governance. However, in the four First Ministers conferences with First Nations, Inuit, and Métis Peoples of Canada held in 1983, 1984, 1985, and 1987, there was little agreement. There were even efforts to have matters pertaining to First Nations, Inuit, and Métis Peoples moved out of the Constitution into the preamble where no power would be enshrined to uphold their rights.

Righting Wrongs: The Royal Commission on Aboriginal Peoples

Tensions in the early 1990s between the Government of Canada and First Nations led to creation of the Royal Commission on Aboriginal Peoples (RCAP) which developed a five-volume document totalling over 4,000 pages and 440 recommendations. It comprehensively addressed a spectrum of matters, including housing, education, child welfare, health, youth suicide, recognition of an Aboriginal order of government, creation of an Aboriginal parliament, and development of a new relationship between federal and provincial governments and Aboriginal Peoples (Royal Commission on Aboriginal Peoples 1996).

The Federal Government responded in 2007, with a report entitled "Gathering Strength;" however, it neglected to implement any recommendations. In 1998, the United Nations Committee on Economics, Social and Cultural Rights, and in 1999, the United Nations Humans Rights Committee, expressed concern that Canada had not taken decisive and urgent action to implement the recommendations of the RCAP report (Hurley and Wherrett 2000). In 2006, the Assembly of First Nations concluded there had been "clear lack of action on the key foundational recommendations of RCAP and a resultant lack of progress on key socio-economic indicators. *Based on our assessment, Canada has failed in terms of its action to date*" (Assembly of First Nations 2006, italics in original). They gave an A for acting on one of the 60 key areas reviewed, the establishment of a National Aboriginal Day enacted by the Governor General on June 13, 1996. The rest of the areas' grades ranged from B+ to F. A total of 37 areas received a failing grade. These failing grades, combined with international recognition of Canada's inaction, are indicative of the federal government's stance in regards to First Nations Peoples. To create change has required great efforts by the First Nations, primarily through the court system, evidenced through First Nations Peoples challenge of the government in the area of residential school compensation.

Residential School Compensation

In the early 1990s, the Grand Chief of the Assembly of Manitoba Chiefs, Phil Fontaine, publicly disclosed his experience of sexual and physical abuse in the residential schools (Fromm 1990). This prompted other disclosures and court challenges on the abuse First Nations, Inuit, and Métis Peoples suffered as children in residential schools. As a response, the Minister of Indian Affairs issued a statement of regret on June 7, 1998, to those who were abused in residential schools. A $350 million fund was established in 1998 to address the aftermath of the residential schools, which finally closed in 1996 (Aboriginal Healing Foundation 1998, Indian Affairs and Northern Development 1997). Over the following years, tens of thousands of former students participated in class action lawsuits filed against the church-run schools and the Federal government who funded them. After failed efforts to address these claims out of court, the Government of Canada and the Assembly of First Nations established an agreement in principle in November 2005 outlining how to address compensation for more than 80,000 surviving individuals who attended residential schools (Agreement in Principle 2005). This Indian Residential Schools Settlement Agreement was initiated on September 19, 2007 with five key areas: 1) a Common Experience Payment (CEP) for all eligible former students of Indian Residential Schools (IRS); 2) an Independent Assessment Process (IAP) for claims of sexual or serious physical abuse; 3) measures to support healing; 4) commemorative activities; and 5) the establishment of a Truth and Reconciliation Commission (TRC)—Aboriginal and Northern Affairs and Development (nd). The agreement was supported with $1.9 million in funding from the Federal government.

The issue of compensation and healing was gaining national attention. On June 11, 2008, the Prime Minster issued a formal apology in the House of Commons, along with statements from the Leader of the Official Opposition, the leader of the third political party in the House of Commons, and First Nations, Métis, and Inuit political leaders (Parliament of Canada 2008). While an apology was made in 1998 by a Minister of Indian Affairs, this 2008 apology marked acknowledgement from all political parties that Canada, as a nation, recognized the oppression imposed by the residential schools. Part of this recognition included establishment of the TRC, which opened its doors in April, 2010. The goals of the Commission were identified as:

a. acknowledge Residential School experiences, impacts and consequences;
b. provide a holistic, culturally appropriate, and safe setting for former students, their families, and communities as they come forward to the Commission;
c. witness, support, promote, and facilitate truth and reconciliation events at both the national and community levels;
d. promote awareness and public education of Canadians about the IRS system and its impacts;
e. identify sources and create as complete an historical record as possible of the IRS system and legacy. The record shall be preserved and made accessible to the public for future study and use;
f. produce and submit to the Parties of the Agreement a report including recommendations to the Government of Canada concerning the IRS system and experience, including: the history, purpose, operation, and supervision of the IRS system, the effect and consequences of IRS (including systemic

harms, intergenerational consequences, and the impact on human dignity), and the ongoing legacy of the residential schools;

g. support commemoration of former Indian Residential School students and their families in accordance with the Commemoration Policy Directive (Truth and Reconciliation Commission nd).

As of 2012, the Commission was halfway through the mandated period of operations, conducting hearings and making presentations across the country.

Child Welfare Services as an Example of Contemporary Policy Making

The area of child welfare policy development has been greatly influenced through First Nations Peoples challenging the Canadian government. Prior to the 1950s, under federal jurisdiction, child welfare within First Nations was left to the extended family, or the federal Indian agent in each reserve who would generally send children to the residential schools. Changes to the Indian Act in 1951 allowed provincial services to be delivered on reserves. As the residential schools were failing to assimilate First Nations children, child welfare was seen as a new system of assimilation (Johnson 1983).

Provincial jurisdiction over services coincided with a significant increase in the number of children in the child welfare system in the 1950s and 1960s. By the 1970s, thousands of First Nations children had been taken into care and many were adopted out to white, middle-class families in other provinces and countries. When the numbers of First Nations children taken into foster care are included, one in three First Nations children were being separated from their families (Fournier and Crey 1997). By 1981, in Manitoba, one out of two children placed for out-of-province adoption were First Nations, Métis, or Inuit.

Condemnation by First Nations leaders and others led to a public inquiry and moratorium on out-of-province adoptions of Aboriginal children (Hamilton and Sinclair 1991). This inquiry confirmed the child welfare system was implementing a form of cultural genocide (Kimelman 1985) and recommended significant changes, including returning First Nations children to their communities and families, supporting First Nations agencies to provide services to members off-reserve, strengthening the role of extended family in child welfare processes, non-Aboriginal adoption as a last resort, and ensuring "affirmative action" in agency hiring processes. Further inquiries highlighted significant changes necessary within the child welfare system in Manitoba specifically (Hamilton and Sinclair 1991). However, this report remained shelved for nearly 10 years.

In 2000, the Government of Manitoba revisited this report in relation to child welfare and entered negotiation with First Nations and Métis representatives to establish the Aboriginal Justice Inquiry-Child Welfare Initiative (AJI-CWI). The AJI-CWI identified several goals, including recognition of First Nation Peoples' right to control development and delivery of child and family services to their peoples throughout Manitoba and to restructure the Child and Family Services system. In 2006, four child welfare authorities were created: the First Nations of Northern Manitoba Child and Family Services Authority, the First Nations of Southern Manitoba Child and Family Services Authority, the Métis Child and Family Services Authority, and the General Child and Family Services Authority. Authorities were given responsibility to administer and provide child and family services in ways reflective of the cultures of the people served, and to design and manage services by setting their own service standards to supplement existing provincial standards. The greatest change of this new structure was the ability of First Nations and Métis Peoples to provide services to their own peoples living off-reserve.

While First Nations Peoples increased their control over child welfare services, concerns remain. For example, funding agreements established for this new system outlined that the federal government would provide funds for services to children and families residing on reserve at the time of intervention, while the province would provide funds for services for children and families residing off reserve. In 2007, the First Nations Child and Family Caring Society of Canada and the Assembly of First Nations filed a complaint with the Human Rights Commission alleging:

> The federal funding policy discriminates against First Nations children on reserve on the basis of race (being status Indian) and residency (on reserve location) by knowingly providing them with inequitable levels of child welfare funding resulting in unequal benefit under child welfare laws. (First Nations Child and Family Caring Society 2007)

The federal government made significant efforts to stop this human rights case from being heard through legal technicalities, appeals, and changing the Chairperson. It was decided in Federal Court that the Human Rights Tribunal should examine evidence that First Nations children were being discriminated against through underfunding of on-reserve child protection services (*Canadian Human Rights Commission v. Attorney General of Canada et al.* 2012).

Common Themes across Sectors

The legislative and political dynamics exemplified through child welfare are not uncommon. First Nations Peoples also experience disparities in education and socio-economic status. Despite decades of calls for greater control of education for First Nations people by First Nations people (Manitoba Indian Brotherhood 1971, National Indian Brotherhood 1973, Assembly of First Nations 2010, Senate Standing Committee on Aboriginal Peoples 2011), the federal government continues to act unilaterally and cut such things as education for First Nations Peoples living off-reserve and post-secondary educational assistance (Ward

1986). In 1996, the federal government unilaterally capped educational funding at 2 percent, a rate lower than inflation, in spite of First Nations Peoples being the fastest growing segment of the Canadian population. This cap remains today, resulting in increasing shortfalls in educational funding.

In 2008, the federal government announced, "The government will spend $70 million over two years to improve First Nations education by encouraging integration with provincial systems" (Department of Finance 2008, cited in First Nations Education Council 2009), raising First Nations concerns that the focus was on assimilation as opposed to First Nations control. Two years later, the federal government announced it was partnering with the Assembly of First Nations to create a panel of experts "to explore and advise on the development of options, including legislation, to improve elementary and secondary education outcomes for First Nation children who live on-reserve" (Government of Canada and Assembly of First Nations 2010), but by October of 2012 the Assembly of First Nations had withdrawn from the process citing that the federal government was acting behind closed doors and developing a one-size-fits-all solution to the education crisis (Canadian Press 2012). The federal minister confirmed that Ottawa will continue to push forward with its legislation while also stating that legislation has not been drafted (Canadian Press 2012).

In the area of health and social economic status, First Nation leaders have called for greater attention to the health disparities between First Nations Peoples and the rest of the Canadian population. There appeared to be positive development through the Kelowna Accord. The ten-year plan provided a commitment of over five billion dollars to close the gap between First Nations, Métis, and Inuit Peoples' health and socio-economic health statuses in relation to the rest of Canada. Confirmed by all parties in November 2005, the agreement covered such areas as housing, economic opportunities, education, and health (Patterson 2006). However, before implementation the negotiating government fell from power. Though the new federal government committed to meeting the targets of the Kelowna Accord, successive budgets have reflected no financial commitment (CBC News Online 2006). Words of support have not translated into action.

Canada's Colonialism and Social Work's Role in Decolonization

Assimilation and colonialism are recurring themes in Canadian social policy for First Nations Peoples. There are several definitions of colonialism. For example, Boehmer (1995) explained that colonialism involves settlement, exploitation of local resources, and governance of Indigenous Peoples of the occupied lands. Gandhi (1998) defined colonialism as "the historical process whereby the 'West' attempts systematically to cancel or negate the cultural difference and value of the 'non-West'" (16). Said (1994) defined it as "the implanting of settlements on distant territory" (9). Horvath (1972) initiated one of the most thorough discussions on colonialism in which he identified the following characteristics:

1. Domination is the control by individuals or groups over the territory and/or the behavior of other individuals or groups.

2. Intergroup domination is the domination process in a culturally heterogeneous society; intragroup domination occurs in a culturally homogeneous society.

3. Colonialism is that form of intergroup domination in which settlers in significant numbers migrate permanently to the colony from the colonizing power. (50)

While these definitions have contributed to a greater understanding of the phenomenon, the voice of First Nations Peoples is not well reflected in these definitions. The following definition is a response to this absence: Colonialism is the evolving processes where we, as peoples of this land, face impositions—from genocide, to assimilation, to marginalization—of views, ideas, beliefs, values, and practices by other peoples at the cost of our lives, views, ideas, beliefs, values, practices, lands, and/or resources. It is when we, as peoples of this land, are stopped, hindered, cajoled, and/or manipulated from making and enacting decisions about our lives, individually and as a group, because of being a person of the peoples of this land. These decisions include how we are going to be who we are, and how, if at all, we are going to incorporate the ideas, beliefs, values, and practices of other peoples (Hart 2008). With this definition in mind, the historical and ongoing processes of colonialism in the lands now referred to as Canada become more clearly evident.

Canada has a history of trying to protect, civilize, and assimilate First Nations Peoples (Tobias 1999). From the time of the Royal Proclamation to the contemporary period where policies are unilaterally developed by non-First Nations Peoples, the settler society has been trying to: 1) access benefit and profit from the land and resources of Ininiwi-Ministik; 2) remove First Nations Peoples from "being in the way" of these benefits and profits; and 3) remain guilt free of any association with the oppression of First Nations Peoples.

The ultimate control over peoples is to dismiss their existence. Since it is unacceptable within the settler worldview to physically destroy various peoples, the next best means of dismissal is to destroy who they are and their connection to their past. Assimilation, an ideal means to this end, allows the façade of a benevolent state while maintaining the goal of removing the peoples. Assimilation requires that First Nations abilities and contributions be ignored, and that the people be objectified. Objectification is established through the creation of a mythical portrait where the people are described as inferior and incapable in order to dehumanize and rationalize the need to care for, protect, and assimilate (Memmi 1991). By ignoring their strengths and abilities, recreating the image, settler society justifies their actions of imposition. These impositions include predetermining the policies that First Nations Peoples must follow, particularly policies created without First Nations input. These actions are colonial.

Recognizing Our Responsibilities

While colonial oppression is clearly evident to those oppressed, lack of information about experiences and perspectives of the oppressed hinders Canadians' understanding of how they participate and maintain colonial oppression. Privileges and benefits remain largely unexamined. As discussed at the beginning of this chapter, it is through our learning of history that this begins. We must ask ourselves, whose history are we learning and for what purpose? Whose voices are excluded and by what method? Consideration of how this maintains a system that oppresses is critical to support this dismantling.

In the field of social work, for example, social workers carry such privilege and yet many remain unaware of how the profession has acted to support oppression. The profession has spoken about the need to address the oppression (Canadian Association of Social Workers 1994). Social work involves addressing the relationship between individuals and societies. While the common fallback position for many social workers is to change the individual to fit society, such actions alone will not stop oppression of Indigenous Peoples; it only allows some peoples to navigate within the oppressive systems. A stronger foundation is necessary to dismantle oppression, particularly colonial oppression. Social workers writing, implementing, and critiquing social policy must be vigilant to deconstruct the blatant and hidden cultural hegemony evident in Canadian social policies.

The following tasks require attention, not only by those within the social work profession, but by all who become aware of this entrenched oppression and work to dismantle these histories. The list of supportive tasks, not meant to be exhaustive but to provide a framework for forward movement, includes: 1) educating self about oppression in general, and colonial oppression specifically; 2) learning about the untaught First Nations history; 3) developing critical reflexive skills, as well as critical analysis skills; 4) honestly looking at one's unconscious participation and/ or erroneously informed participation in the oppression; 5) educating others on oppression through social action, informal dialogues, and sharing of information; 6) developing an understanding of First Nations Peoples, cultures, perspectives, and experiences; 7) creating space for First Nations contributions and developments which requires encouragement, acceptance of differences, and concrete support; 8) challenging the profession of its privileges, whether those privileges stem from the types of practices that are utilized, the theoretical perspectives that are taught and learned, or the values and belief system that is followed; 9) supporting the continuing development of Indigenous social work practice, perspectives, and theories; and 10) making space for Indigenous participation in all segments of the profession. This must accompany a commitment to maintain supportive relationships with Indigenous Peoples.

Positive, supportive relationships take time to develop and maintain. Decolonizing processes also take time since it is about rebuilding a relationship that has been wrought with judgments, violence, distrust, hurt, and anger. We must remember that relationships involve at least two parties. As such, both the oppressed and the privileged in the colonial relationship must be involved in decolonization processes. This requires inward reflexivity towards personal responsibilities as both oppressed and privileged address this colonial relationship.

The words of Anishinaabe activist and scholar Leanne Simpson need to be considered: "Our social movements, organizing, and mobilization are stuck in the cognitive box of imperialism and we need to step out of the box, remove our colonial blinders and at least see the potential for radically different ways of existence" (2011, 149). As Dene professor Coulthard (2008) stated, we also must "turn away" from the "assimilative lure of settler-state recognition" (201). This means moving beyond the commonly accepted perspectives and practices forwarded by settler policies.

As Cree writer Neal McLeod (2007) explained, this involves the process of *mamâhtâwisiwin*, the process of tapping into the life force within and around us as a means to move beyond the ordinary and rethink the world around us. This process, when coupled with critical reflection, could be considered Indigenous transformative praxis. Through such reflection, we can see, as Coulthard (2008) noted, that, "our cultures have much to teach the Western world about the establishment of relationships within and between people and the natural world that are profoundly non-imperialist" (201). By all people honoring the relationship, and recognizing First Nations Peoples, our histories, as well as First Nations gifts and contributions, we can move beyond the uninformed, oppressive ideas we are repeating and create positive changes for not only First Nations, but all peoples.

References

Aboriginal Affairs and Northern Development Canada (nd). Settlement Agreement. Retrieved November 5, 2012, from http://www.aadnc-aandc.gc.ca/eng/110010 0015638/1100100015639.

Aboriginal Healing Foundation 1998. Aboriginal Healing Foundation completes election of directors; Board to manage $350 million healing fund. June 23. Retrieved November 5, 2012, from http://www.ahf.ca/downloads/pr-june-23 -1998.pdf.

Agreement in Principle 2005. Retrieved November 5, 2012, from http://www. residentialschoolsettlement.ca/AIP.pdf.

Assembly of First Nations 2006. *The Royal Commission on Aboriginal Peoples at 10 Years: A Report Card.* Ottawa: Assembly of First Nations. Retrieved November 5, 2012, from http://www.cbc.ca/news/background/aboriginals/pdf/ afn_rcap.pdf.

Assembly of First Nations 2010. *First Nations Control of First Nations Education.* Ottawa: Assembly of First Nations. Retrieved November 5, 2012, from http:// www.afn.ca/uploads/files/education/3._2010_july_afn_first_nations_control_ of_first_nations_education_final_eng.pdf.

Boehmer, E. 1995. *Colonial and Postcolonial Literature: Migrant Metaphors.* New York: Oxford University Press.

Canadian Association of Social Workers 1994. The social work profession and the Aboriginal Peoples: CASW presentation to the Royal Commission on Aboriginal Peoples. *The Social Worker/Le Travailleur Social*, 62(4), Winter 1994, 158.

Canadian Human Rights Commission v. Attorney General of Canada et al. 2012. Federal Court. Retrieved November 15, 2012, from http://www.fncaring society.com/sites/default/files/fnwitness/T-578-11%20Order%20English%20 %28April%2018%2C%202012%29.pdf.

Canada Newswire 2009. Prime Minister Harper denies colonialism in Canada at G20. September 29. Retrieved November 17, 2012, from http://www.news wire.ca/en/story/534215/prime-minister-harper-denies-colonialism-in-cana da-at-g20.

Canadian Press 2012. Harper government's First Nations education plan collapses. CBC News, Politics. October 4. Retrieved November 15, 2012, from http:// www.cbc.ca/news/politics/story/2012/10/04/pol-cp-first-nations-education- plan-collapse.html.

Cardinal, H. 1969. *The Unjust Society*. Edmonton: M.G. Hurtig Publishers.

CBC News Online 2006. Upgrading the Kelowna agreement. CBC News, In Depth (November 21). Retrieved November 15, 2012, from http://www.cbc. ca/news/background/aboriginals/undoing-kelowna.html.

Chansonneuve, D. 2005. *Reclaiming Connections: Understanding Residential School Trauma among Aboriginal People*. Ottawa: Aboriginal Healing Foundation.

Coulthard, G. 2008. Beyond recognition: Indigenous self-determination as prefigurative practice. In *Lighting the Eighth Fire: The Liberation, Resurgence, and Protection of Indigenous Nations*, edited by L. Simpson. Winnipeg: Arbeiter Ring Publishing.

DeMeo, J. 2006. Peaceful versus warlike societies in pre-columbian America: What do archaeology and anthropology tell us? In *Unlearning the Language of Conquest: Scholars Expose Anti-Indianism in America*, edited by D.T. Jacobs. Austin: University of Texas Press.

Dickason, O.P. 2002. *Canada's First Nations: A History of Founding Peoples from Earliest Times* (3rd edition). Don Mills, ON: Oxford University Press.

Dieter, C. 1999. *From Our Mother's Arms: The Intergenerational Impact of Residential Schools in Saskatchewan*. Etobicoke, ON: United Church Publishing House.

Dupuis, R. 2002. *Justice for Canada's Aboriginal Peoples*. Toronto: James Lorimer and Company.

First Nations Child and Family Caring Society of Canada 2007. Assembly of First Nations and the First Nations Child and Family Caring Society launch human rights complaint. *Newsletter*, Spring. Retrieved November 14, 2012, from http://www.fncaringsociety.com/sites/default/files/newsletters/Newslette rSpring2007.pdf.

First Nations Education Council 2009. Paper on First Nations education funding. February. Retrieved November 15, 2012, from http://www.cepn-fnec.com/PDF/etudes_documents/education_funding.pdf.

Fontaine, T. 2010. *Broken Circle: The Dark Legacy of Indian Residential Schools.* Calgary: Heritage House Publishing Company.

Fournier, S. and Crey, E. 1997. *Stolen from our Embrace: The Abduction of First Nations Children and the Restoration of Aboriginal Communities.* Vancouver: Douglas and McIntyre.

Frideres, J. and Gadacz, R. 2008. *Aboriginal Peoples in Canada* (8th edition). Toronto: Pearson Prentice Hall.

Frideres, J. and Gadacz, R. 2011. *Aboriginal Peoples in Canada* (9th edition). Toronto: Pearson Prentice Hall.

Fromm B. (Host). 1990. Guest Phil Fontaine. In *The Journal.* October 30. Toronto: Canadian Broadcasting Company. Retrieved November 5, 2012, from http://www.cbc.ca/archives/categories/politics/parties-leaders/phil-fontaine-native-diplomat-and-dealmaker/shocking-testimony-of-sexual-abuse.html.

Gandhi, L. 1998. *Postcolonial Theory: A Critical Introduction.* New York: Columbia University Press.

Government of Canada. 1969. *Statement of the Government of Canada on Indian Policy.* Ottawa: Queen's Printer. Retrieved August 31, 2012, from http://www.aadnc-aandc.gc.ca/eng/1100100010189/1100100010191.

Government of Canada and Assembly of First Nations. 2010. News release—Creation of panel: Government of Canada and Assembly of First Nations announce the creation of a panel of experts engagement on First Nations elementary and secondary education. December. Retrieved September 11, 2013, from http://www.aadnc-aandc.gc.ca/eng/1291988144856/1291988281925.

Hamilton, A. and Sinclair, M. 1991. *Report of the Aboriginal Justice Inquiry of Manitoba.* Retrieved November 15, 2012, from http://www.ajic.mb.ca/volumel/recommendations.html#Aboriginal%20Peoples%20and%20the%20Child%20Welfare%20System%20in%20Manitobahttp://www.ajic.mb.ca/volumel/recommendations.html#Aboriginal%20Peoples%20and%20the%20Child%20Welfare%20System%20in%20Manitoba.

Hart, M.A. 2008. *Understanding Oppression: An Aboriginal Perspective.* Presented at "Understanding Oppression: Becoming an Ally Community Workshop," November, Winnipeg, MB. Invited.

Hawthorn, H. 1966. *A Survey of the Contemporary Indians of Canada: Economic, Political, Educational Needs and Policies.* Vol. 1. Ottawa: Queen's Printer Press, 1966–1967. Retrieved September 11, 2013, from http://www.ainc-inac.gc.ca/ai/arp/ls/phi-eng.asp.

Hawthorn, H. 1967. *A Survey of the Contemporary Indians of Canada: Economic, Political, Educational Needs and Policies.* Vol. 2. Ottawa: Queen's Printer Press, 1966–1967. Retrieved September 11, 2013, from http://www.ainc-inac.gc.ca/ai/arp/ls/phi-eng.asp.

Horvath, R.J. 1972. A definition of colonialism. *Current Anthropology*, 13(1), 45–57.

Hurley, M., and Wherrett, J. 2000. PRB 99-24E: The report of the Royal Commission on Aboriginal Peoples. Parlimentary Research Branch. Retrieved November 5, 2012, from http://www.parl.gc.ca/Content/LOP/ResearchPublications/prb99 24-e.htm.

Indian Affairs and Northern Development 1997. *Gathering Strength: Canada's Aboriginal Action Plan*. Ottawa: Minister of Public Works and Government Services Canada. Retrieved November 5, 2012, from http://www.ahf.ca/downloads/gathering-strength.pdf.

Indian Chiefs of Alberta 1970/2011. Citizens Plus. *Aboriginal Policy Studies*, 1(2), 188–281. Retrieved August 30, 2011, from http://ejournals.library.ualberta.ca/index.php/aps/article/view/11690/8926.

Jennissen, T. and Lundy, C. 2011. *One Hundred Years of Social Work: A History of the Profession in English Canada 1900–2000*. Waterloo: Wilfred Laurier University Press.

Johnson, P. 1983. *Native Children and the Child Welfare System*. Toronto: Canadian Council on Social Development and James Lorimer and Company.

Kimelman, Judge E.C. 1985. *No Quiet Place: Review Committee on Indian and Metis Adoption and Placements*. Manitoba Community Services.

Leslie, J.F. 2002. The Indian Act: An historical perspective. *Canadian Parliamentary Review*, 25(2), 23–7.

Manitoba Indian Brotherhood 1971. *Wahbung: Our Tomorrows*. Winnipeg: Manitoba Indian Brotherhood, http://amc.manitobachiefs.com/images/pdf/wahbung%20-%20position%20paper%20-%20a%20return%20to%20the%20beginning%20for%20our%20tomorrows.pdf.

Mann, C.C. 2005. *1491: New Revelations of the Americas before Columbus*. Toronto: Random House of Canada.

McLeod, N. 2007. *Cree Narrative Memory: From Treaties to Contemporary Times*. Saskatoon: Purich Press.

Memmi, A. 1991. *The Colonizer and the Colonized*. Boston: Beacon Press.

Métis National Council 1983. *A brief to the Senate Standing Committee on legal and constitutional affairs*. September 8. Ottawa.

Miller, J.R. 2000. *Skyscrapers Hide the Heavens: A History of Indian–White Relations in Canada* (3rd edition). Toronto: University of Toronto Press.

Milloy, J.S. 1991. The early Indian acts: Developmental strategy and constitutional change. In *Sweet Promises: A Reader on Indian–White relations in Canada*, edited by J.R. Miller. Toronto: University of Toronto Press, 145–54.

National Indian Brotherhood 1973. *Indian Control of Indian Education*. Policy Paper presented to the Minister of Indian Affairs and Northern Development. Ottawa: Assembly of First Nations. Retrieved November 15, 2012, from http://64.26.129.156/calltoaction/Documents/ICOIE.pdf.

Native Women's Association of Canada (nd). *Aboriginal Women's Rights are Human Rights*. Ottawa: Native Women's Association of Canada. Retrieved

August 31, 2012, from http://action.web.ca/home/narcc/attach/AboriginalWo
mensRightsAreHumanRights.pdf.

Parliament of Canada 2008. 39th Parliament, 2nd Session. June 11. Retrieved
September 11, 2013, from http://www.parl.gc.ca/HousePublications/Publicati
on.aspx?DocId=3568890&Language=E&Mode=1&Parl=39&Ses=2.

Patterson, L.L. 2006. *Aboriginal Roundtable to Kelowna Accord: Aboriginal
Policy Negotiations, 2004–2005.* Political and Social Affairs Division,
Parliamentary Information and Research Service, Library of Parliament.
Retrieved September 11, 2013, from http://www.parl.gc.ca/Content/LOP/Re
searchPublications/prb0604-e.htm.

Royal Commission on Aboriginal Peoples 1996. *Report of the Royal Commission
on Aboriginal Peoples.* Retrieved November 5, 2012, from http://www.coll
ectionscanada.gc.ca/webarchives/20071124125216/http://www.ainc-inac.gc.
ca/ch/rcap/sg/sg1_e.html.

Said, E. 1994. *Culture and Imperialism.* New York: Vintage Books.

Senate Standing Committee on Aboriginal Peoples 2011. *Reforming First Nations
Education: From Crisis to Hope.* Retrieved November 15, 2012, from http://
www.parl.gc.ca/Content/SEN/Committee/411/appa/rep/rep03dec11-e.pdf.

Simpson, L. 2011. *Dancing on our Turtle's Back: Stories of Nishnabeg Re-creation,
Resurgence, and a New Emergence.* Winnipeg: Arbeiter Ring Publishers.

Titley, B. 1992. *A Narrow Vision: Duncan Campbell Scott and the Administration
of Indian Affairs in Canada.* Vancouver: UBC Press.

Tobias, J.L. 1999. Protection, civilization, assimilation: An outline history of
Canada's Indian policy. In *Sweet Promises: A Reader on Indian–White
Relations in Canada,* edited by J.R. Miller. Toronto: University of Toronto
Press, 127–44.

Trigger, B. 1985. *Natives and Newcomers: Canada's "Heroic Age" Reconsidered.*
Kingston and Montreal: McGill-Queen's University Press.

Truth and Reconciliation Commission (nd). Our Mandate. Retrieved November 5,
2012 from http://www.trc.ca/websites/trcinstitution/index.php?p=7.

Union of BC Indian Chiefs 1970. *A Declaration of Indian Rights: The BC
Indian Position Paper.* Vancouver: Union of BC Indian Chiefs. Retrieved
August 31, 2012, from http://www.ubcic.bc.ca/files/PDF/1970_11_17_Decla
rationOfIndianRightsTheBCIndianPositionPaper_web_sm.pdf.

United Nations Human Rights Committee 1981. Communications CCPR/C/DR
(XIII)/No. R.6/24.

Venne, S. 1997. Understanding Treaty 6: An Indigenous perspective. In *Aboriginal
and Treaty Rights in Canada,* edited by M. Asch. Vancouver, BC: UBC Press,
173–207.

Ward, S. 1986. Indian Education: Policy and Politics, 1972–1982. *Canadian
Journal of Native Education,* 13(2), 10–21.

PART II
Social Work:
Past, Present, and Future

The social work profession evolved during a time of major transformation for Indigenous Peoples in the United States and Canada. While the status of Indigenous Peoples vis-à-vis the settler societies that came to surround them was being shaped by colonization and resulting social policies, social work was establishing its domain among other helping professions. Built on a foundation of both social justice and individualistic interventions designed to help people adapt to and flourish within their social environments, the social work profession has a history of being paternalistic and a method of social control used to assimilate Indigenous Peoples. On the other hand, it is a profession with tremendous promise and an advocacy bent, capable of helping to empower and bring about real social change for Indigenous Peoples.

This section provides three chapters with varying perspectives on social work and Indigenous Peoples. Tamburro and Tamburro provide a detailed overview of helping practices that existed among Indigenous populations prior to colonization, as well as how the social work profession crafted its interactions with these populations. Prue uses historical records to trace the profession's standpoint or attitude toward Indigenous Peoples. Both these chapters reflect a largely negative and difficult history between social workers and Indigenous Peoples. McEachern also recounts the difficulties that Indigenous social work students have faced in bridging the profession with their own experiences and the needs of their communities. In addition to this negative history, however, McEachern challenges us to look at the possibility of a better future in which the social work profession realizes its potential to truly assist and advocate for Indigenous Peoples. Using a cross-cultural lens she describes how one particular social work program reaches out to Indigenous Peoples in ways that help them use the best of western education blended with Indigenous knowledge and community strengths to build a better future for Indigenous communities.

Chapter 3

Social Services and Indigenous Peoples of North America: Pre-Colonial to Contemporary Times

Andrea Tamburro and Paul-René Tamburro

This chapter provides a historical context for social services with Indigenous Peoples. The way in which Indigenous Peoples of North America have provided and received social services has dramatically shifted over the past 500 years. For 300 years after contact with Europeans (about 1500 to 1800) Native Americans continued to provide for their own needs. Many Indigenous ways of helping persist; however, Indigenous Peoples now also have contact with social workers and Western ways of helping.

Traditional Supports, Ways of Helping, and Healing

Originally, Indigenous Peoples provided for the social welfare needs of their own communities and assisted newly arrived colonists from Europe. Colonists encountered systems where women were in leadership roles, councils operated with democratic principles, and extremes of wealth and poverty did not exist. Native American social systems provided an alternate worldview and influenced the American constitution, representative government, Marxism, socialism, and the women's rights movement. These ideas, if they existed in the "Old World," were only theory until European colonists encountered them in action in the Americas (Dickason and McNab 2009, Gage 1893, Johansen 1982, Johansen Grinde Jr and Mann 1998, Weatherford 1988).

In the first 200 years of contact with the European societies, Native American populations maintained systems that were culturally adapted to maintain the health of their communities. For example, loss of family members and associated grief could be mediated through ceremonies, including adoption. The literature is replete with examples of the adoption of women and children into Native American societies (Axtell 1975). The records on many adoptions include comments on the grief felt by European women and children and African slaves forced to return to their European communities after treaty negotiations. It was clear that some became accustomed to Native American society and felt their needs were met there.

> Captives who returned to write narratives of their experiences left several clues
> to the motives of those who chose to stay behind. They stayed because they
> found Indian life to possess a strong sense of community, abundant love, and
> uncommon integrity—values that the English colonists also honored, if less
> successfully. But Indian life was attractive for other values—for social equality,
> mobility, adventure. (Axtell 1975, 88)

In Europe and early American societies, social institutions were developed
to take care of the needs of communities and their members. Examples include
prisons, jails, schools, brothels, poor houses, "insane" and other asylums,
orphanages, and standing militaries. Such institutions did not exist in traditional
Indigenous communities. Indigenous societies did not develop institutions that
separated groups of people from the rest of the community to the extent European
communities did (Dickason and McNab 2009, Miller 1997, O'Brien 1989).

In contrast to European cultures, Indigenous children were considered important
members of communities. Throughout the Americas, various extended family
networks existed so no child was left without family. The concept of kinship was
so important that many relationship terms were utilized. Even in treaty-making
with the newly arrived Europeans, terms such as "brothers," "grandmother," and
"fathers" were regularly used.

Observers of Indigenous Americans commented on the lack of violence and
coercion directed toward children and women, strategies used to keep control in
the hands of men in European communities. "There are no beggars amongst them,
nor fatherlesse children unprovided for ... Their affections, especially to their
children, are very strong" (Williams 1643, 29).

The emotional and psychological well-being of the community was maintained
through participation in dance and song "therapies," often based on acting out
dreams. Healing reflected therapeutic uses of all the senses so that music, dance,
visual stimulus, olfactory stimulus through smudging, herbal medicines, and talk
therapy were all combined to assist the healing of mind, body, and spirit.

Many traditional ways of helping are now utilized by social workers as clinical
approaches (Baskin 2011, Hart 2001, 2002, Pace and Smith 1990). These forms of
healing were utilized in the Americas long before they became part of the Western
tradition. Methods of physical healing were quickly copied by Europeans as they
learned of the many herbal medicines used in the Americas. Food provision was
also a source of help for starving Europeans as many new agricultural products,
domesticated by Indigenous Peoples, flooded Europe, greatly increasing the life
expectancy and health of the average European (Weatherford 1988).

Many Social Changes

Various diseases not known before colonization caused the death of vast numbers
of Indigenous Peoples. During the first three centuries of European contact,

epidemics led to huge population declines. The exact number of deaths is unknown, but projections range from 40 percent to 90 percent in various communities (Dickason and McNab 2009).

During the 1600s, and first half of the 1700s, there was an active slave trade by several European nations in the eastern half of North America. Wars of colonial expansion led to many Indigenous captives being enslaved. Accurate numbers of Native Americans forced into slavery are unavailable, but during this 150-year period possibly hundreds of thousands became slaves in the Canadian and American colonies. More slaves were sent to Europe, the Caribbean, and Africa, where African slaves were traded for Indian slaves. The Spanish, English, and French were all involved in the slave trade. Although rarely noted, the French in Canada had such an active trade that the term "panis" (pawnee) became a specific term for people enslaved from the Mississippi river area and sold in Quebec (Dickason and McNab 2009). Based on historical records, Gallay (2002) projected between 24,000 and 51,000 Southern Native Americans were enslaved by the British between 1670 and 1715.

Indigenous Peoples across the continent also faced starvation and accompanying physical consequences such as disease and malnutrition. Vast numbers of deer in the eastern woodlands were decimated through over-hunting by Europeans. Thousands of deer skins, and beaver and other pelts were sent to Europe by the time of the American Revolution (Bonvillian 2001). As European Americans spread across the continent in the 1800s, immeasurable herds of American bison were destroyed, initially for commercial purposes, then in a calculated attempt to destroy the economic base of the Plains Indian Peoples (Bonvillian 2001). Likewise, Native American Peoples were removed from coastal and river areas, thus losing their food supply (Bonvillian 2001).

The introduction of alcohol to Indigenous communities north of Mexico happened concurrently with the reduction of land and resources among First Nations Peoples. This introduction had negative physical and social consequences (Duran Duran and Yellow Horse Brave Heart 1998, Thatcher 2004). In the 1700s and 1800s, alcohol was used as an important gift item at treaty negotiations where land transfers were made. Representatives of treaty delegations in both the US and Canada mentioned the importance of alcohol to these negotiations. When people were forced into the restrictive environments of reservations and reserves, the use of alcohol continued as a form of self-medication and addiction due to social disintegration (Dickason and McNab 2009, Thatcher 2004).

From 1800 until the close of the nineteenth century, Native American Peoples in both Canada and the US were forced onto reservations in the US (known as reserves in Canada). This confinement disrupted traditional lifestyles and changed self-supporting communities to communities dependent on services from colonial governments.

In the 1830s, the US Supreme Court interpreted the constitution by ruling that rather than being sovereign, tribes were self-determined, domestic dependent nations (Deloria and Lytle 1984, Prucha 1990). This unique status requires social workers to understand how treaties, court cases, and governmental policies affect Indigenous Peoples in ways distinct from other diverse groups. In exchange for treaty concessions, the federal government accepted a trust responsibility, a promise of education, health care, and supplies (Deloria and Lytle 1984, Jaimes 1992, Shelton 2004). Services provided by the Canadian and US governments during the reservation period included distribution of food and other commodities, provision of education in the form of forced residential schooling, and health services.

There are exceptions to these policies. There are some Native Americans who did not achieve recognition by the Federal Government, as is the case for approximately 30 state-recognized tribes and hundreds of Native American groups petitioning for federal or state recognition. Without recognition, Indigenous groups have no access to Native-specific services, negotiated through treaties.

Indigenous communities have attempted to maintain their own social service systems throughout the past 200 years, despite the imposition of external systems. Social services continue to be adapted and delivered in culturally defined ways. For example, during the first hundred years of the reservation system, commodities distributed by government officials were often redistributed through giveaways organized by community leaders to ensure everyone in the community received a fair share.

Reduction of Traditional Helping and Increase of Western Social Services

For generations, Indigenous Peoples in the US and Canada were controlled through confinement on reservations, banning spiritual ceremonies, and forcing children to attend Christian boarding schools. The goal of these policies was political and economic colonization leading to assimilation (Robbins 1992). Captain Richard Pratt, who started the Indian Boarding School model in the US with adult prisoners of war in Florida, coined the phrase "kill the Indian, save the man" (Davis 2002, Morel 1997). After the US civil war, American Indian children, ages six through sixteen, were required to attend boarding or day school (Jaimes 1992). The experiences of Indigenous children at these schools have been described as cultural genocide, because the schools helped destroy the cultures and life-ways of Indigenous Peoples (Chrisjohn et al. 2003, Manuel and Posluns 1974, Weaver 2005). Students were punished for speaking their languages, practicing their cultures, or conducting ceremonies. They were forced to conform to a military, regimented, Christian lifestyle. By 1887, there were 227 boarding schools in the US operated by the Indian service, with an additional 64 operated mostly by churches (Tyler 1973).

The US and Canadian governments treated Indigenous Peoples as their wards. One of the positions created by the Indian Act (1876) in Canada was the Indian Agent, who was appointed by the government to oversee all First Nations people on reserves. In the US, Indian Agents also had responsibilities to ensure the interests of the US government in treaty negotiations. In Canada, and in many cases in the US, especially by the late 1800s, these government representatives held the roles of judge, police, and surveyor (Dickason and McNab 2009, Prucha 1994).

The US Indian Boarding School model was adopted by Canada through the Indian Act of 1876. The Canadian residential school system forced the three groupings of Canada's Indigenous Peoples, Indian, Métis, and Inuit, to surrender their children from age four through high school (Brant Castellano et al. 1986, MacDonald 2007, RCAP 1996). The damage to Indigenous Peoples has been acknowledged as multigenerational trauma and provides a foundation for many of the issues Indigenous Peoples currently face. Recently, Canadian social workers have come under criticism for utilizing boarding schools as placement agencies for children needing foster care (Blackstock 2009).

Under the Department of War, in the early 1800s, some health services were provided for Indigenous Peoples living near forts. Their care, provided by military physicians, was sporadic. Funding for smallpox vaccinations was passed by the US Congress in 1832. More formalized health services were provided in 1836 to the Ottawa and Chippewa Tribes (IHS 2005). Medical services shifted from military control under the War Department to the Department of Interior in 1849. The first separate appropriation for Indian Health Services was in 1911 (IHS 2005).

Some treaties between the US or Canada and Indigenous Peoples included the provision of medical supplies and the services of physicians. Based on the federal trust doctrine, the Snyder Act of 1921 authorized the Bureau of Indian Affairs to spend federal funds for the education and health care of American Indian people (IHS 2005). The Snyder Act (1921) is described as the "basic authorization for Federal health services to US tribes. It identified the 'relief of distress and conservation of health of Indians' as one of the Federal functions" (IHS 2005, 8). In 1924, as part of the Snyder Act, all American Indians were granted dual citizenship, regardless of where they lived; Indians were citizens of their own nations and also citizens of the US (Deloria and Lytle 1984). Even though they were US citizens, some states still denied American Indian people the right to vote in elections (Bruynell 2004).

The Meriam Report (1928), written by The Institute for Government Research, a private for-profit company, conducted a study of the circumstances of people living on reservations. This report focused on reservation-based needs such as tribal administration, health, and education, including Christian education. This report recommended increased funding, more and better-educated health-care personnel, and clinics on reservations. Senate and House Committee hearings on Indian Affairs provided the background needed to make extensive changes in the 1930s and 1940s (Tyler 1973). This report organized information into one document and provided a template for Indian administration (Tyler 1973).

The Bureau of Indian Affairs developed a career path for social workers. These social workers provided a variety of services to reservation and urban Indian communities. During the Great Depression, President Franklin D. Roosevelt appointed several people with social service backgrounds to help develop the

New Deal. One of these, Harold Ikes, Secretary of the Interior (which included Indian Affairs), was an urban social reform activist from Chicago (Kunitz 1971). Roosevelt also appointed John Collier, who served as Commissioner of Indian Affairs from 1933 to 1945 (Kunitz 1971, Tyler 1973). Collier was a community organizer with the People's Institute in New York City (Fisher 1977, Kunitz 1971).

In his first year as Commissioner, Collier accelerated the transfer of children from boarding schools to day schools in their home communities. He also ended the ban on the practice of American Indian spiritual ceremonies and encouraged the continuation of Indigenous cultures (Tyler 1973). Under Collier's influence, Congress passed the Indian Reorganization Act (The Wheeler-Howard Act, 1934) and reversed the allotment of Indian lands, which Collier identified as destructive for Indigenous Peoples (Prucha 1990). This Act funded economic development and vocational education for Indian children, encouraging a tribal constitution for self-government, and granting incorporation to tribes so that they could manage their own lands. It established the right to form businesses and other organizations, a system of credit, and vocational education (Kunitz 1971, Prucha 1990). This reorganization was intended to reinstate self-determination and local problem-solving by Indigenous Peoples in the US; however, according to Walch (1983) the goal of the Act remained assimilation by changing Indian communities to become more westernized.

Under the New Deal, 489 new positions were added to the Indian Service, all filled by American Indian people (Tyler 1973). The Civilian Conservation Corps, established by President Roosevelt in 1933, included 72 work camps in 15 Western states for American Indians (Tyler 1973). These programs and military service in World War II brought income and training to American Indian communities.

Residential schools in Canada continued to remove Indian children from their communities until 1974, when control was relinquished to the First Nations. Most of the schools were run by religious denominations contracted by the government. Indigenous spiritual and cultural practices were outlawed until the 1950s in Canada, including possible jail sentences for Indian dancing (Dickason and McNab 2009, Frideres and Gadacz 2008). Indigenous Canadians were granted voting rights in 1961; however, women did not gain rights equal to men until the passage of Bill C-31 in 1984, which was extended to more descendants in 2009 (Changes to the Indian Act affecting Indian Registration and Band Membership *McIvor v. Canada* 2009, Dickason and McNab 2009). The Indian Act (1876) established a status system to control benefits from the government. Under the status system, if an Indian man married a non-Indian, she gained Indian status and they could live on the reserve. However, until 1984, an Indian woman marrying a man without Indian status would lose her Indian status and could no longer live on reserve land. Any Aboriginal person might lose status by attending college, working off-reserve, or serving in the military (Dickason and McNab 2009). Many non-status Indian people were forced to urban ghettos.

After the Meriam Report (1928), several inquiries were conducted, including those done by the Hoover Commission (1948) and the American Medical

Association. The findings included elevated infant death rates and infectious diseases resulting in premature death. Based on these reports, public health advisors were assigned to work with Indian Tribes. In 1954, all health functions were transferred to the Surgeon General of the US Public Health Service. Additional studies indicated that the health-care facilities were "marginal at best" (IHS 2005, 8). The Health Services for American Indians Study (1957) recommended a formal federal Indian health program, resources developed in consultation with individual Indigenous communities, and services provided without discrimination. Based on these recommendations, health services, health-care facilities, and prevention programs were improved and private services were added.

During the termination period (1950s and 1960s), mainstream social workers and social programs began to work with the influx of Indigenous Peoples into urban areas. Social workers assisted the relocation by providing counseling and job training for one year after relocation. Adjustment services provided in some areas included assistance shopping in stores, using banks, post offices, child care, health care, food marketing, money management, job skills, basic education, family life, and social skills training (Tyler 1973). In urban centers today, social workers continue to assist American Indians who were forced or voluntarily relocated, and with their descendants.

Social Programs of the 1960s and Beyond

In Canada, during the 1960s, the federal government began to pay provincial social welfare agencies and foster homes to remove Indigenous children from their families. Since poverty was a major feature of most Indian communities due to generations of economic and social neglect, out-of-home placements increased dramatically, with many children going to homes in the US. This period of time, termed the "60s Scoop," is a critically important period for social workers to understand since adoption out and residential school abuse are frequently discussed by Canadian Indigenous clients in the social service system (Blackstock 2009, Blackstock et al. 2006, Sinclair 2007, 2009).

In the United States, termination and relocation helped mobilize American Indian organizations (Deloria and Lytle 1984). The Manpower Development Training Act (1963) was made accessible to American Indians, leading to a total of 89 public works projects on 21 reservations. Between 1950 and 1968, 1,200 industries began to employ 4,000 to 5,000 American Indians. These are the first examples of American Indian people accessing mainstream governmental programs since the New Deal. Community organizing was also active in Canada, inspired by intellectual leaders such as George Manuel, who called Indigenous Peoples worldwide "the Fourth World," to describe them as outside the system of the First, Second, and Third world countries (Manuel and Posluns 1974).

During this time period, the Indian Health Service began to include tribal input to manage health services, increased training, nursing, nutrition, and a healthy environment (IHS 2005). Also, research and development became a goal for the Indian Health Service to increase effectiveness, efficiency, and community participation (IHS 2005).

The American Indian Civil Rights Act (1968) was intended "to further integrate IRA-type [Indian Reorganization Act] governance into the functioning hierarchy itself," creating more governmental control and oversight (Robbins 1992, 102). Throughout the nineteenth and twentieth centuries, many Native Americans had their money held in trust by the Bureau of Indian Affairs (BIA). A 1996 class action lawsuit charging US government mismanagement of trust funds shut down this process. When this case was settled, tribes were awarded $3.4 million dollars, a fraction of what disappeared (Buck 2006, Cobell 2011).

The Self-Determination and Education Assistance Act (1975) offered tribes the choice to assume the control of their own governments and educational services or to continue to allow administration by the BIA (Prucha 1990). Under this Act, the US government supplied some funding for tribal support, training, and transition. The IHS continued to operate and the Indian Health Care Improvement Act (1976) was implemented to improve the health of American Indian people and increase participation in health-centered programs, including a scholarship program, health facilities, sanitation systems for Indian homes, and reimbursement through Medicare and Medicaid (IHS 2005). Tribes were encouraged to take over their own health-care programs and to integrate Western and Indigenous forms of healing (1996 Accountability Report, Bureau of Indian Affairs, Policy, Management and Budget 1996).

For the past half-century, many self-help and native-run sobriety programs have been initiated within communities, often with great success. Many spiritually oriented cultural revival movements spread across the US and Canada and include abstinence from alcohol as a major component. Thatcher (2004) describes culturally based systems within Native communities that offer an alternative to alcohol. These programs may include the use of ceremonies such as the sweat lodge, along with typical approaches such as self-help and residential treatment (Thatcher 2004).

Social workers in the United States experienced a major shift with passage of the Indian Child Welfare Act of 1978. Since jurisdiction over children of federally recognized tribes in the United States was now with their community, government funds were promised to set up reservation-based social work systems for child welfare. In Canada, there was a similar reaction to the "60s Scoop" (Blackstock 2009, Sinclair 2007). Today, social workers in both the United States and Canada need to understand child welfare policies specific to Indigenous children in order to protect the rights of these children, families, and communities.

Provinces have substantial power over Indigenous Peoples in Canada in comparison to states in the US. In 1996, all health and social services for Indigenous Peoples were transferred to the provinces. Therefore, the First Nations in Canada now negotiate with provinces to receive Indigenous-centric child welfare and other social services (Hick 2004, Walmsley 2005).

Urban Indian community centers and other self-help organizations developed in the US during the 1970s and 1980s to provide social services within Native American urban communities. In Canada, a similar movement occurred in the development of Indian Friendship Societies. At first, urban Indian community centers in the US and Friendship Societies in Canada provided social services in these settings through natural helping Indigenous networks. Later, they developed positions for professionally trained social workers.

More recently the Patient Protection and Affordable Care Act (PPACA) reinstated and made permanent the Indian Health Care Improvement Act (IHCIA) which had been allowed to lapse January, 2010 (Heisler and Walke 2010). The PPACA also established direct payments from Medicare, Medicaid, and other third-party insurers. The IHCIA established a national policy to deliver health service with a goal of improving healthcare delivered by the Indian Health Service thus improving the health status of American Indian people (Heisler and Walke 2010).

Native Americans in the Helping Professions

During the 1970s, Indigenous social workers began to publish in mainstream journals such as *Social Work* (Farris and Farris 1976, Good Tracks 1973, Lewis and Ho 1975). The first 20 to 30 years of published content on Indigenous Peoples, in both Canada and the US, focused heavily on child welfare. The issue of Indigenous children taken from their communities has been and continues to be an issue of cultural destruction in the US and Canada (Blackstock 2009, Blackstock et al. 2006, Sinclair 2009). Survival of the community is the ultimate goal of Indigenous Peoples (Wilkinson 1980).

The CSWE-sponsored (Council on Social Work Education) American Indian Task Force Report by Mackey (1973) indicated that there were very few professionally educated Indigenous social workers. During the 1970s, the US government supported the education of a few Indigenous Masters of Social Work (MSWs). Unfortunately, the social work curriculum often does not meet the needs of students who plan to work in Indigenous communities because it remains Eurocentric (Brown et al. 1983, Shaughnessy and Brown 1979, Weaver 1999). There is still much work to be done to include Indigenous knowledge, skills, and values into social work (Tamburro 2010).

In 1980, *Social Casework, The Journal of Contemporary Social Work* devoted an issue to Indigenous concerns. Today, an increasing number of texts and conferences encourage the decolonization of social work and the inclusion of Indigenous world views (Baskin 2011, Graveline 1998, Sinclair et al. 2009, Tamburro 2010, Weaver 2005). An example is the inclusion of content on two-spirit people, which provides a post-colonial perspective of gender. Several Indigenous cultures include the concept that a person may have more than one gender spirit, considered by some to be a special gift with certain ceremonial responsibilities

(Brown 1997, Jacobs et al. 1997). Also, social workers are becoming more aware of the value of Indigenous forms of healing such as sweat lodges, longhouse and smoke house ceremonies, pipe ceremonies, Sundances, Native American Church ceremonies, the Medicine Wheel, and ceremonies at pow-wows and urban centers (Tamburro 2010).

The needs and opportunities for Indigenous social workers continue to increase, but there is still little content in schools of social work devoted to Indigenous issues or Indigenous social work faculty or students (Cross et al. 2009). In Canada, social work content on Aboriginal Peoples is required as part of accreditation. Most schools of social work in Canada have from one to three courses devoted to Indigenous content. At this time in the US, no recognition is given in the CSWE standards for the inclusion of American Indian-specific content in curricula as is Aboriginal content in Canada and Australia (AASW 2010, CASWE 2012).

Recognizing the need to examine Native American issues in social work education, CSWE created a Native American Task Force in 2007 (Cross et al. 2009). A review of 55 textbooks and of CSWE archives identified gaps in the literature (Cross et al. 2009). The Task Force identified the need to increase integration of Native American content in the curriculum (Cross et al. 2009). Research in Canada supports these findings (Tamburro 2010). The Task Force reported that there is a need for social work graduates to understand issues facing the Indigenous Peoples of North America. They recommended all social work students develop knowledge, skills, and values to work effectively with Native Americans. Also, Native American students need additional supports to succeed in high school and higher education, including social work. The need is great, there are groups within social work pressing for more inclusion, but there is a great deal more progress needed in this area.

Conclusion

Initially, the Indigenous Peoples of North America had thriving economies, social support, and healing systems. Colonization brought many problems, including diseases, alcohol, guns, and a worldview that supported the domination and oppression of Indigenous Peoples. These elements, along with wars, loss of land, intentional cultural destruction by colonizers, and loss of self-determination, brought destructive lifestyle changes to the Indigenous Peoples, creating multigenerational trauma. Industrialization, boarding schools, and the systematic removal of Indigenous children from families caused further cultural disruption.

Despite the many social changes, Indigenous North American cultures continue to grow. Indigenous communities and peoples continue to heal. The Seven Generations model takes into account that significant change takes seven generations. It demonstrates that, although change may be hard and slow, it is also achievable. Social work as a profession needs to be a part of this change. We look forward to a time when Indigenous world views and approaches will be more integrated into the North American social system. There is much to gain by adding Indigenous knowledge to our current Eurocentric helping system.

References

1996 Accountability Report, Bureau of Indian Affairs, Policy, Management and Budget 1996. Retrieved from http://www.doi.gov.

AASW 2010. Australian Social Work Education and Accreditation Standards. Retrieved November 10, 2011, from http://www.aasw.asn.au/document/item /100.

Axtell, J. 1975. The White Indians of colonial America. *The William and Mary Quarterly*, 23(1).

Baskin, C. 2011. *Strong Helper's Teachings: The Value of Indigenous Knowledges in the Helping Professions.* Toronto, ON: Canadian Scholars' Press Inc.

Blackstock, C. 2009. The occasional evil of angels: Learning from the experiences of Aboriginal Peoples and social work. *First Nations Child and Family Review*, 4(1), 28–37.

Blackstock, C., Cross, T., George, J., et al. 2006. Reconciliation in child welfare: Touchstones of hope for Indigenous children, youth, and families. Retrieved September 11, 2013, from http://www.cecw-cepb.ca/publications/640.

Bonvillian, N. 2001. *Native Nations: Cultures and Histories of Native North America.* Upper Saddle River, NJ: Prentice Hall.

Brant Castellano, M., Stalwick, H., and Wien, F. 1986. Native social work education in Canada: Issues and adaptations. *Canadian Social Work Review*, 4, 166–84.

Brown, E.F., Lewis, R.G., Compton, J., and Mackey, J.E. 1983. American Indian content in social work curricula: A challenge for the 1980s. In *Mental Health and People of Color: Curriculum Development and Change*, J.C.I. Chun, P.J. Dunston and F. Ross-Sheriff (eds). Washington, DC: Howard University Press, 157–76.

Brown, L.B. 1997. Women and men, not-men and not-women, lesbians and gays: American Indian gender style alternatives. In *Two-Spirit People: American Indian Lesbian Women and Gay Men*, L.B. Brown (ed.). Binghamton, NY: Haworth Press, 5–20.

Bruynell, K. 2004. Challenging American boundaries: Indigenous people and the "gift" of citizenship. *Studies in American Political Development*, 18(1), 30–43.

Buck, C. 2006. "Never again": Kevin Gover's apology to the Bureau of Indian Affairs. *Wicazo Sa Review*, 21(1), 97–126.

CASWE 2012. CASWE-ACFTS Accreditation Standards. Retrieved May 29, 2012, from http://www.caswe-acfts.ca.

Changes to the Indian Act affecting Indian Registration and Band Membership *McIvor v. Canada* 2009. Retrieved September 11, 2013, from http://www.ainc-inac.gc.ca/br/is/smm-eng.asp.

Chrisjohn, R., Wasacase, T., Nussey, L., et al. 2003. Genocide and Indian residential schooling: The past and present. In *Canada and International Humanitarian Law: Peacekeeping and War Crimes in the Modern Era*, R.D. Wiggers and A.L. Griffiths (eds). Halifax, NS: Dalhousie University Press.

Cobell, E. 2011. Cobell case wins final approval in major victory for Native Americans. *Indian Country Today*. Retrieved September 11, 2013, from http://ndnnews.com/2011/06/cobell-case-wins-final-approval-in-major-victory-for-native-americans/.

Cross, S.L., Brown, E.F., Day, P., et al. 2009. *Task Force on Native Americans in Social Work Education: Status of Native Americans in Social Work Higher Education*. Washington, DC: Council on Social Work Education, 44.

Davis, S.L. 2002. Captain Richard Henry Pratt, Founder of the Carlisle School for Indian Students. *Buffalosoldier*. Retrieved September 11, 2013, from http://www.buffalosoldier.net/CaptainRichardH.Pratt.htm.

Deloria, V., Jr. and Lytle, C. 1984. *The Nations Within: The Past and Future of American Indian Sovereignty*. New York: Pantheon Books.

Dickason, O.P. and McNab, D.T. 2009. *Canada's First Nations: A History of Founding Peoples from Earliest Times*. Don Mills, ON: Oxford University Press.

Duran, B., Duran, E., and Yellow Horse Brave Heart, M. 1998. Native Americans and the trauma of history. In *First Nations Education in Canada: The Circle Enfolds*, M. Battiste and J. Barman (eds). Vancouver: UBC Press, 60–76.

Farris, C.E. and Farris, L.S. 1976. Indian children: The struggle for survival. *Social Work*, 21(5), 386.

Fisher, R. 1977. Community organizing and citizen participation: The efforts of the People's Institute in New York City, 1910–1920. *Social Service Review*, 51(3), 474–90.

Frideres, J. and Gadacz, R. 2008. *Aboriginal Peoples in Canada*. Toronto: Pearson Prentice Hall.

Gage, M.J. 1893. Women, church and state: A historical account of the status of women through the Christian ages: With reminiscences of the Matriarchate. Retrieved from http://archive.org/details/womanchurchstate00gagerich, 544.

Gallay, A. 2002. *The Indian Slave Trade: The Rise of the English Empire in the American South, 1670–1717*. New Haven, CT: Yale University Press.

Good Tracks, J.G. 1973. Native American non-interference. *Social Work*, 19, 30–35.

Graveline, F.J. 1998. *Circle Works: Transforming Eurocentric Consciousness*. Winnipeg, MB: Fernwood Publishing.

Hart, M.A. 2001. An Aboriginal approach to social work practice. In *Social Work Practice: Problem Solving and Beyond*, T. Heinonen and L. Spearman (eds). Toronto: Irwin, 231–56.

Hart, M.A. 2002. *Seeking Mino-pimatisiwin: An Aboriginal Approach to Helping*. Halifax, NS: Fernwood Publishing.

Heisler, E.J. and Walke, R. 2010. Indian Health Care Improvement Act provisions in the Patient Protection and Affordable Care Act (P.L. 111-148). Congressional Research Service.

Hick, S.H. 2004. *Social Welfare in Canada*. Toronto, ON: Thompson Educational Publishing.

IHS 2005. The first 50 years of Indian Health Service: Caring and curing. Retrieved from http://www.ihs.gov.

Jacobs, S., Thomas, W., and Lang, S. (eds). 1997. *Two-Spirit People: Native American Gender Identity, Sexuality, and Spirituality*. Chicago: University of Illinois Press.

Jaimes, M.A. (ed.). 1992. *The State of Native America: Genocide, Colonization, and Resistance*. Boston, MA: South End Press.

Johansen, B.E. 1982. Forgotten Founders: Benjamin Franklin, the Iroquois. Retrieved September 11, 2013, from http://www.ratical.org/many_worlds/6 Nations/FFintro.html.

Johansen, B.E., Grinde Jr., D.A., and Mann, B.A. 1998. *Debating Democracy, Native American Legacy of Freedom*. Santa Fe, NM: Clear Light Publishers.

Kunitz, S.J. 1971. The social philosophy of John Collier. *Ethnohistory*, 18(3), 213.

Lewis, R. and Ho, M.K. 1975. Social work with Native Americans. *Social Work*, 20(5), 379–82.

MacDonald, D. 2007. First Nations, residential schools, and the Americanization of the Holocaust: Rewriting Indigenous history in the United States and Canada. *Canadian Journal of Political Science*, 40(4), 995–1015.

Mackey, J.E. 1973. American Indian Task Force Report. New York: Council on Social Work Education.

Manuel, G. and Posluns, M. 1974. *The Fourth World: An Indian Reality*. Don Mills, ON: Collier Macmillan Canada Ltd.

Miller, J.R. 1997. *Shingwauk's Vision: A History of Native Residential Schools*. Toronto, ON: University of Toronto Press.

Morel, M.K. 1997. Captain Pratt's school. *American History*, 32(2), 26–36.

O'Brien, S. 1989. *American Indian Tribal Governments*. The Civilization of the American Indian Series. Norman, OK: University of Oklahoma Press.

Pace, J.M., and Smith, A.F.V. 1990. Native social work education: Struggling to meet the need. *Canadian Social Work Review*, 7(1), 109–119.

Prucha, F.P. 1994. *American Indian Treaties: A History of Political Anomaly*. Los Angeles: University of California Press.

Prucha, F.P. (ed.). 1990. *Documents of United States Indian Policy* (2nd edition). Lincoln, NE: University of Nebraska Press.

RCAP 1996. Royal Commission on Aboriginal Peoples of 1996. Ottawa: Government of Canada, Indian and Northern Affairs.

Robbins, R. 1992. Self-determination and subordination: The past, present, and future of American Indian governance. In *The State of Native America: Genocide, Colonization, and Resistance*, M.A. Jaimes (ed.). Boston, MA: South End Press.

Shaughnessy, T. and Brown, E.F. 1979. Developing Indian content in social work education: A community-based model. In *Multicultural Education and the American Indian*, J.R. Young (ed.). Los Angeles, CA: UCLA American Indian Studies Center, 157–70.

Shelton, B.L. 2004. Legal and historical roots of health care for American Indians and Alaska Natives in the United States (Vol. February): The Henry J. Kaiser Family Foundation.

Sinclair, R. 2007. Identity lost and found: Lessons from the sixties scoop. *First Peoples Child and Family Review: A Journal on Innovation and Best Practices in Aboriginal Child Welfare, Administration, Research, Policy & Practice*, 3(1), 65–82.

Sinclair, R. 2009. Identity or racism: Aboriginal transracial adoption. In *Wicihitowin: Aboriginal Social Work in Canada*, R. Sinclair, M.A. Hart, and G. Bruyere (eds). Winnipeg: Fernwood Publishing, 89–112.

Sinclair, R., Hart, M.A., and Bruyere, G. (eds). 2009. *Wicihitowin: Aboriginal Social Work in Canada*. Winnipeg: Fernwood Publishing.

Tamburro, A. 2010. *A Framework and Tool for Assessing Indigenous Content in Canadian Social Work Curricula*. Education Doctorate, Simon Fraser University, Surrey, BC. Retrieved September 11, 2013, from https://theses.lib.sfu.ca/thesis/etd6119.

Thatcher, R.W. 2004. *Fighting Firewater Fictions: Moving Beyond the Disease Model of Alcoholism in First Nations*. Toronto: University of Toronto Press.

Tyler, S.L. 1973. *A History of Indian Policy*. Washington DC: US Bureau of Indian Affairs, Department of Interior, 342.

Walch, M.C. 1983. Terminating the Indian Termination Policy. *Stanford Law Review*, 35(6), 1181–215.

Walmsley, C. 2005. *Protecting Aboriginal Children*. Vancouver: University of British Columbia Press.

Weatherford, J. 1988. *Indian Givers: How the Indians of the Americas Transformed the World*. New York, NY: Crown Publishers.

Weaver, H. 1999. Indigenous people and the social work profession: Defining culturally competent services. *Social Work*, 44(3), 217–25.

Weaver, H. 2005. *Explorations in Cultural Competence: Journeys to the Four Directions*. Toronto, ON: Nelson.

Wilkinson, G.T. 1980. On Assisting Indian People. *Social Casework*, 61(8), 451–4.

Williams, R. 1643. *A key into the language of America: or, An help to the language of the natives in that part of America, called New-England: Together, with briefe observations of the customes, manners and worships, &c. of the aforesaid natives, in peace and warre, in life and death. On all which are added spirituall observations, generall and particular by the authour, of chiefe and speciall use (upon all occasions,) to all the English inhabiting those parts; yet pleasant and profitable to the view of all men*. London: Printed by Gregory Dexter.

Chapter 4

A Standpoint View of the Social Work Profession and Indigenous Peoples in the United States: From the Profession's Origins through its First Century

Robert E. "Bob" Prue

This chapter addresses social work's philosophy towards Indigenous Peoples over its development as a profession. Primary sources for this essay were limited to the computer searchable archives of the Proceedings of the National Conference on Charities and Corrections, later called the National Conference on Social Welfare (NCCC/SW) for the years 1874 to 1982, maintained by the University of Michigan (2002). The NCCC/NCSW archives were searched using three keywords: American Indian, Indian, and Native American. The frequency of reference to those terms is sufficiently small that each instance is represented here. The understanding of social work's thinking and activities with Indigenous Peoples from the 1980s until the present were obtained from two sources: one, a Council on Social Work Education publication titled *Social Work with the First Nations: A Comprehensive Bibliography with Annotations* (White 2001), and the other Social Work Abstracts (EBSCOhost 2009, SilverPlatter Information 2000). Social Work Abstracts was searched using the phrases "Indian," "American Indian" or "Native American" or "First Nations" or "Indigenous." That search returned 453 citations. These sources were used to explore social work's thought and actions regarding the well-being of Indigenous Peoples through current times. Standpoint theory is used to examine three distinct historical phases of the profession and examine the relationship of well-being to control of social and health services.

Standpoint Theory

Standpoint theory is especially suited to analyzing power inequities between classes of people. Standpoint theory states that a group's social, historical, and cultural position is a generator of knowledge. This stands in contrast to the classic sociological approach of dispassionate and removed observations, collectively agreed upon by a jury of "peers." As Dubois pointed out, the Academy of Peers is represented primarily by one standpoint and has been one mechanism by which cultural oppression has been systematic, excluding the voices and contributions of minority groups in the history of a whole society (Allan 2005). Standpoint is not only an idea by which people can understand a grouping of experiences shared by a class of people, it can be used to advance social change as a "technical theoretical device that can allow for the creation of better (more objective, more libratory) accounts of the world" (Hartsock 1998, 236).

This paper assumes that the most accurate and complete knowledge of a social situation or condition is vital for social work interventions to be maximally effective. Not only having differing perspectives, the oppressed and oppressor groups often have opposing understandings of the world.

> The dominant group's view will be partial and more superficial. It is in the dominant group's interest to maintain, reinforce, and legitimate this dominance and understanding of the world, regardless of how incomplete it may be … In contrast, the perspective from subordinate groups' life has the potential to be more complete. Marginalized populations have fewer interests in maintaining ignorance about how the social order actually works and fewer reasons to invest in maintaining or justifying the status quo than do the dominate groups. (Swigonski 1994, 391)

Rather than striving for a single objective "truth" about human existence, standpoint theory assumes classes of people differ and sometimes conflict in their understandings. For example, many conceive Indigenous Peoples as a singular group, when in fact they are diverse. They consist of thousands of family/clan-centric geopolitical groups, each with their own histories and relationships both with each other and with colonizing forces. Similarly, the colonizer is not a monolithic entity; it is Latin, Anglo, Catholic, Protestant, capitalist. Common themes do unify the two broad groups, colonized and colonizer, into separate and identifiable standpoints. One is the common experience of oppression and marginalization of Indigenous Peoples and the other a legacy of privilege for the oppressor. Indigenous Peoples have a shared experience sufficiently similar "to have the possibility of coming to understand their situations in ways that can empower their oppositional movements" (Hartsock 1998, 241). For an investigation that traverses the grounds of colonization and genocide, a method developed with conflict and oppression in mind is critical. While most social workers, both now and then, might not think themselves in conflict with Indigenous Peoples, a lack of understanding of the perspectives of Indigenous Peoples has unleashed the best of intentions to unwitting destructive ends.

Finally, social work as a profession itself is not a single entity. This was particularly true during its formative years. The Conference on Charities and Corrections had representatives from a wide variety of vocations and institutions including ministers, prison officials, government officials, and social activists. The Flexner report of 1915 confirms a lack of a unified professional theory (Austin 1983). Only in the 1950s did a more unified voice begin to crystallize. Two organizations emerged with the primary responsibility of defining and advancing social work practice and education. The National Association of Social Workers formed out of a "merger of the American Association of Social Workers and other practice specialty organizations in an effort to create a unified voice for social work" (Mizrahi and Davis 2008, 329), whereas the Council on Social Work Education (2012) formed from groups responsible for the advancement of social work education.

The Conference of Charities and Corrections in Context

Since there was not an organized profession providing ethical guidance, the standpoint of those addressing the Conference reflects the orientation of the vocations represented: soldiers, ministers, academics, and social reformers. Information about Indigenous Peoples came to the fledgling profession in the form of reports from the field by military and other US government agents, missionaries, and anthropologists. Each of these sources has its own standpoint biases regarding the best interests of Indigenous Peoples. The military had charge to first subdue and then contain Indigenous Peoples. Missionaries were loyal first to Churches, who were intent on converting Indigenous Peoples to Christianity. Missionaries colluded with the US Federal government's effort to destroy Indigenous culture by compulsory boarding school attendance. Early anthropologists were not only government agents, sent to document the "vanishing races," but were also members of "the dominant social class traveling into an environment to study the 'primitives' in their 'native environments' … 'cultured' peoples go[ing] 'into the field' to study indigenous people from another country presupposes that the people are 'primitive' and in some sense lesser than the dominant social class [inside quotes in the original]" (Singer 2003, 4).

Setting the parameters for this critique of social work's performance regarding the Indigenous Peoples can be overly simplistic: using either/or thinking—the Indigenous standpoint and the Euro-American standpoint. However, in reality it is much more complex, and overlapping at times. The Indigenous standpoint included the voices of tribal leaders, others in government service, and Christian Indians. The Euro-American view has primarily Christian and secular sub-divisions, with the secular including government, academic, and professional standpoints.

Social Welfare's First Notice: The 1887 and 1892 Conferences

The National Conference first focused its attention on Indigenous Peoples in 1887, along with other groups of color. A committee on Indian policy was developed, which delivered its first report in 1892. Two groups of European Americans articulated the earliest attention to the needs of Indigenous Peoples. The Christian missionary acted out of religious obligation to convert, but colluded with government forces to disenfranchise any group that remained non-Christian. "[I]t would of course be competent for a Christian nation, through its fundamental law, to exclude entirely from the benefits of immigration and citizenship all heathen people" (University of Michigan 2002, 163). A secular voice, primarily of US government operatives enforcing federal policy, included many who had been part of the war against and occupation of tribal peoples. The government standpoint also contains a decided Christian bias, whether from a former military man rationalizing slavery and genocide as good fortune for Africans and Indians, by giving them the opportunity for US citizenship and a Christian life—"inscrutable are the ways of Providence" (University of Michigan 2002, 50)—or of a social worker justifying the Indian Allotment Act: "you will see, therefore, that you cannot civilize the Indian—that is you cannot bring him into line with our civilization—you cannot Christianize him, until you have run this furrow right across the tribal circle" (University of Michigan 2002, 178).

Fundamental to standpoint theory is how control of subordinate voices and activities supports the status quo, which privileges the dominate group. The lone and indirect voice of an Indigenous person is quoted at the conference. That voice clearly served the purpose of the Christian minister reporting and reflected the Western bias in its choice: "I stood among the Choctaws a few days ago, and heard an Indian, well dressed, well educated, with a perfect command of the English language, make a plea in behalf of his race; and his argument [was] for Christian education for his people" (University of Michigan 2002, 184).

Regardless of source, every presenter's standpoint included a clear Euro-centric bias and a belief in race superiority. The glaring issue of mistreatment of the Indigenous Peoples and Africans was glossed over because "there was originally sufficient reason for this in the fact that they were untutored savages" (University of Michigan 2002, 163). Additionally, the welfare of people of color was not seen as an opportunity to right past injustice or be good Americans and Christians, but appears to be more of a grudging national duty, "as both belong to races intellectually inferior, undeveloped, and uncivilized, the United States owe it to themselves and to them—having, at the outset of the government, declared all men free and equal" (University of Michigan 2002, 163–4).

Though in the minority, dissenting opinions from whites regarding the treatment of Indigenous Peoples are found in these early discussions. The immorality of the differential treatment of Indians, Africans, and European immigrants was not lost to some of the conference, the "cordiality with which America has welcomed the oppressed of every land ... hardly extends to the aborigines on their own soil, nor to the Africans whom we dragged in chains and slavery from their native land" (University of Michigan 2002, 163). Philip C. Garrett, who chaired the first Special Committee on Indians in 1892, was critical of US policy, stating: "[I]t might even be instructive, in our assumed superiority, to consider the policy *of the Indians*" (University of Michigan 2002, 23, italics in original). Garrett could have been a standpointist, recognizing that Indigenous Peoples would develop policy to better meet their own needs and that the outsiders' position had only developed a "policy towards the Indians [that] is hostile, unjust and lacking in humanity" (University of Michigan 2002, 23). He highlighted the inconsistency in US thinking: "we praise patriotism, and then we recognize the Indian tribes as separate nationalities, and abuse and destroy them because they defend their customs and hunting grounds" (25). That same year, William F. Slocum, President of Colorado College, advocated for individualized education for Indians based on their circumstances, capacities, and interests. He also cautioned the conference to not "transform them into Anglo-Saxon or Puritan Christians ... but remember that they are Indian, and should preserve those national peculiarities and ideas which have always attracted the interest and admiration of all" (University of Michigan 2002, 72).

The Blindness Caused by Power

One tenet of standpoint theory is that privilege blinds advantaged groups, enabling them to be openly inconsistent. During the 1892 reports to the National Conference regarding the needs of Indigenous Peoples, there are numerous instances where participants state a point then contradict their contentions. Regarding Indian lands and title: "We have recognized the Indian's right of occupancy [followed shortly by] the Indian does not legally own his land" (1887, 175). At other times the truth loses out to political expediency. Ethnologist Alice Cunningham Fletcher described the Indian as "thoroughly organized in his life, in his tribal relations" (1887, 175), then in detail describes structured agricultural, social, and ceremonial life. Fletcher does an abrupt about face, advocating for destruction of the tribal system. Fletcher was a close associate of Senator Henry Dawes and a chief architect of the Dawes Act (Mark 1988), an Act responsible for the dispossession of most lands that Indians still held (Greenwald 2002). Fletcher describes social systems within the Seneca and Omaha peoples that are simultaneously collectivist, while supporting individual land stewardship. Understanding the Indigenous Peoples' conceptions of land ownership or stewardship is important in understanding the motivations of whites in promulgating legislation related to the dispossession of Indian lands.

Captain R.H. Pratt (commandant of the Carlisle Training School for Indians), in a moment of honesty, describes for the conference the brutal reality of military subjugation, the open land deceptions, and the hatred demonstrated by whites (University of Michigan 2002, 46–50). He recognized "because of our savage example and treatment of them" (51–2), Indigenous Peoples "have no notion of joining us and becoming a part of the United States" (54). Instead of understanding their plight, Pratt demonizes, claiming Indigenous Peoples' "whole disposition is to prey upon and hatch up claims against the government" (54). Even the supportive Special Committee Chair on Indians, Phillip C. Garrett, has his moments of obvious blindness. "But what, again, is the use of teaching them history, and illustrating thereby the value of republican government, if they are immediately placed under the autocratic rule of the agent," "better to scatter young Indians among industrious whites, effacing, if need be, their Indian identity forever" (University of Michigan 2002, 28). Garrett presents his point as the lesser of two evils, which allows him both the standpoint of the moral high ground, while acting with indifference.

The Oppressed as Oppressor

Both clarity and distortion of vision can occur within an individual when standpoints of race and gender collide (McIntosh 1998). Alice Fletcher, a social reformer who clearly grasped the misogynistic attitudes of her male mentors, failed to fully grasp her own Euro-centrism. Ms Fletcher, who persevered despite her male mentors' belief that an ethnographic investigation in Indian Country was beyond the capabilities of a woman, uses this experience to understand that "the most I did know was that we had behaved badly to the Indians, and it was from the Indian side that I faced my race and met the Indian question. It was not a pleasant thing to do. I have often said that I learned more of my own race than of the Indian race" (University of Michigan 2002, 179). Fletcher failed to grasp the standpoint of Indigenous Peoples, evidenced by her support of the Dawes Act, during a time when tribal nations opposed it. "Fletcher's allotment and other benevolent works have been regarded as a grievous error in the administration of Native American lands and peoples" (Smithsonian Institution 2003). This damage by a well-meaning helper cannot be over-emphasized.

1893–1927: A Time of Little Interest

Hastings H. Hart, President of the National Conference, recognized the unique political relationship of Indigenous Peoples with the Federal government. He claimed, "there is a special propriety in the discussion of the Indian question by the National Conference of Charities and Correction for the reason that the Indians are the wards of the general government, and not of any State or local organization" (University of Michigan 2002, 27). There was little impact on the Conference's actions.

In the years from 1893 to 1927 the National Conference rarely mentions Indigenous Peoples. The delegate from Indian Territory/State of Oklahoma mentioned that the Five Civilized Tribes were operating their own orphanages and schools. During this time, efforts were being put forward by members of the conference to both diminish and support the rights of Indigenous Peoples. Rev. W.B. Sherrard of South Dakota reported on the efforts to "encode into policy a means to more easily terminate parental rights of Indians once children have been removed" (1896, 57). Herbert Walsh of the Indian Rights Association reported on efforts through legal and policy reform (primarily in the Indian Service) to prevent the loss of additional Indian lands and property to whites (1896, 394). There was one call for action to investigate federal jails in Indian Country (University of Michigan 2002, 240). Several times Indians were mentioned in stereotypical and derogatory ways (1900, 451; 1903, 240), but Indigenous Peoples also received positive mention for their method of redistribution of wealth. Northwestern Indians were admired as a model of how to distribute goods while controlling individual greediness (1905, 469–70). In a broader discussion of racism, the discussion shifted from cultural incompatibility to economic exploitation as causative factors (1922, 102).

Standpoint Theory: Who Controls the Story?

Central to standpoint theory is the ability of the oppressor group to recast events into terms more favorable to the status quo. One brief anecdote shines a light on the ease with which a dominant group is able to discount the standpoint of subjugated people. The story was of Indigenous prisoners sent back to their reservations because of predicted imminent death from tuberculosis. Later, when visiting the reservation, "the officer found them to be alive. When asked if they were the ones who had been sent home to die, 'Yes,' was the reply, 'but our medicine man is greater than yours. He cured us. We are all well.' And so it was found to be. The sunlight and breath of the pines, the freedom and the life in the open had wrought this miracle. They were cured" (University of Michigan 2002, 153). When given a direct report about an Indigenous person's situation, it was completely discounted. It must have been the *miracle* of sunlight and free living, rather than the skilled medicine man, that effected the cure. The truth of whether the healing had been wrought by sunshine or a medicine man is secondary to the disregard for the experience reported by the person who lived it.

1927–1935: Social Welfare Again Takes Notice

The 1927 Proceedings contain the first conference-level report of a field social worker informing the national membership of a direct practice activity with Indigenous Peoples. Henrietta J. Lund reported on casework on the Blackfoot Reservation (341). Her report of activities includes family-centered concepts, such as friendly visiting and training mothers: "The keynote of the family work which we had endeavored to undertake: helping them to help themselves" (University of Michigan 2002, 342). Her report also includes an emphasis on community building activities, such as partnering with local leadership: "[T]he development of forces of leadership in the field of social service work on the reservation has been one of the first problems to be encountered" (University of Michigan 2002, 342). In fact, she credits success in accomplishing more than just direct relief with "gaining the confidence and understanding of this little group" (University of Michigan

2002, 341) and collaborating with Indigenous leadership. Ms Lund illustrates the leader's grasp of social welfare principles, stating that Blackfoot leader Long Time Asleep provided her with "a discourse on the theory and practice of case work that one seldom hears expounded from more learned lips" (University of Michigan 2002, 342). She also reports Long Time Asleep emphasized the importance of working with the strengths of the community and culture, "the need of a better understanding of the instinctive life and native equipment of [my] people and the essential elements lacking in their environment [and] the value of bringing out local leadership and of sharing responsibility were emphasized" (University of Michigan 2002, 342). Rather than blaming inherent incapacity or cultural deficits of the Blackfoot People, Ms Lund normalizes the conditions across cultures and ascribes causality to economic conditions, "as far as the problems [on Blackfoot Reservation] are concerned, they are practically the same there as elsewhere" and stem out of the effects of "dire poverty" (University of Michigan 2002, 342).

The standpoint of the US at this time was of European racial and cultural superiority. The National Conference reflected these ideas and supported social policies aimed at denying equal treatment of Indigenous Peoples because of "serious questions of racial capacity" (University of Michigan 2002, 552). There also existed countervailing white voices. Lewis Meriam, Director of Survey of Indian Affairs, discounted the notion that whites were superior to Indians. Stating, while "modern psychological tests seem to indicate that the whites have a somewhat superior intelligence, [that] possibly the tests tend to favor the whites. The almost universal testimony of persons who have worked with Indians and who have known them well is that they have plenty of intelligence for working purposes" (University of Michigan 2002, 549).

Meriam called for social workers to "demand that the government shall recognize in full its obligations towards its Indian wards, that it will furnish them with a social service abreast of the best rendered any people" (University of Michigan 2002, 548), and that "full consideration should be given to the wishes of Indians" (University of Michigan 2002, 553–4). Meriam recommended reversal of the policy of forced acculturation into Western-styled civilization, stating that there was no good reason not to support the desires of tribes such as "the Rio Grande Pueblos [who] do not want to be absorbed. For more than four hundred years they have been in contact with the whites and yet they retain much of their distinctive culture, modified to be sure, but none the less treasured and revered. It would be a great mistake to attempt to force them into a new channel" (554). The Meriam report not only advocates a strong message to steer a different course in Indian policy, it also demonstrated social work's power to influence public policy: "the Meriam report has resulted in increases in appropriations" (University of Michigan 2002, 632) for social services for Indigenous Peoples. This period of social welfare history sees the beginning of a standpoint consensus between Indigenous Peoples and the majority regarding the needs of Indigenous Peoples, at least around the issues of local control, partnering with local leadership, and supporting local ways of doing things as important components of what is in the best interests of Indigenous Peoples.

Indigenous Peoples Address the Conference

The years 1927 to 1933 saw members of Indigenous Nations stating their opinions on what was happening in their jurisdictions and what was needed for their peoples. With Indigenous Peoples, standpoint theory must also be understood within the context of colonization. On one hand, the cooptation of Indigenous Peoples for the purpose of representing those people to the mainstream is a common tactic of colonizers (Churchill 1992). On the other, the prominent Oglala spiritual leader Black Elk was purported to have consciously embraced elements of Western and Catholic culture as part of an overall survival strategy for his people (Hollar 1995). It is, therefore, important to understand who these Indigenous Peoples presenting to the National Proceedings were by what they were presenting, perhaps over whom they were representing.

With the exception of Chief Ben Dwight, these Indigenous Peoples were not political leaders in their communities, but in some cases were representatives of the US Government or of Christian denominations: groups that had long held goals of changing or eliminating Indigenous Peoples, cultures, and beliefs. All were evidently college educated. Winnebago scholar Henry Roe Cloud (University of Michigan, 2002), who earned two bachelor-level degrees (psychology and philosophy) and a Master's degree in Anthropology from Yale (Tetzloff 2003), spoke; as did W. David Owl (University of Michigan 2002) of the Baptist and Presbyterian Indian Churches, of the Cattaraugus Reservation. In 1931 both Ruth Muskrat Bronson, a Cherokee employed by the Indian Services, and Ben Dwight, the Principal Chief of the Choctaw Nation, "a Columbia man, with advanced training at Stanford" spoke (University of Michigan 2002, 622).

Standpoints: Indigenous and Mainstream

As diverse as this group is in vocation and background, they express several clear themes regarding the needs of Indigenous Peoples. They derided the need for continued ward status for Indigenous People, which prevented individuals and groups from acting in their own best interests in financial and legal matters. Roe Cloud was clear that "the ward status of Indians have left them worse off" (University of Michigan 2002, 562). Muskrat Bronson said ward status caused "genuine harm" (University of Michigan 2002, 638). Owl described the Iroquois as "weary of the thoroughly paternalistic method of dealing with his race" (University of Michigan 2002, 625) which caused failures in social policy and program.

They have not been permitted to make their own decisions in matters which mean substantial progress in the affairs of life. Schools have been planted among them, hospitals are established for their benefit, decisions are handed down to them, all these frequently without their consent or without any willingness on their part to support them. (University of Michigan 2002, 625–6)

Working with the strengths and aspirations of Indigenous Peoples, as groups and individuals, was another clear theme. Discussing economic self-sufficiency of his Nation, Chief Dwight thought it wise for his people to pursue farming and fruit production "since the Choctaw nation is [in] an agricultural section [of the country] and the Choctaw people are primarily agriculturists, it is paramount that the farming industry be used as the cornerstone for the reconstruction program" (University of Michigan 2002, 679–80). Questioning the rationale for the wholesale abandonment of the agricultural training and supports, Roe Cloud cited successful Indian Service farming programs among the Pima, Hopi, and Pueblo, who had long ago "mastered the art of dry farming and irrigation" (University of Michigan 2002, 561).

The Indigenous speakers cited poverty and oppression, not their cultures, as the source of their problems. According to Muskrat Bronson, "there is nothing especially Indian in most of our problems; in our delinquencies; our illegitimate babies; our mental deficiencies. They are just human problems that all groups everywhere have to face, and our great objective for the Indian must be exactly the same as it is in all social work for all other groups—to make him self-sustaining and independent, emotionally, economically, and socially" (University of Michigan 2002, 641). Chief Dwight indicated that the health problems of the Choctaws were not specifically Indian, but related to poverty (University of Michigan 2002, 680–81). By the 1930s, social work had substantially embraced psychoanalytic theory, which emphasized character flaws and individual failure. These early Indigenous social leaders are clearly attempting to steer social work away from that path, at least as it concerns race and culture.

The mainstream social welfare standpoint also articulated the importance of local Indigenous control. Julia Lathrop cited the need to have an Indian presence in field research into Indian needs, not only for the purpose of "opening doors" to Indigenous communities, but also as "a guarantee of good faith of the survey" (University of Michigan 2002, 642). The lack of local control had not only caused failure to buy into schemes to help Indigenous Peoples, but also contributed to the failure to reassume local control. May Louise Mark, Professor of Sociology, had strong words concerning continued ward status: "In denying the Indians a chance to decide their own affairs, haven't we denied them a chance to develop? Haven't we cheated them out of their normal growth? … we blame them for lacking ambition; yet we insist on planning their lives. It is sheer foolishness for us to expect to find economic incentive under such circumstances" (University of Michigan 2002, 617). Participants continued reiterating the importance of local control regarding child welfare (University of Michigan 2002, 617), public health

(University of Michigan 2002, 628), and general social services (University of Michigan 2002, 589). The Conference also recognized the limited progress the profession had made with Indigenous Peoples. However, "for various reasons, the organized social work movement has had little opportunity to play a part in the government's service to Indians" (University of Michigan 2002, 602). "Social work as a movement has not penetrated the areas where Indians live ... has been little interested or has had limited opportunity to demonstrate its usefulness to the Indian field" (University of Michigan 2002, 609).

1960s to 1980s: Indigenous Social Workers Demand their Own Voice

From the mid 1930s until the late 1960s, the profession paid little attention to Indigenous Peoples. While understandable during World War II, this was inexcusable during the post-war period, when not only was forced boarding school education continued, but new assimilationist schemes of coercive relocation from reservations and attempts to terminate treaty responsibility were implemented by the US Federal government.

What brought Indigenous Peoples back into the focus of the National Conference was Indigenous people themselves. This period saw Indigenous social workers insisting their voice be heard. During the 1969 conference, "disruptions were planned by a variety of protest groups, [including one led] by Chief Thunderhawk from North Dakota, representing the American Indians" who described the plight of Indigenous Peoples as being due to "the war perpetrated on the American Indians by the Bureau of Indians Affairs" (University of Michigan 2002, 189). The conference responded by placing a panel of Indigenous social workers on the agenda in 1972, headed by Evelyn Blanchard, Indian Health Services social worker. This panel outlined a vision of social work with Indigenous Peoples that provides a link from the thinking of Indigenous social leaders of the 1930s to the kind of thought found in the present. Like their predecessors in the 1930s, this panel denied that the social problems of Indigenous Peoples were due to culture. Central to their statement of causes of social problems were the effects of colonization and oppression. "The fibers that held us together have been systematically attacked and many have broken. We see as our responsibility the task of catching these loose fibers, tying them together, and supporting those which have remained intact" (Proceeding 1972, 266). In that statement of causation they also state the nature of the work to be accomplished: supporting existing strengths and rebuilding communities. Addressing the non-Indigenous social work role in Indigenous communities, the panel implored those interested in working with Indigenous Peoples to "step out of [the] protected role of social worker [and] be encountered as a human being" (University of Michigan 2002, 277).

1980s to Present: Indigenous Social Welfare Thinking

The National Association of Social Workers has taken an unambiguous standpoint of the value of culture. The profession's *Code of Ethics* states that "social workers should understand culture and its function in human behavior and society, recognizing the strengths that exist in all cultures" (NASW 1999, 9). That understanding of culture and its function in Indigenous human behavior and societies has been moving away from concepts such as teaching bicultural competence to Indigenous Peoples as a mechanism to cope with an oppressive society (LaFramboise and Rowe 1983). Contemporary writers focus on the need for social workers to become culturally competent (Weaver 1997a, McDiarmid 1983, Weaver 1999) and to understand the diversity among Indigenous Peoples (Earle 1998, Long and Nelson 1999.

A Contemporary Standpoint of Indigenous Social Workers

Indigenous social work scholar Hilary Weaver used a survey to capture the broad standpoint of Indigenous social workers. She found that in order to be culturally competent with Indigenous Peoples, the social worker needs to: know the history of the client's people, understand that individual's or group's understanding of their own Indigenous identity, and be able to conceptually understand and work with the issues of dual citizenship and sovereignty (Weaver 1998). Weaver found criticism in the status quo approach to diversity and cultural competence. One student's observation was that the "professors viewed cultural content as less important and should be taken as elective—of no real value in professional practice" (Weaver 2000, 421). Indigenous scholars were clear that diversity was an important part of the educational preparedness of the future social work professional. "I strongly advocate for longer courses to help students achieve a greater understanding of diversity" (Yellow Bird 1999a, 22). Cultural competence is clearly lacking when viewed from an Indigenous standpoint.

Indigenous Peoples are in a process of defining social work practice that is not just culturally competent, but is a product of the culture it assists. "The distinct needs and cultural paradigms of Aboriginal peoples call for the creation of unique Aboriginal models of social work practice" (Allgaier et al. 1993 quoted in Summers and Yellow Bird 1995, 455). One example is the use of the traditional Lakota methods for addressing historical grief and trauma (Yellow Horse Brave Heart 1998). The Tohono O'Odham Nation has developed an approach to social well-being based on the O'Odham Himdag or their traditional ways of being (Woods et al. 2002). The Iroquois promote a "program that increasingly addresses matters of substance abuse prevention in Native youth based on an increasing understanding of indigenous culture" (Skye 2002, 118).

With a helping approach that emerges from unique Indigenous cultures and traditions, the role of the non-Indigenous social worker becomes more narrowly and locally defined. The use of the Sahnish genesis story by a member of that Nation can be a powerful tool for healing, but a non-Sahnish social worker attempting the same would be viewed as lacking credibility, competence, or even as exploiting that tradition's spirituality (Canda and Furman 1999). These ideas emerge from the very heart of the concepts of sovereignty and a communal identity.

> Sovereignty is an issue that has been here since non-indigenous people first came to the Americas. We existed as members of independent, sovereign nations then. We exist as members of independent sovereign nations now. The least that others can do is to respect that fact. (Weaver 1997a, 17)

Social work with Indigenous Peoples cannot be apolitical, the geopolitical and historical realities must be competently understood and interventions geared to multilevel change. Though more narrowly defined, the role of non-Indigenous social work continues. No Indigenous author advocated for a complete separation of social work based on status. Non-Indigenous social workers are still clearly needed and wanted in Indian Country: "[N]on-Natives must be aware of their power to influence the actions of their own government and people. This power can be used to create positive change" (Weaver 2000, 19), when their intentions are community oriented (Weaver 1997b).

The emphasis on individual problems has been long rejected by Indigenous social workers in favor of an approach that focuses on social justice. The current generation of Indigenous social work thought was succinctly stated by Michael Yellow Bird:

> I [don't] think we [need] social workers coming into our territories to save us through copious amounts of psychotherapy or by feeling sorry for us. But, what we need is social workers willing to stand with us and help us maintain our sovereignty and nationhood. (1999a, 18)

Passage of the Indian Child Welfare Act (ICWA) is a major accomplishment aligned with social work's social justice role, yet more work remains to be done. Limb et al.'s (2004) study of 49 ICWA eligible cases in a single state showed compliance with ICWA provisions, despite a deficit in awareness of ICWA provisions by state social workers, who also differed in their understanding of ICWA compared to tribal social workers. Nationally, however, Carter (2008) found that Native American children were over-represented in group/residential facilities and under-represented in kinship care compared to the rest of the population; this contrary to the aims of ICWA.

Conclusion: Where Does the Profession Go from Here?

The history of social work through the 1960s reflects periods of intense interest in Indigenous Peoples, punctuated by long periods of neglect. The power of a status quo is palpable, but not omnipotent. In 1892 the infant profession found itself with a duty to Peoples just emerging from military genocide. The emerging social work profession was a product of the same society that perpetuated that genocide, so it is not surprising that it has taken a century for Indigenous Peoples to begin to take control of their own social services. Indigenous control of their own lives has been an essential component in the process of reversing ongoing cultural genocide. In the century since the fledgling profession first emphasized the importance of Indigenous control of social welfare services, only episodic efforts to reach that goal have materialized.

Indigenous Peoples increasingly define the social work agenda for themselves, by an indigenization of social welfare principles and practices and movement toward the development of social welfare systems based on traditional values and methods. The development of indigenized social welfare programs hinges on the availability of adequately trained Indigenous social workers. This will require increasing the ranks of Indigenous social workers at all levels—educators, researchers, administrators, and direct practitioners. In order to truly be a product of Indigenous control these social workers would ideally come from Indigenous higher education systems.

The shortage of social work programs in Indigenous colleges is problematic. There are just two CSWE-accredited BSW programs at tribally controlled colleges: Oglala Lakota College in Kyle, Pine Ridge Reservation, South Dakota, and Salish Kootenai College in Pablo, Flathead Indian Reservation, Montana. Schools of social work with established relationships with tribal colleges should work towards creating partnerships that result in tribal colleges having programs that meet their defined needs. Schools of social work located in areas with large Indigenous populations should foster such relationships. While tribal regions remain distant and scattered, technology makes it possible to link peoples in ways unknown less than a decade ago. An investment in distance education to link tribal colleges with Indigenous scholars could facilitate social work infrastructure that is more accessible to Indigenous Peoples.

The role for non-Indigenous social work continues to be vital. Indigenous social workers have defined a role that includes political advocacy interventions, with the caution that the role of advocate for Indigenous Peoples can have destructive results when the social worker does not clearly understand and support the Indigenous worldview. This understanding of Indigenous worldview is not being adequately addressed with the current system that focuses on diversity and cultural competence. Social workers working with Indigenous social policy need to possess a high degree of competence with the complex dynamics of colonization and the diverse cultural reality of Indigenous Peoples, in addition to a general understanding of the needs of human beings living under conditions of poverty and oppression.

References

Allan, K. 2005. *Explorations in Classical Sociological Theory: Seeing the Social World*. Thousand Oaks, CA: Pine Forge Press.

Austin, D.M. 1983. The Flexner myth and the history of social work. *Social Service Review*, 57(3), 357–77.

Canda, E.R. and Furman, L.D. 1999. *Spiritual Diversity in Social Work Practice: The Heart of Helping*. New York: Free Press.

Carter, V.B. 2008. Comparison of American Indian/Alaskan Natives to non-Indians in out-of-home care. *Families in Society*, 90(3), 301–8.

Churchill, W. 1992. *Fantasies of the Master Race: Literature, Cinema and the Colonization of American Indians*. Monroe, ME: Common Courage Press.

Council on Social Work Education 2012. Home Page. Retrieved August 31, 2012, from http://www.cswe.org.

Earle, K.A. 1998. Cultural diversity and mental health: The Haudenosaunee of New York State. *Social Work Research*, 22(2), 89–99.

EBSCOhost 2009. Social Work Abstracts (Database). Retrieved 31 December, 2009, from http://laurel.lso.missouri.edu/record=e1000251-S3.

Greenwald, E. 2002. *Reconfiguring the Reservation: The Nez Perces, Jicarilla Apaches, and the Dawes Act*. Albuquerque: University of New Mexico Press.

Hartsock, N.C.M. 1998. *The Feminist Standpoint Revisited and Other Essays (Feminist Theory and Politics)*. Boulder: Westview Press.

Hollar, C. 1995. *Black Elk's Religion: The Sun Dance and Lakota Catholicism*. Syracuse, NY: Syracuse University Press.

LaFramboise, T.D. and Rowe, W. 1983. Skills training for bicultural competence rationale and application. *Journal of Counseling Psychology*, 30(4), 589–95.

Limb, G.E., Chance, T., and Brown, E.F. 2004. An empirical examination of the Indian Child Welfare Act and its impact on cultural and familial preservation for American Indian children. *Child Abuse & Neglect*, 28(12), 1279–89.

Long, C.R. and Nelson, K. 1999. Honoring diversity: The reliability, validity, and utility of a scale to measure Native American resiliency. *Journal of Human Behavior in the Social Environment*, 2(1/2), 91–107.

Mark, J.T. 1988. *A Stranger in her Native Land: Alice Fletcher and the American Indians*. Lincoln: University of Nebraska Press.

McDiarmid, G.W. 1983. Community and competence: A study of an Indigenous primary prevention organization in an Alaskan village. *White Cloud Journal*, 3(1), 53–74.

McIntosh, P. 1998. White Privilege: Unpacking the invisible knapsack. In *Re-visioning Family Therapy: Race, Culture, and Gender in Clinical Practice*, M. McGoldrick (ed.). New York: Guilford Press, 147–52.

Mizrahi, T. and Davis, L.E. 2008. *The Encyclopedia of Social Work*, 20th edition. Washington: NASW Press and Oxford University Press.

NASW 1999. *Code of Ethics*. National Association of Social Workers. Retrieved September 12, 2013 from http://www.naswdc.org/pubs/code/default.asp.

SilverPlatter Information 2000. Webspirs Development Team. ERL Webspirs (Version 5.1). Retrieved from http://web5.silverplatter.com.www2.lib.ku.edu:2048/webspirs/start.ws?customer=kuwebsp&databases=SWAB.

Singer, J. 2003. Feminist standpoint theory. *Verdad*, Winter, 1–10.

Skye, W. 2002. E.L.D.E.R.S. gathering for Native American youth: Continuing Native American traditions and curbing substance abuse in Native American youth. *Journal of Sociology and Social Welfare*, 24(1), 117–35.

Smithsonian Institution 2003. Camping With the Sioux: Fieldwork Diary of Alice Cunningham Fletcher. Retrieved October 1, 2003, from http://www.nmnh.si.edu/naa/fletcher/foreword.htm.

Summers, H. and Yellow Bird, M. 1995. Building relationships with First Nations communities and agencies: Implications for field education and practice. In *Social Work Field Education: Views and Visions*, G. Rogers (ed.). Dubuque, IA: Kendall/Hunt, 548.

Swigonski, M.E. 1994. The logic of feminist standpoint theory for social work research. *Social Work*, 39(4), 387–94.

Tetzloff, J. 2003. Encyclopedia of North American Indians: Cloud, Henry Roe. Retrieved October 6, 2003, from http://college.hmco.com/history/readersco mp/naind/html/na_007700_cloudhenryro.htm.

University of Michigan 2002. National Conference of Charities and Corrections (continued as) National Conference on Social Welfare Proceedings (1874–1982). Retrieved August 31, 2003, from http://hti.umich.edu/n/ncosw/.

Weaver, H.N. 1997a. Training culturally competent social workers: What students should know about native people. *Journal of Teaching in Social Work*, 15(1/2), 97–111.

Weaver, H.N. 1997b. Which canoe are you in? A view from a First Nations person. *Reflections*, 3(4), 12–17.

Weaver, H.N. 1998. Indigenous people in a multicultural society: Unique issues for human services. *Social Work*, 43(3), 203–11.

Weaver, H.N. 1999. Indigenous people and the social work profession: Defining culturally competent services. *Social Work*, 44(3), 217–25.

Weaver, H.N. 2000. Culture and professional education: The experience of Native American Social Workers. *Journal of Social Work Education*, 36(3), 415–28.

White, J.Z. 2001. *Social Work with the First Nations: A Comprehensive Bibliography with Annotations*. Alexandria, VA: Council on Social Work Education.

Woods, T.K., Blaine, K., and Francisco, L. 2002. O'odham Himdag as a source of strength and wellness among the Tohono O'odham of Southern Arizona and Northern Sonora, Mexico. *Journal of Sociology and Social Welfare*, 24(1), 35–53.

Yellow Bird, M. 1995. Spirituality in First Nations storytelling: A Sahnish-Hidatsa approach to narrative. *Reflections*, 1(4), 113–24.

Yellow Bird, M. 1999a. Radical, skewed, benign, and calculated: Reflections on teaching diversity. *Reflections: Narratives of Professional Helping*, 5(2), 12–22.

Yellow Horse Brave Heart, M. 1998. The return to the sacred path: Healing the historical trauma and historical unresolved grief response among the Lakota through a psychoeducational group intervention. *Smith College Studies in Social Work*, 68(3), 287–305.

Chapter 5

Reflecting Out of the Box:
Locating Place and Practice in
the Decolonization of Social Work

Diane McEachern

This chapter is a reflective perspective of over 15 years of social work practice in a rural, remote area of Alaska inhabited for over 10,000 years by Indigenous tribes such as the Yup'ik and Cup'ik people. Life and work in this region is continually full of eye-opening experiences and reflective opportunities for someone such as me, a non-Indigenous woman, social worker/educator, working primarily within Indigenous communities. As a social worker who, within this region, transitioned from direct community practice to professor within a university classroom, my reflective journey has been challenging, ongoing, and, ultimately, transformational.

In this chapter I explore the intersection of adult learning and social work education, specifically related to adult Indigenous people and situated within the western region of Alaska. I will do so weaving together key reflective touchstones from my experiences working cross culturally as a Peace Corps Volunteer, community social worker in rural Alaska, and as an Assistant Professor teaching and learning from adult Indigenous students within an innovative college program. The chapter begins with the geographic and education contexts that frame the content. A review of the treatment of Indigenous populations in adult learning and international social work fields follows. Key experiences that knit together an approach to cross-cultural work are explored and insights from teaching social work and learning from adult Indigenous students conclude the chapter.

Geographic and Education Context

At about one-fifth the size of the United States, Alaska is the largest state in the union. The western region, the location for this chapter's discussion, is about the size of Ohio. Scattered throughout this flat, slough- and lake-filled tundra are 56 Alaska Native villages with a total population of around 25,000. Village populations range from 80 to 1,000, with most around 450. Western Alaska is home primarily to the Yup'ik and Cup'ik people, whom archeologists estimate have survived and thrived in this spectacular geography for over 10,000 years (see http://www.akhistorycourse.org/articles/article.php?artID=148, last accessed September 12, 2013).

There are no road systems in this region, so all travel is by small plane, boat, and snow machine. Survival in this environment has required the full flourish of human ingenuity, intelligence, and spiritual depth. Where a visitor might see a vast, flat, seemingly empty space, Yup'ik and Cup'ik people see a cultural and spiritual place full of stories and experiences animated by intricate knowledge of how to live well in such a challenging but rich landscape. For the Yup'ik and Cup'ik people, the last 150 years of their history have taxed this worldview, although creative resiliency and naturally embedded strengths remain readily apparent. This pattern is similar to that experienced by native populations throughout North America.

Like Native Americans throughout the United States and Aboriginal groups in Canada, Indigenous Peoples of the western region of Alaska have not been spared the imposition of powerful outside forces. In the early part of the twentieth century, diseases brought in by those from outside the region killed approximately 60% of the Native population. In the western region, whole villages and entire kin groups perished (Napoleon 1996). The tuberculosis epidemic in the 1930s, for example, was responsible for the deaths of one out of three Alaskan Natives (Fellows 1934).

The state of Alaska also instituted an educational system in which Native children were punished for speaking their Indigenous language and were sent away from home to western boarding schools, some as early as first grade and often to the lower 48 states. The disruption included not only the removal of young people from their families and communities, but also the violation of culturally related ways of learning, resulting in the particularly damaging consequence of the westernization of their education. Indigenous Peoples in western Alaska have weathered what have essentially been, both in terms of policy and practice, attempts to dismantle the very fiber of their cultural, spiritual, psychosocial, and intellectual selves.

At the same time, Alaska Natives were being subjected to missionary influences—often linked to education—that designated most of their spiritual practices as "heathen" and uncivilized (Freed and Sampson 2004). These spiritual practices, which could have provided a measure of healing and a sense of well-being in order to cope with the aggressive and formidable colonial changes forced upon them, were "disallowed" or denigrated. It is little wonder that indicators of a people in distress—substance abuse, suicide, domestic violence—begin to occur with heartbreaking and epidemic frequency. These symptoms appeared in the form of breakdowns in the safety and well-being of the Yup'ik and Cup'ik people that had been cultivated and ensured by their particular cultural constructs for thousands of years. It was recognition of these alarming conditions that set the stage for the development of an education response from the university.

In 1990, a working group of elders, Native leaders, and university faculty held a series of meetings to develop a culturally relevant and academically sound program aimed at rural Alaskan Natives doing social service work. The goal of the co-created curriculum was to develop a program grounded in the Alaska Native rural context. In 1993, the University of Alaska-Fairbanks (UAF) faculty senate approved Rural Human Services (RHS) as a 34-credit certificate program. By 2008 the program, located in three different campuses, had graduated 356 rural human service providers working in over 171 communities and villages throughout Alaska. At the Kuskokwim campus (KuC) in Bethel, the RHS program promotes a particular pedagogical design which has greatly influenced my own thinking about not only teaching, but the discipline of social work.

The small town of Bethel, Alaska, is the hub of the western region. Headquarters for all major social service institutions that serve the 56 villages within the region are located there. Bethel is also the location of the KuC campus, which is housed within the College of Rural and Community Development (CRCD) of UAF. The RHS college certificate program at the KuC campus is designed as a cohort model (20–25 students) of education delivery, and the adult students who join the cohorts are primarily Indigenous Alaskans from rural villages throughout the western region. They are funded to fly in one week a month for two academic years. The instructional team includes elders. Most of the adult students have not been in a formal educational setting for between 10 and 30 years.

The RHS program is designed so that to succeed and flourish, students need to bring their whole selves into the classroom. This necessarily includes their spiritual, cultural, emotional, and historical selves. The RHS education experience stands in sharp contrast to that of their younger days in school, in which their cultural values were to be left at the door, unwelcome. Programs designed with cultural sensitivity and respect are rare within university settings. However, where they do exist, increases in Indigenous retention and completion rates are apparent. Canadian Professors Ball and Pence (2006) wrote of a similarly designed early childhood education program that evolved what they referred to as a "generative curriculum model." Their education commitment holds central the community and culture of the participating Indigenous adult students and strives for a model that transforms their "training from a prepackaged, didactic process to one that is open-ended and participatory. It means engaging in dialogue, co-constructing curricula that will further a community's own ... goals" (15). The principles they outline are in sync with the way the RHS program was designed and how it continues to transform with each new cohort.

A useful way of understanding the educational framework utilized by the RHS program is Wenger's (1998) concept of a "community of practice" (CoP). Communities of practice emerged from Lave and Wenger's (1991) work on participation as learning. Like Freire's (1998) "banking model" critique of the classroom environment and pedagogical practices, Lave and Wenger (1991) viewed the patterns of teaching in which teachers transmit knowledge to more or less passive learners as problematic. Instead, they positioned learning as embedded in wider social and historical practices, which interact to generate valued practices within a given community. Lave and Wenger (1991) also introduced the concept of "situatedness" which informs the "relational character of knowledge and learning" (33). This concept nicely dovetails with Indigenous students' values of the interconnectedness of all things and the importance of how a person ought to relate to the world. Additionally, how a person relates to his or her own mind is important. The Yup'ik worldview holds that thoughts are powerful entities that must be carefully reflected upon, managed, and expressed. This perspective finds resonance with Freire's (1998) comment that "our being in the world is far more than just 'being.' It is a 'presence,' a 'presence' that is relational to the world and to others" (25). Similarly, the Yup'ik worldview supports one's consciousness and awareness to personal conduct as it relates to the world around them.

The RHS program is designed to accentuate this relational worldview. In doing so the classroom environment couples cultural values with ideas around learning in community to encourage, as Stein (2002) describes, "[a] social practice; a group of people representing the diversity of a community come together to create local knowledge from in-depth study of local situations and put what they learn into practice to bring about a desired future" (27). In order for these Indigenous adult students to experience a more formal educational process that bears little connection to any they have experienced in the past requires attention to specific program design elements. Given the oppressive colonial education system most rural Alaskan Natives have endured, finding ways of re-conceptualizing and enacting education with Indigenous adults was a primary goal of the RHS program development.

Further, the RHS program has particular features built into the classroom:

- Experiential education: Hands-on activities, small group discussions, large group collaborative activities, dialogue as a key to creating knowledge together, and incorporation of Elders in a traditional manner.
- Holistic learning environment: Students call upon their emotional, spiritual, historical, intellectual, cultural, and artistic selves to engage with course content.
- Community learning environment: A powerful cultural strength and source of comfort and well-being is that of the collective learning process in which mutual support, connection, and a sense of cultural unity is encouraged.
- Elder participants: For each course, the program hires two Elders who provide cultural grounding, encouragement, and stories that connect the course content to the culture. In the Yup'ik culture, Elders are the living embodiment of "historical or generational healing" and offer students wisdom about enduring life's struggles.
- Relationship as a form of empowerment: Students are encouraged to explore the relationship between personal change and community change.

Adult Learning and International Social Work

In the first edition of *Learning in Adulthood*, Merriam and Caffarella (1991) did not mention Indigenous populations at all and only noted in a cursory manner issues of culture and cross-cultural studies. They explained that, whereas "cross cultural studies have been completed in the anthropological tradition, this material has rarely been incorporated into the adult development literature" (113). In the 2008 edition of the same text, they pointed to the need for more astute cross-cultural attunement. While a necessary contribution, this chapter paid scant attention to an explicitly Indigenous population. Nonetheless, the authors highlight four themes that constitute key epistemological features noted in ongoing and growing scholarship about Indigenous populations. These features can be summarized as non-Western and, as such, emphasize interdependence; learning done in community; holistic aspects of learning, including emotional components, being as important as cognitive approaches; and informal learning as a core part of the learning experience for Indigenous Peoples (Cajete 1994, Merriam and Caffarella 2008, Reagan 2005).

Rather than a discourse on racism specifically, Indigenous scholarship often focuses on colonialism. This allows for a clear trigger to a historical legacy which often binds together Indigenous populations in terms of domination, and also policies of explicit and tacit genocide (Semali and Kincheloe 1999). These are populations in which their knowledge production and transmission have been isolated and relegated to "superstition" or "primitive," terms which reinforce a dominant western knowledge base. Anti-colonial theorizing rises out of alternative paradigms, which are in turn based on Indigenous concepts and analytical systems with cultural frames of reference (Reagan 2005, Dei et al. 2000, Semali and Kincheloe 1999, Wilson 2008). Another angle with which to pursue a space for Indigenous voices and world views might be to consider those adult learning theories and practices which, while not specifying "Indigenous" possibilities, still posit a kind of pedagogy that allows space and consideration for a worldview that is not familiar to a dominant western-based discourse.

The adult learning field has research and praxis which have cultivated and promoted methods of dialogue, empowerment, and participatory processes that are more inviting to Indigenous populations. Brookfield's (1986) analysis of "community action learning groups," Shor's (1992) "empowering education," Freire's (1998) "dialogic model," and Cranton's (2006) model of "transformative learning" are a few of the scholars who have mapped out theoretical approaches that are less alienating to those from Indigenous communities. More explicit to Indigenous Peoples has been the work of Vella (2002) Merriam et al. (2001) and Merriam (2007), who applied some of these ideas and processes to their work in Indigenous communities, both within the United States and internationally. These scholars' work attempts to build concepts aware that when knowledge systems are rigidly held and myopic, our knowledge of ourselves, our communities, and our institutional contexts remain partial. Minnich (2005) writes that "if we uncover where and how knowledge is partial, we open spaces for other modes of knowing and knowledge systems" (268). Into those open spaces, Indigenous populations, who in the past would have been considered "partial humans," now bring a full and complex contribution to both Indigenous contexts and social work education.

Discourse within the field of international social work underscores current arguments in adult education that encourage a critical evaluation and deconstruction of social work as a profession. In particular, Askeland and Payne (2006) critique international social work and promote an "anti-colonial" education practice. Askeland and Payne make a link to adult educator Stephen Brookfield, who notes that a pedagogy that is participatory and empowering avoids "the process whereby ideas, structures and actions come to be seen by the majority of people as wholly natural, preordained, and working for their own good, when in fact they are constructed and transmitted by powerful minority interests to protect the status quo that serves those interests" (Brookfield 1995, 15). Strong analysis and critical study come out of Canada from Canadian social work scholars Haug (2005) and Razack (2002, 2003), who likewise deconstruct international social work as a discipline, noting its western foundation and structure that continues to be imposed on diverse populations internationally, thus forwarding an ongoing hegemonic force. Haug (2005) asserts the need for social work to encompass a definition of the field that is "expanded so that a broad diversity of forms of social work based on a multiplicity of social care traditions are included" (132). Social work as a profession, then, did not develop unfettered by the prevailing colonial ideas about the superiority of western ideas and practices. Some of those practices include the move towards more clinical, individualistic, and Medicaid-structured services. This has left gaps in community (macro), culturally diverse, and social justice-based practice (Specht and Courtney 1994).

The Western model of social work and the corresponding education of social workers is often part of a colonization process with practices that are not readily transferable to other countries and cultures, let alone always suitable for North American Indigenous communities. Indigenous social work scholars participate in the decidedly "anti-colonial" debates that revolve around not only international social work curriculum but also what is taught to Indigenous students and how it is taught. They argue for ongoing critical examination of social work's claims and responses to problems of cultural and developmental relevance (Battiste 1998, Weaver 2008, Gray et al. 2008, Youngblood Henderson 2000). Going to the heart of the debate, they call for a "decolonization" of social work and it was this call that provided me a much needed impetus with which to sort through my own "place" in this dialogue. As a social work provider and educator, I needed to become more vigilant, thoughtful, and curious about what it meant for me to join in this decolonization work.

Cross-Cultural: Philippines, Ibaloi People

Part of my identity is that of a white non-Indigenous woman who has lived in the western region of Alaska for almost 15 years. I also find myself in a peculiar position of both an "outsider" and an "insider" to the RHS program. I am, culturally, an "outsider" while at the same time, within the context of the RHS program; my role has been more of an "insider." Those positions, insider and outsider, represent particularly developed lenses, and I have selected an experiential thread that helps tie together these variant roles in a cohesive way. An experience I had while a Peace Corps Volunteer living in a remote mountainous region of the Philippines, and later recalled while living in an Alaskan Yup'ik village 20 years later, has influenced and continues to inform my education work in the RHS program.

Hiking through the mountain forest back to the Philippine village of Bagong, it was becoming dark. I was hiking at the front of a long line of Ibaloi people, a tribe living in the mountainous region of Northern Luzon. We had attended a feast and were returning home. It was customary to have me hike near the front; a courtesy shown to "outsiders" in order to ensure the pace remained comfortable and not too fast. As dusk moved to darkness, a man tapped me on the shoulder and asked if I would move to the last spot in the line. Somewhat startled I dropped out and moved to the rear and asked him why. He told me that the *anitos* (spirits that inhabit all things) sometimes snatch the last person in line. I felt a chill and quickly asked him, "What about me?" He smiled and said the *anitos* would never snatch me because, according to him, "You don't believe." Fortunately, I was not snatched but I did look over my shoulder during that hike home. At the time I marveled at how this man held two seemingly contradictory ideas in his mind without confusion or the need to fit either into a closed and rational system. I sensed this was a particular kind of cross-cultural moment. I had experiences 20 years later when living in a Yup'ik village outside of Bethel that helped crystallize another layer of meaning to this story.

Cross-Cultural: Alaska, Yup'ik Village

My first three years in western Alaska were spent living in a small (population 650) Yup'ik Eskimo village. At the time I was their school social worker. While I did travel to other assigned villages throughout the region, more time was spent with the village I lived in. Working with K-12 children within the school building quickly became unsatisfying. I knew that children essentially bring their family and their community with them to school every day. Taking to heart that realization, I began to extend my social work practice out of the school and into the community, focusing first on families. I sat at many kitchen tables, eating dried fish dipped in seal oil, listening to parents tell me about their children. One of the first questions I would ask a parent was, "What would you like the school to always remember about your child?" I would also ask the parent to share with me a story from when their child was a baby. Parents' primary experience when hearing from the school was when their child was misbehaving. These two simple questions brought a noticeable relaxation and, many times, tender and culturally rich stories. I absorbed these conversations and worked them through my mind and work experiences with the intention of broadening my understanding of not just cultural considerations but also the kinds of damaging education impositions that have been, at times, rocking the villages. Through ongoing dialogue with parents and extended families, a natural pathway developed for me to follow that led to working more closely with the village's own providers of social services.

I distinctly remember the day I walked to the end of the village where the small blue ramshackle social services building was. I walked in and there were a few people in their offices. They greeted me politely but remained somewhat cool and distant. I was later told that they were in shock that the school social worker had actually come to their offices. That had never happened before and they had no idea how to interact with me. Yet the roles they played in their community were critical partners to my role. One was the community suicide prevention counselor, another was the Youth outreach counselor, a third was the Wellness Counselor, and a fourth the Indian child welfare (ICWA) worker. Within this particular school district of 24 K-12 village schools, we were about to create a collaborative cross-cultural work life that had not been tried anywhere else in the region.

We began a slow process of building rapport and trust with one another. Over time, we decided we wanted to form a village-based multidisciplinary team (MDT). We began outreach to those people in the village who could join our team. There was a small health clinic staffed with nine Community Health aides. We offered a stress management workshop to them and from that came a pattern of meeting with them once a month. Since no one could talk about specific cases due to confidentiality, we instead talked about the ethics of self-care when working in social services. Two of the health aides were selected by their peers to join the MDT. An elder joined as well. The village police officer agreed to periodically join if invited, when we needed his expertise. After almost three years of deliberate but steady work, the village MDT consisted of 10 members who met regularly. My autonomy had eventually given way to an alignment of my work with these key practitioners.

As our group grew we often discussed my role with the team in order to reduce any tendencies for dependency or disempowerment. Essentially, I asked them to design my skills, training, and degree to fit their needs. My stance was that those areas of my professional life did not belong solely to me but could be molded by them to best fit their needs. These discussions were vibrant and enlightening to all of us. One of the team members spoke about his surprise at both the idea and the real experience of my involvement being that of joining rather than coercing them, albeit nicely, or otherwise depositing information and expecting them to comply. Those meetings were full of good humor and teasing, a sure sign of connection with Yup'ik people. I remember one time when I was late for our weekly meeting. They called up to the school and insisted, "Where are you, we're all here!" I jokingly asked if I could get away with some "Yup'ik time" and they laughed and said that, in fact, no I could not because I was not Yup'ik. It was an interesting and refreshing insight to me that no one wanted me to be Yup'ik. They wanted me to be the "outsider" that I am and, I soon learned, with good reason.

This community, like most of the 56 villages in the Western region, had high incidents of domestic violence, child sexual abuse, and death by suicide. The village MDT realized they needed to find a way to have what would be difficult discussions about these sensitive social issues. In a small rural Native community it was often uncomfortable and inappropriate for people to talk openly about such sensitive topics. These issues would be challenging for any MDT members to initiate discussion about. Without doubt the individual team members had all been impacted by these tragic kinds of events as well. Discussions would have to be done with great care. Mindfulness of the historical context was also a salient consideration.

When we discussed my role at the meetings, they were clear that facilitation was important. The team also wanted an education process and I needed to, at times, take the role of a teacher. One woman said something that took me back 20 years to that time I hiked at the end of the line with the Ibaloi people. She explained that part of my role was to bring up these key issues, sit back, and the team would proceed with discussion. She added that as a trusted "outsider" I could get away with bringing tough issues to the team for discussion. Our agreement was that if I would be willing to find a way to initiate dialog, they would participate in discussing what many found frightening, shameful, and, at times, overwhelming. They appreciated that as an "outsider" from the lower 48, I could be more "blunt," and within the context and purpose of our meetings this characteristic was valued. I realized that my "outsider" status could be useful to them and they found a way to put it to work. The Ibaloi people had used my "otherness" as a cloak to protect them from the *anitos*, and did so without also putting me at risk. So too had the village MDT found a way to have my "otherness" perform a necessary service, one they designated and controlled. I learned a valuable lesson that I carried with me into the university.

Cross-Cultural: Kuskokwim Campus, University of Alaska

As I entered the university setting I sought a perspective that allowed for my "otherness" but also molded it towards a "goodness of fit." I had interpretive barriers to face, reflect upon, and redefine. There are many critical moments of doing this and I will share three as transformative examples. One involved elders in the classroom, another was how I interpreted the adult Indigenous students, and finally the need for me to become aware of what, exactly, was at stake for my students.

Elders

The start of each two-year RHS cohort was always powerful for the students
and for me. Walking into the classroom with 25 adult Indigenous students and
at least two elders, the anxiety and apprehension of the students was, and still is,
almost palpable in those first few courses. Some are flooded with memories of
education long ago when they needed, essentially, to leave much of their cultural
and historical selves at the door in order to succeed in a western-oriented school
setting. They were not the only nervous ones. When I glanced over at the two elders,
my own nerves jumped. I had my syllabus, experiential activities, and curriculum
for the week but, in the beginning, I had not learned how to work with elders in
the classroom. I was uncomfortable with them because I had not grown up with
elders and my understanding of their cultural role was shallow at best. A concern
for me was whether they would detract from the curriculum learning outcomes
embedded in the syllabus. Would they take the class in a direction unrecognizable
to my teaching goals for the week? Sometimes I caught myself dreading their time
to speak and I noted my internal impatience. It was important to me, as I sifted
through reactions such as these, to engage a reflective process that promoted my
taking responsibility for those reactions. My impulse to control the classroom was
colonial in the guise, or, one could say, protection, of "institutional curriculum
integrity." It was also born of my own fears. In his book, *The Courage to Teach*,
Parker Palmer (1998) writes, "If we embrace the promise of diversity ... we face
... the fear that a live encounter with otherness will challenge or even compel
us to change our lives" (38). He goes on to say that "otherness always invites
transformation" (39). And so it was with me. I was fearful of losing control of the
classroom, of making cross-cultural errors in front of students, and of my own
distance from understanding elders. It would be my responsibility to own those
fears and find a way to transform them and myself.

I drew upon two values within Yup'ik culture that I witnessed often in my
travels, life, and work in villages as paths for this transformation. My stance
became one of careful listening and observing, two characteristics I often observed
with Yup'ik people. These two Yup'ik values guided me as I embraced my fears.
As I observed students, I noticed that they seemed to relax when elders spoke.
That is, my own apprehensions were rarely, if ever, mirrored by students. I settled
into a feeling of humility as I detected a synergy between the elders and students
that, initially, I did not share. I listened carefully to elder stories and relaxed my
struggle to pinpoint elements that fit the week's curriculum. During breaks, I sat
with the elders and asked their advice on next directions to take with the class or
just enjoyed being with them. It took time but slowly I changed.

I clearly recall the day, about two years into my teaching, when both elders
were not in class during the first morning. This rare occurrence was due to doctor's
appointments and they would be in class after lunch. After lunch the two elders
arrived and a wave of relief flooded my body. Tension I had carried throughout the
morning that I was not aware of drained out of me and I took delight in greeting

them. I also felt grateful that I grew within me a genuine appreciation and need for the elders' presence in my classes. As a non-Indigenous woman I found an authentic, slowly cultivated way of *being* with Yup'ik elders.

From Clients to Colleagues

The social issues that beset the region infiltrate the classroom. RHS students are front-line social service providers who live and work in remote villages and are impacted directly or indirectly by the difficulties of the region. In the RHS classroom, learning and healing are coterminous experiences. Learning contributes to healing and healing adds to learning. This holistic orientation dovetails with Yup'ik culturally infused beliefs about the interrelated nature of life and experience. And it makes for a dynamic classroom. Students sift new information through their own life experiences and develop skills along with reflecting upon ways their own lives have been impacted by the same issues their communities face. RHS uses talking circles, small support group discussions, and journaling as tools to aid students with integrating healing, learning, and new skill development. As an instructor in this environment it took me some time to understand the co-mingling of learning and healing. My ongoing reflexivity uncovered another aspect of how, as a social worker, I perceived this process of engagement students experienced, and this awareness startled me.

When considering my social work education, certainly there were courses geared towards cross-cultural understanding and "cultural competency." There would be chapter readings outlining "best practice" with particular population groups—all of which were minorities. I often wondered if this encouraged a bias in me that the designated "helper" was not a minority, but instead someone white, like me. It was through teaching and interacting in the RHS classroom that I discovered an additional bias, that is, of viewing the designated "client," in this context, as Alaska Native. I began to interrogate my own interpretations of what I witnessed in the classroom. Did I see my adult Indigenous students as "clients" in some way? With healing and learning inseparable, could I understand that dynamic through a culturally respectful framework rather than the fallback duality of "client" and "clinician?" I felt challenged by this insight because I knew that I could sway in the direction of clinical duality. The easy clinical rubric that allowed me to be the distant "clinician" and students the vulnerable "client" needed to be unpacked and re-conceptualized. Anthropologist Ruth Behar in her book *The Vulnerable Observer: Anthropology that Breaks Your Heart* (1996), describes the significance of "life history and life story ... merging as a key form of approaching and transforming reality" (27). Over time, I was unable to maintain a precise distance; I was learning not only about my students, but also myself. This organic experience of learning about myself through my students and, too, learning about my students through myself culminated in realizing that rather than the "designated client," I understood the adult students as my current, developing, and future *colleagues*.

Education, Empowerment, and Survival

Rather than a career path or résumé builder, participation in RHS was for many a route towards *saving their people*. When I first heard students periodically making this kind of comment about the angle their commitment to learning took, I was startled. In my academic life as a student, I had not heard classmates say this, much less thought of it in this way myself. Certainly, as social work students, my classmates and I wanted to "help others," but I had not heard anyone contextualize their social work education in terms of *survival as a people*. The RHS students often reflected upon and contextualized their learning beyond themselves, through their classroom, and upon their communities. This in turn dovetails with Freire's (1987) idea that "transformation is possible because consciousness is not a mirror of reality, not a mere reflection, but is reflexive and reflective of reality" (13). Spiraling back and forth through their own and their communities experiences while *in community* with other Indigenous learners was not only empowering for students but, for many, life changing, as well as enabling a more hopeful vision for their communities and tribes. The stakes were high and I often struggled to keep up, move beyond my syllabus, and allow those high stakes to educate me.

Conclusion

A reflective practice has been a thread that allows for transformational space to learn, change, and confront often mistaken and harmful interpretations. Rather than narrow dichotomies of western vs non-western, Indigenous vs non-Indigenous, or teacher vs student, I discovered an ongoing *living* way to use reflexivity to peer out beyond those boxes. Helping guide those reflections were a diverse range of critical scholars and also my Indigenous adult students and elders. I recognized over time that those Indigenous "voices" and "wisdom" were not enough, but that, in fact, social work as a profession cannot change in better ways without Indigenous *leadership* and *guidance*. This contributes to an interdisciplinary avenue for what Dei (2000) refers to as "academic decolonization" of, I would argue, *both* adult learning and social work as necessary for *all* students.

References

Askeland, G. and Payne, M. 2006. Social work's cultural hegemony. *International Social Work*, 49, 731–45.

Ball, J. and Pence, A. 2006. *Supporting Indigenous Children's Development*. Toronto: UBC Press.

Battiste, M. 1998. Enabling the autumn seed: Toward a decolonized approach to Aboriginal knowledge, language, and education. *Canadian Journal of Native Education*, 22, 16–27.

Behar, R. 1996. *The Vulnerable Observer: Anthropology that Breaks Your Heart.* Boston: Beacon Press.

Brookfield, S. 1986. *Understanding and Facilitating Adult Learning: A Comprehensive Analysis of Principles and Effective Practices.* San Francisco: Jossey-Bass.

Brookfield, S. 1995. *Understanding and Facilitating Adult Learning: A Comprehensive Analysis of Principles and Effective Practices.* San Francisco: Jossey-Bass.

Cajete, G. 1994. *Look to the Mountain: An Ecology of Indigenous Education.* Skyland, NC: Kviaki Press.

Cranton, P. 2006. Transformative Learning. In *International Encyclopedia of Adult Education*, L.M. English (ed.). New York: Palgrave Macmillan, 630–37.

Dei, S.G. 2000. Rethinking the role of Indigenous knowledges in the academy. *International Journal of Inclusive Education*, (4)2, 111–32.

Dei, S.G., Hall, L., and Rosenberg, D. (eds) 2000. *Indigenous Knowledge in Global Contexts: Multiple Readings of our World.* Toronto: University of Toronto Press.

Fellows, F.S. 1934. Mortality in the native races of the Territory of Alaska, with special reference to tuberculosis. *Public Health Reports*, 49, 289–98.

Freed, C. and Sampson, M. 2004. Native Alaskan dropouts in western Alaska: Systemic failure in Native Alaskan school. *Journal of American Indian Education*, 43(2), 33–45.

Freire, P. 1987. The dream of liberating education. In *A Pedagogy for Liberation: Dialogues on Transforming Education*, I. Shor and P. Freire (eds). Westport, CT: Bergin & Garvey, 13–15.

Freire, P. 1998. *Pedagogy of Freedom: Ethics, Democracy and Civic Courage.* New York: Rowman and Littlefield.

Gray, M., Coates, J., and Yellow Bird, M. (eds) 2008. *Indigenous Social Work Around the World: Towards Culturally Relevant Education and Practice.* Farnham: Ashgate Publishing.

Haug, E. 2005. Critical reflections on the emerging discourse of international social work. *International Social Work*, 48(2), 126–35.

Lave, J. and Wenger, E. 1991. *Situated Learning: Legitimate Peripheral Participation.* New York: Cambridge University Press.

Merriam, S. (ed.) 2007. *Non-Western Perspectives on Learning and Knowing.* Malabar, FL: Krieger Publishing Company.

Merriam, S. and Caffarella, R. 1991/2008. *Learning in Adulthood: A Comprehensive Guide.* San Francisco: Jossey-Bass.

Merriam, S., Lee, M-Y., Kee, Y., et al. 2001. Power and positionality: Negotiating insider/outsider status within and across cultures. *International Journal of Lifelong Learning*, 20, 405–16.

Minnich, E. 2005. *Transforming Knowledge.* Philadelphia: Temple Press.

Napoleon, H. 1996. *Yuuyaraq: The Way of the Human Being.* Alaska: Alaska Native Knowledge Network, University of Alaska Fairbanks.

Palmer, P. 1998. *The Courage to Teach.* San Francisco: Jossey-Bass.

Razack, N. 2002. *Transforming the Field: Critical Anti-racist and Anti-oppressive Perspectives for the Human Services Practicum.* Halifax: Fernwood Publishers.

Razack, N. 2003. Critical race discourse and tenets for social work, with Donna Jeffery. *Canadian Social Work Review,* 19(2), 257–72.

Reagan, T. 2005. *Non-Western Educational Traditions: Indigenous Approaches to Educational Thought and Practice.* New Jersey: Erlbaum Associates.

Semali, L. and Kincheloe, J. (eds) 1999. *What is Indigenous Knowledge: Voices from the Academy.* New York: Falmer Press.

Shor, I. 1992. *Empowering Education: Critical Teaching for Social Change.* Chicago: University of Chicago Press.

Specht, H. and Courtney, M. 1994. *Unfaithful Angels: How Social Work has Abandoned its Mission.* New York: The Free Press.

Stein, D. 2002. Creating local knowledge through learning in community: A case study. In *Adult Learning in Community* (95), D. Fall, D. Stein, and S. Imel (eds), 27–41.

Vella, J. 2002. *Learning to Listen, Learning to Teach: The Power of Dialogue in Educating Adults.* San Francisco: Jossey-Bass.

Weaver, H. 2008. Indigenous social work in the United States: Reflections on Indian tacos, trojan horses and canoes filled with Indigenous revolutionaries. In *Indigenous Social Work around the World: Towards Culturally Relevant Education and Practice,* M. Gray, J. Coates, and M. Yellow Bird (eds). Burlington, VT: Ashgate Publishing, 72–81.

Wenger, E. 1998. *Communities of Practice: Learning, Meaning, and Identity.* Cambridge, UK: Cambridge University Press.

Wilson, S. 2008. *Research is Ceremony: Indigenous Research Methods.* Halifax/ Winnipeg: Fernwood Publishing.

Youngblood Henderson, J.S. 2000. Challenges of respecting Indigenous worldviews in Eurocentric education. In *Voice of the Drum: Indigenous Education and Culture,* R. Neil (ed.). Manitoba, Canada: Kingfisher Publications, 59–80.

PART III
Indigenous Peoples across the Life Cycle

Balance is a central theme across Indigenous cultures. It is important for an individual to maintain balance as the essence of well-being within his or her own life. Additionally, a balance exists among different components of our families, communities, and across the life cycle. The issues that affect the well-being of youth affect families and communities, as do the issues that affect the well-being of elders. Wellness is important in all components to insure the well-being of the whole Indigenous society.

This section of the book begins with an examination of the well-being of Indigenous youth presented by Day. The well-being of youth is the central building block for the future of Indigenous nations. Two chapters examine the challenges of Native families. The Lucero and Bussey chapter provides a discussion of the importance of family preservation. The González and González-Santin chapter examines the Indian Child Welfare Act and how to maintain cultural integrity for Native youth and families under circumstances where children are removed from their families. The final Day chapter concludes this section with a discussion of the role of elders in Native communities.

Chapter 6

Raising Healthy American Indian Children: An Indigenous Perspective

Priscilla A. Day

The kinship unit is very powerful. I want my descendants to have a strong sense of who their ancestors were and to understand that they have a responsibility to be a conduit for our culture. That is the only hope we have of ensuring the essence of our culture will continue ... (Medicine 2004, 65)

The kinship unit noted above and the connection between descendants and ancestors is central to the transmission of culture and raising healthy American Indian/Alaska Native children. The term "culturally restorative practice" was developed by Simard (2009) in her work with Weechi-it-te-win Family Services, a First Nation Family Services program in Canada. According to Simard, culturally restorative practice is a way to "rebuild" Indigenous systems. This kind of research is about "the process of acquiring knowledge from the ancestral knowledge keepers within the First Nation community, and using this knowledge for the betterment of the community" (3).

American Indian/Alaska Natives believe that our children are gifts from the Creator and are sacred. As such, they are to be loved and cherished (Peacock and Wisuri 2006). "Traditionally, we believe our children enter this world as precious spirits to be taken care of and nurtured through life's changes from an infant to a child, a child to an adolescent, from adolescence to adult and then into another sacred role, that of elder" (Day 2011, 39). In order for this transition to occur, children must be raised with the values, beliefs, and practices of their tribal community and family (Simard and Blight 2011). While there is a plethora of material available for mainstream parents about raising healthy children on everything from nutrition to trauma, little exists for American Indian parents and others like social workers, teachers, and health-care professionals who would like to learn about what a healthy American Indian child looks like in today's world. "As parents, we all want our children to lead a better life than we did. A life full of opportunity for better education, expanded job choices, and of course, a life in a family system that can care for and offer safety and security for that child, to pass on family stories, norms, values and beliefs" (Day 2011, 40). This chapter recounts some of those stories and beliefs.

Quite a bit is written about the role of historical trauma on communities and resulting issues of chemical dependency, family violence, health and mental health issues, and chronic poverty (Brave Heart 2004). While these issues have impacted the ways Indigenous Peoples, traditional parenting values remain in our communities and some are presented here. Most of the examples used are from the Anishinaabe (aka Ojibwe or Chippewa) culture as a way to illustrate how one tribal nation defines healthy Native children.

Defining Ourselves

While there is little documentation about Indigenous parenting and support networks, we know that children have always been viewed as sacred. We also know that war, disease, boarding schools, and child welfare practices were designed to destroy tribal culture and family ways (Brave Heart 2004). All of these practices served to interfere with Indigenous parenting skills. "Policies were designed systematically … to deconstruct traditional Indian family and social systems and reconstruct Indian identity in the likeness of mainstream society child welfare" (Red Horse et al. 2001, 17).

It is important to provide context about the physical challenges faced in tribal communities. The literature is full of information about physical health of Indian children, childhood obesity, diabetes, FAS/E, depression, infant mortality, low birth weight, and other health concerns. Overall, American Indian/Alaska Natives suffer disproportionately from infant death (second highest rate); diabetes (second highest rate); the highest liver disease and cirrhosis (related to alcoholism); and unintentional death (Office of Health Policy 2011). American Indian/Alaska Natives have some of the highest rates of childhood obesity in the United States (Adams et al. 2005) and overall food insecurity of any population (Gunderson 2006). Some researchers have speculated that poor nutrition and lack of exercise came about when American Indian/Alaska Natives were forced onto reservations, where diets changed from traditional healthy foods to processed foods high in starch and fats and activity levels became more sedentary (Story et al. 1999). All of these health issues provide challenges in raising healthy American Indian/ Alaska Native children.

Another area that impacts raising healthy American Indian/Alaska Native children is the high rate of poverty. According the Annie E. Casey Foundation, American Indian youth live in poverty at rates much higher than white youth: 35 percent vs 5.9 percent respectively (Snipp 2002). The National Center for Children in Poverty has developed a "Young Child Risk Calculator." Children raised in an environment with these factors are more likely to have poor outcomes such as high dropout rates, engaging in high-risk behavior, and having poor health and developmental outcomes. The Center found "economic hardship paired with any of the listed risk factors may indicate a greater chance of poor outcomes. Children with three or more risks are exceptionally vulnerable." The risk factors are: households without English speakers, coming from a large family, low parental education, residential mobility, having a single parent, having a teen mother, and having an unemployed parent (National Center for Children in Poverty 2012).

Many American Indian/Alaska Native families have three or more of these risk factors and may live in geographical areas with high unemployment. "Poverty impacts children in numerous harmful ways and has been shown to be a contributing factor to high out-of-home placement, low educational attainment, homelessness, increased contact with child welfare, juvenile justice and other institutions where they experience harsher outcomes than white youth" (Day 2011, 41). These health disparities, chronic poverty, and a history of discrimination from the larger society, can make raising American Indian/Alaska Native children challenging. It is important for American Indian/Alaska Native families to have support. American Indians/Alaska Natives traditionally had family and cultural structures that provided parents with assistance in child rearing (Poupart et al. 2000, Rheault 1999, Simard and Blight 2011).

Cultural Identity

Part of raising healthy children is to help them have a firm understanding of who they are in relationship to the world around them. Culture plays an important role in helping a child to know who they are and to feel grounded in the world (Weaver 2001). This is true for all children. Children who understand their role in their families and in the world are more likely to be resilient than children who don't (Association of Alaska School Boards nd). While government policies and practices tried to take culture and cultural practices away from Indigenous Peoples, tribal values and practices remain in many communities (Poupart et al. 2000, Rheault 1999). These practices provide children with health and well-being.

Simard and Blight (2011), two First Nation Anishinaabe women, wrote about cultural identity, attachment, and working in a culturally appropriate way with Indigenous Peoples. They interviewed Indigenous First Nations staff in Canada to document cultural meanings around raising and working with children in a culturally healthy manner. They use the term "Aboriginal," which is a common way of referring to First Nation people. They describe the importance of framing Indigenous concepts in Native worldview.

> It is important to understand that through an Aboriginal lens, all things are related on a spiritual level. A primary difference between Aboriginal worldview— *Aki naanaagadawaabiwi* and Non-Aboriginal theories of development is that everything in Aboriginal worldview—*Aki naanaagadawaabiwi* is based on the spirit whereas the concept of spirituality or the spirit is often overlooked in Non-Aboriginal theories of development. (5)

They use their traditional language to better understand these concepts. Meaning is embedded in cultural language and is not able to be fully captured in English translation. American Indian/Alaska Natives generally believe that a child was put on the earth to fulfill a sacred purpose. This purpose becomes clear as they interact with family, community, and participate in spiritual practices (Rheault 1999).

Cultural identity is interwoven with how one sees the world. Worldview can be described as either linear or relational. If one sees the world in a linear fashion things seem to fall into line in an independent, systematic way. If one views the world in a relational manner, events are shaped by other events and relationships that are not necessarily linear. Most Native people raised within a cultural setting view the world through a relational lens (Rheault 1999). Cross (2010) says,

> Balance and harmony in relationships between multiple variables, including spiritual forces, make up the core of the thought system. Every event is understood in relation to all other events regardless of time, space, or physical existence. Health exists only when things are in balance and harmony. (2)

Children raised using a relational worldview have different experiences and perspectives on health, wellbeing, family, and spiritual connections.

Cultural identity is developed through social learning norms that exist within specific cultural groups. Cultural identity is developmental and is learned in social constructs of family, environment, and culture. One's sense of identity changes as one has more experiences and develops a sense of shared identity (Rheault 1999, Weaver 2001). These constructs embrace cultural values, tribal language, traditional teachings passed down through centuries, ceremonies, connection to a land base, shared history, and accumulated wisdom (Rheault 1999).

Most Indigenous Peoples understand the connection between health and well-being and maintaining balance within the mental, emotional, spiritual, and physical aspects of one's life. This is important within the individual self, one's family and extended family, and within one's tribal community (Simard and Blight 2011). Living life on a good path means making sure children have meaningful interaction with extended family, community, and culture. "In tribal practice, family preservation involves bringing families in balance with community, spiritual, and other natural relationships" (Red Horse et al. 2001, 22). This is put into practice when family, extended family, and tribal community members support families during times of stress. Living a good life starts before birth in how a mother takes care of herself and her developing child, and it continues throughout life and even after death when a person is sent into the next world in the proper spiritual way (Rheault 1999). This is all done within the context of a tribal community.

According to Simard, "Mino-bimaadiziwin is a word that means well-being of a person, and describes a sacred way of life for the Anishinaabe. Aboriginal people understand to succeed in the present-day multicultural world the child must be spiritually grounded in Mino-bimaadiziwin" (Simard 2009, 8). The term "mino-bimaadiziwin" is often translated as meaning living a good life or walking on a good path. In order to do this, a child must be grounded in their cultural identity, including living in a spiritual way and abiding by cultural values and teachings. "When referring to *Mino-Bimaadiziwin* it is understood that the spirit is the essence and the way of being. I am a spirit having a human experience" (Rheault 1999, 95). These teachings are passed on through stories and interactions with other Indigenous people in everyday life and ceremony. Knowledge is passed on orally through the generations and is intertwined in relationships with family, clan, and cultural community (Poupart et al. 2000, Rheault 1999, Simard and Blight 2011).

Sovereignty

The concept of sovereignty is critical in understanding American Indian/Alaska Native families and communities. American Indian/Alaska Natives retained rights that are political, but also relevant to self-determination as tribal entities and in terms of religious freedom and the practice of traditional beliefs. The political status of tribes has resulted in the passage of policies like the Indian Child Welfare Act (ICWA) and American Indian Religious Freedom Act, both passed in 1978. These and many other policies are possible because of the unique political status tribes have retained. The ICWA was passed to stem the removal of American Indian children from their families and community. If they must be removed, they are to go to an extended family member, a member of their own tribe, or, as a last resort, into a non-Indian home (Poupart et al. 2000; Red Horse et al. 2001). It is clear that this Act is not being implemented as intended, as the removal of American Indian/ Alaska Native children remains high (Day 2011, Red Horse et al. 2001).

Tribes have been fighting to maintain their sovereign rights since European contact. The practice of removing American Indian/Alaska Native children through boarding schools and child welfare removals was used to force assimilation. "Historically, the attempts to undermine tribal sovereignty, destroy tribal cultures, and force the assimilation of American Indian people through their children were often masked in the language and practice of child welfare" (Geary and Day 2010, 3). Unfortunately, while awareness has improved, the practice of child removal from tribal communities continues to be problematic (Poupart et al. 2000, Day 2011).

Tribal self-determination is embedded in the recognition of sovereignty and tribal norms (Red Horse et al. 2001). "At base, sovereignty is a nation's power to self-govern, to determine its own way of life, and to live that life—to whatever extent possible—free from interference" (Cobb 2006, 118). Being truly sovereign is to insure that one's culture will continue (Cobb 2006). There is no more important way to ensure cultural survival than through the care and well-being of children. Deloria (1995) describes tribal sovereignty as internal and external.

Internal Sovereignty

When people think about tribal sovereignty, they most often think about the external domain. This applies to government-to-government relations between tribal governments and state and federal governments. Internal sovereignty is equally important. Internal sovereignty recognizes that not only do tribal people have a unique political status, but we also have unique cultural ways that have provided us with strength and continuity through the centuries. This internal sovereignty is practiced across the world by Indigenous Peoples. It is this internal sovereignty that is seen when tribal groups exercise this right through the practice of Indigenous ways, especially in the practice of Indigenous religions. The practice of Indigenous ways within families and communities is often hidden from the public view (Poupart et al. 2000). "American Indian elders advise that support and preservation of Indian families rests as much on retaining cultural integrity of tribal life as it does on the exercise of sovereign political power" (Red Horse et al. 2001, 16). It is internal sovereignty—the transmission of tribal culture throughout all aspects of tribal life—that supports raising healthy Indigenous children.

American Indian Family Systems

The Indigenous family would be called an extended family in mainstream vernacular. While this captures some of what an Indigenous family is, family in a tribal sense is much more than that. Indigenous families are "blood relatives," but they are also comprised of "cultural families" who are bonded through clans, ceremonies, and cultural adoption. These cultural families provide a much larger nurturing system of support (Red Horse et al. 2001). It is important to understand the role these systems play in supporting parents to raise healthy children. "Nurturing systems include extended family and kin systems, traditional healing systems, and other tribal customary supports. In most aspects of tribal social services, families, communities, spirituality, and other natural support elements are integrated components of a holistic nurturing system" (Red Horse et al. 2001, 17).

American Indian/Alaska Native family systems have been preserved through the years despite attempts to destroy them. They remain strong because there are three reinforcing areas that work together to maintain "socio-cultural standards." They are institutional domains, sustaining systems, and nurturing systems (Red Horse et al. 2001)—see Figure 6.1.

Institutional domains consist of tribal governments and other supporting external structures. For example, in Minnesota there are 11 distinct tribes, each with its own unique government with elected officials, tribal codes, policies, and laws. These tribal governments are supported by the Minnesota Indian Affairs Council where all 11 tribes meet to discuss common issues. Then there is the Minnesota Chippewa Tribe, which consists of the Anishinaabe tribes only. These structures surround the other domains and are the first line of defense in terms of treaty and external matters. Institutional domains exist for Indigenous Peoples worldwide.

Sustaining systems are composed of primarily tribal programs. Because every tribe is unique, the array of services varies greatly. They may consist of Headstart

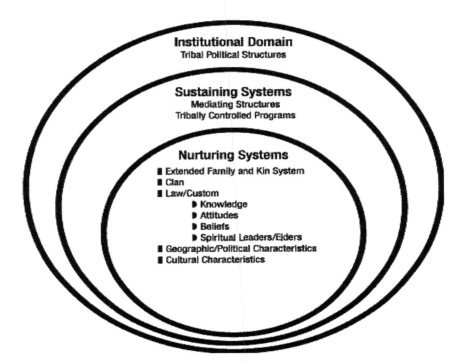

Figure 6.1   Nurturing family systems
Source: Red Horse, J.G., Martinez, C., and Day, P. 2001. *Family Preservation: A Case Study of Indian Tribal Policy*. Seattle, WA: Casey Family Programs.

programs, tribal schools, human service and health programs, elderly services, and housing programs. These programs provide families with services that help sustain them and their communities. Some programs are culturally grounded while others are more mainstream in their approach. Sustaining systems are found across the world in Indigenous communities.

Nurturing systems are the cultural core of any tribal community. These systems include family, extended family, cultural family, clans, and the language and traditions of a tribal group. This system is often tied to a land base or geographical region where a tribe's ancestors resided. All of these systems work in tandem to support and sustain a tribal group's culture and assure its continuity.

Raising Healthy American Indian/Alaska Native Children

While each tribe is unique and has its own stories and ways of transmitting cultural teachings, Anishinaabe examples and stories are used to provide sufficient detail to be meaningful. Many concepts discussed may be generalizable to other tribal groups.

In order to understand a culture, it is important to understand basic elements of it. Key Anishinaabe concepts as articulated in Anishinaabemowin (the language of the Anishinaabe people) are as follows: 1) *ishpendaagokin* (values); 2) *azhawinamaadiwin* (language and communication patterns); 3) *izhiningodogamig* (family orientations); 4) *noojimotwaawin (an) gaye izhichigewin* (healing beliefs and practices); 5) *izhitwaawin* (religion); 6) *ozhichigan(an), niimi'idiwin nagamo(an)* (art, dance, and music); 7) *inanjigewin* (diet and food); 8) *izhimamaajiiwin* (recreation); 9) *gigishkigan (an)* (clothing); 10) *mewinzha* (history); 11) *eshpendaagozid* (social status); and 12) *oko'idiwin* (social group interactions) (Simard and Blight 2011, 9).

Simard and Blight (2011) say these "values – *ishpendaagokin* are critical to understand when working in any culture. Helpers must remember, in order for Aboriginal children to thrive within the majority culture, they must be grounded within the structure of their own culture and therefore be attached to the cultural variables and process within their families, communities, and Nation" (14). These variables and this concept of being grounded in cultural identity is the basis for raising healthy Indian children. Each of these variables has important teachings but this chapter will focus on the first three areas—values, language, and family orientation.

Value Development—Ishpendaagokin

Among the Anishinaabeg, there is what is commonly called the Seven Sacred Grandfather Teachings. These values are shared by Anishinaabeg Peoples across the United States and Canada and have been passed down orally for centuries. They are: wisdom, love, respect, bravery, honesty, humility, and truth (Little River Band of Ottawa Indians 2012). While spelling and meanings vary somewhat, they are similar to what Simard and Blight (2011) describe learning from the First Nation elders:

> **Wisdom** – *nibwaakaaawin* – *gikensaasowin* is to acknowledge the opportunity to learn in every moment, to be reflective and to seek to extend knowledge and understanding.

> **Love** – *zaagi-idiwin* – *zheewenidiwin* is to care and cooperate well with others. Love is working toward harmony through kindness and sharing.

> **Respect** – *manaazodiwin* – *ozhibwaadenidiwin* is to maintain high standards of conduct that provides safety for the dignity, individuality, and rights of every living thing.

> **Bravery** – *zoongide'ewin* is to face adversity with integrity and courage by maintaining a strong sense of self and confidence in one's abilities and character.

Honesty – *gwekwaadiziwin* is to be truthful, sincere, and fair through all circumstances.

Humility – *dibasendizowin* – *nookaadiziwin* is to be modest, respectful, and sensitive in relation to all living things, and to know one's status in all of creation.

Truth – *dibasendisowin* – nookaadiziwin is to be genuine and true and know human development as it related to all seven teachings. (14–15)

These are considered to be the values that Anishinaabeg children need to learn in order to live a good life.

Language—Inwewin

Indigenous Peoples throughout the world have experienced a loss in language due to harsh governmental policies, including boarding schools where children were punished for speaking their Native language (Poupart et al. 2000, Brave Heart 2004, Rheault 1999). There has been a resurgence reclaiming Indigenous languages because tribal values and deep understandings about spiritual teachings can't always be translated into English. Native people who grow up with their language have a much deeper understanding of the values and their connection to spirituality and the natural world (Rheault 1999, Simard and Blight 2011, Treuer 2001).

Family Orientation/Natural Protective Network Principle—Inaadiziwin

American Indian/Alaska Native children are born into a nurturing system of care (Poupart et al. 2000, Red Horse et al. 2001). In Anishinaabe culture this natural protective network is called *inaadiziwin* and it includes the "biological family, an extended family, a clan family, a community, and Nation" (Simard and Blight 2011, 16). Knowing who your family is and to whom you are related is important in tribal communities. It is common in tribal communities to be asked when meeting someone for the first time "who are you are related to?" This not only helps a child understand their connection to others but it helps others in the community to know more about the child. It often establishes instant connections.

Besides family and extended family, knowing one's clan and what it represents is an important part of identity. "The clan system is an ancient custom, which has been passed down through many generations" (Simard and Blight 2011, 12). A child is considered related to everyone else who is a member of the same clan. This information guided whom one could marry and many other social connections. This knowledge directs children throughout their life. In Anishinaabe culture, clan is referred to as "doodem." Just as knowing one's relations, clans are an important part of understanding tribal identity (Rheault 1999).

Researchers at the University of Minnesota Duluth (2009) interviewed Anishinaabe elders from several reservations in northern Minnesota asking the question, "What does it take to raise healthy Anishinaabeg kids?" They build upon research conducted by the Search Institute, which has been a leader in researching and providing tools to help children and adolescents succeed in all areas of their lives, family, school, and community (Search Institute 2012). They are known for researching and training in developmental assets that children need to be successful. Their theory is that by consciously increasing developmental assets for youth, high-risk behaviors will decrease. Their research seems to bear this out (Search Institute 2012).

Developmental Assets

According to the Search Institute (2012), there are 40 attributes that enable children to grow up to be healthy, engaged adults. These assets include relationships the child has with others, activities and events they are exposed to and participate in, and their values and ways of coping that help them avoid high-risk behaviors. These behaviors include drug, tobacco, and alcohol usage, sexual activity, and engaging in violence. These behaviors can lead to negative outcomes such as teen pregnancy, dropping out of school, and other problems at home, school, and with law enforcement.

"Levels of assets are better predictors of high-risk involvement and thriving than poverty or being from a single-parent family" (paragraph 5). By studying these phenomena they found that the average young person experiences fewer than half of the 40 assets, and boys experience an average of three fewer assets than girls (Search Institute 2012). Knowing the difference having these assets makes in a young person's life enables parents and community members to consciously increase opportunities for children to have more assets in their life.

Most people agree that raising a child, any child, in a healthy manner is not an easy task. The Center for Regional and Tribal Child Welfare Studies at the University of Minnesota Duluth undertook a research project to ask American Indian community members about developmental assets using the Search Institute's research as a guideline. The elders who participated in the interviews and focus groups identified the phrase "healthy Anishinaabe child" and discussed the parenting and outside support that enables an American Indian/Alaska Native child to be healthy. They said, "Healthy Anishinaabeg (plural) children make good decisions on their own and apply values to their own lives. They have positive self-identifications, are comfortable with who they are, are spiritually connected, and are part of an extended family unit and a cultural community" (paragraph 4). The elders were asked about what constituted support, empowerment, boundaries and expectations, constructive use of time, commitment to learning, positive values, social competencies, and positive identity, and provided stories that illustrated each area.

Support

Elders defined support as "family, extended family, and other caring adults who are actively involved in a child's life." They noted that it is important for children to have "[a]dults communicate to and around the child in a positive way. The community and school show the child they care about him/her. Parents are involved in the child's education" (University of Minnesota Duluth 2009, paragraph 1).

- One of the ways in which a child gets support is that they "should spend time with elders, especially their grandparents." One elder said, "I do as much with my grandson as possible, even little things such as walks, rides, showing him bugs in the woods. Anything that is enjoyable to my grandson" (paragraph 2).
- Another elder told the story of when he was small and one of 10 children in his family. Elders played an important role in helping him to learn what it meant to be a boy and eventually a man. "... in the summer time I would be picking berries and swimming ... the old men taught me how to set nets in the spring for fish, how to clean the fish, and how to cook them in the fireplace ... when my grandpa would go ricing, he would take us kids along ... my grandma made mats out of cedar strips, and I was told to watch her" (paragraph 3).
- The elders stressed the importance of families spending time together doing activities and listening to your children. "Always be home with your child for all those family activities, even if you are tired" (paragraph 4).
- "One thing it takes to raise a healthy child is communication, even if it is by teasing. Small chitchat while doing joint activities is quality time. Pay attention to them, especially the young ones, take them along with you everywhere. Include them as you do your chores and make sure they have some responsibility for the chore being completed" (paragraph 5).

Empowerment

Empowerment was defined as ensuring the child "feels valued and safe in their community, know the importance of helping others and are involved in cultural activities" (University of Minnesota Duluth 2009, Empowerment, paragraph 1).

- An important message about empowerment was that children should be encouraged to explore their world and that people should "create opportunities for them to succeed, and yet allow them to learn from their mistakes" (paragraph 2).
- One elder said, "One of the important things a parent can do is to set up situations where your child can succeed ... these activities are rehearsals for the real life activities they will face" (paragraph 3).

- Another said, "It's very important to praise children, tell them what they did was good to assure them that what they do has value, worth, and importance. Let children learn from their mistakes and let them know everyone makes them. It's important that they learn to get back up after they fall down, don't crucify themselves. Be willing to forgive them" (paragraph 4).
- Many of the elders talked about showing children that they are loved and always treating them with respect. "A good role model loves their children, they are respectful to them and praise them. They also use discipline, but never any discipline that is harsh or cruel." Another elder said, "Once the child feels loved, all the other needs fall into place" (paragraphs 5 and 7).
- Another common theme was that it is important for children to have knowledge of their Ojibwe/Anishinaabe culture, "because it is a source of strength for them." One person said, "Those children that keep their culture do the best at staying healthy" (paragraph 8).

Having Boundaries and Expectations

This is defined as making sure children know what is expected of them and that they have limits set by adults. This concept is important not only at home but also at school and in the community. It also encompasses having positive adult role models available to children, again preferably both at home and in the community. It was also suggested that children learn to have high expectations for themselves, which is learned when adults have high, but reasonable, expectations for them. The elders said this starts with parents being good role models (University of Minnesota Duluth 2009, Boundaries and Expectations, paragraph 1).

- They said, "Parents are good role models when children see them working together. Parents must 'walk the walk' and also work with your child when necessary" (paragraph 2).
- Parents must "provide stable and consistent parenting, with firm schedules, structures, routines, and responsibilities" (paragraph 3).
- One elder gave the example of herself when she was growing up: "As a young child I had a regular schedule or routine. I also stress the same schedule or routine to my own children. My children and I went to bed early and were required to do chores. These were for their own good, so they would accept responsibility and accountability. Even when my sons participated in extra-curricular activities they still had to complete their chores. Sometimes they would come home from school, do the dishes, and then run off to practice" (paragraph 3).
- Making sure children are supervised came up in many discussions. "Parents should pay more attention to their kids. I see kids running around out there, they can do anything they want. They bump into people without excusing themselves. Even at powwows they act up and parents don't tell them to behave" (paragraph 4). Respect for others is expected of children.

Constructive Use of Time

Constructive use of time was described as when "the child engages in creative cultural, community, or school activities; the child is engaged in spiritual and/ or religious activities; the child has a valued role in their family, community, and school" (University of Minnesota Duluth 2009, Constructive Use of Time, paragraph 1).

- Elders talked about the importance of providing "opportunities for children to be outside and in the woods to learn about medicines and survival skills. The cultural teachings involve many medicines, and the children should experience time in the woods to locate these medicines. In the Anishinaabe teachings, there is a natural medicine for any sickness we encounter. A medicine man would fast and he would be told what medicines would help the sick individual" (paragraph 2).
- "Involve children in helpful activities and play. For example, have children take responsibility for watering the houseplants. Be sure to explain how the activity contributes to the plants' growth. Play games with your child— games that involve the mind and physical activity" (paragraph 3).
- Many elders talked about limiting the time kids spend watching TV and playing video games, suggesting instead that they should be involved in cultural programs and ceremonies. "A healthy kid will not have too many bad influences, such as too much TV watching. TVs open up subjects never talked about in traditional times, such as subjects on sexual activity, random killings of others, etc. The more children see, the more they want to do themselves. Kids need to be limited on how much they watch TV or play video games, and what they watch" (paragraph 4).

Commitment to Learning

Commitment to learning was described as a "child [who] has goals and believes that s/he can achieve them, has a positive relationship with their school, enjoys being read to, and cultural activities (crafts, language, ceremonies, etc.) are integrated in their life" (University of Minnesota Duluth 2009, Commitment to Learning, paragraph 1).

- The elders said that it is important to make opportunities for children to learn to speak the Ojibwe language. "The language keeps people straight because the meanings and feelings of the language stress the good life – the red road." In order to learn the language they need "to have the language spoken to them." "Maintaining the culture is important to survival, and we have to use our Ojibwemowin language when we talk to the Creator" (paragraph 2).

- Another important teaching is to "help children to understand their connection to the living world" (paragraph 3).
- Respect includes caring about all living things. "Today the kids do not grow up with knowledge on how to raise, love, or care for animals. When kids are allowed to disrespect the animals, we as a people lose a lot. Those kids are unaware of the connection between the animals and us. Many kids are unaware that the food they eat and the clothes they wear come from the animals" (paragraph 3).
- In order to be successful, children need to be supported to do well in school. "Parents should be involved as their children are engaged in school learning as well as traditional Ojibwe learning." One elder talked about needing to support her children by setting limits and boundaries with children. "Be firm – make sure your kids get their schoolwork done. If they were not getting their work done I would say, 'Get your homework done or I'm coming to class with you!'" (paragraph 4).
- Children need to learn about cultural teachings from elders and grandparents. "As a healthy person, my formal education gave me a foundation to live by. However, my real education came from my grandparents' traditional teachings. They taught me things that formal education never taught" (paragraph 4).

Positive Values

Positive values are defined as a "child shows concern for the wellbeing of others. Kids understand how they are connected to the plants, animals, and human beings around them and the impacts their actions have on the world around them. Children exhibit traditional traits of honesty, integrity, humility, humor, responsibility, respect, kindness, and love" (University of Minnesota Duluth 2009, Positive Values, paragraph 1). These are similar to the grandfather teachings described earlier.

- The elders talked about how "children should be grounded in their community and in Anishinaabe cultural values" (paragraph 2).
- "The traditional religion gives children security and a sense of belonging in the community, a sense of having a community that will accept them" (paragraph 2).
- "Anishinaabeg children should be given an Indian name, and should be taught about the clans" (paragraph 3).
- "Dreams can't be fulfilled until you know who you are and why you are here. The clans offer these teachings" (paragraph 3).
- "Make sure to use your Indian name and clan to be recognized" (paragraph 3).
- Parents and other adults need to practice living in a good way to serve as healthy role models. "Kids copy parents, so if you have bad or unhealthy

behaviors such as smoking, drinking and using drugs, they will see that" (paragraph 4).

- "One of the most important things parents can do for their kids is to keep them chemically free. You must be a role model, and be chemically free yourself to be effective and believable. You have to walk the walk" (paragraph 4).
- "Model humility, sharing, respect for elders, and humor so kids can learn them" (paragraph 5).
- "Show kids how to take care of others first, then themselves. They should know how to forgive even when it's hard and they should not talk down to people. Talk about healing in a good way, that is an important teaching" (paragraph 5).
- "Humor is a main connecting fiber that helps us defuse personal stuff, it is a good survival mechanism. Humor helps us connect and show affection. Humor and optimism can turn children into healthy adults" (paragraph 5).

Social Competencies

Social competencies were described as a "youth who is able to plan and make good decisions, they get along well with others, understand and appreciate their own culture as well as the cultures of others, they demonstrate leadership and healthy conflict resolution skills" (University of Minnesota Duluth 2009, Social Competencies, paragraph 1).

- One elder said, "Young Anishinaabeg children need to be familiar with ceremonies and spiritual practices" (paragraph 2). This means learning the cultural protocols so that they know how to ask for help and what to do at ceremonies.
- "I remember seeing my grandfather use tobacco for ceremonial purposes. I remember my grandmother and great-grandmother smoking their pipes for ceremonial purposes and for praying. Those two women always made sure tobacco was purchased when someone went to town to buy something" (paragraph 2). It is important to always have tobacco and to use it.
- "Ceremonial practices are good. I teach my kids about the proper use of tobacco, and when and where to pray with tobacco. My children also participate in other ceremonies and see the amount of work required to conduct a ceremony" (paragraph 2).
- Adults need to model respect with their children. "Help children learn by listening to their questions and by being patient with them. A healthy child is curious and their questions should be considered important" (paragraph 3). Children learn about the world and how to behave with others by the relationships they have with their family and community.

Positive Identity

Positive identity was described as "children who feel good about themselves, are hopeful about their future, believe they can make a difference in the world around them, and feel connected to their family, culture, and tribe" (University of Minnesota Duluth 2009, Positive Identity, paragraph 1).

- Positive identity occurs when children feel loved. "Tell your children when you are pleased with them" (paragraph 2).
- "To help your children develop positive self-esteem, praise them. Don't condemn them for mistakes, but rather assure them that they are learning and that they are not expected to be experts the first time. Really praise them when they accomplish something" (paragraph 2).
- "Encourage the interests children discover on their own, and teach kids to be authentic and true to themselves" (paragraph 3).
- Adults need to guide children to move toward the purpose for which they were put on the earth. "When a child wants to be someone else rather than who they are, tell them 'no' and 'just be yourself'" (paragraph 3).
- "To help kids develop positive self-esteem, we have to encourage them to be themselves, and that who they are is ok. Help the children succeed, even if it is only in small successes, and be sure to praise them ... Spend time with them to help them discover their uniqueness and strengths" (paragraph 3).

Conclusion

Findings from the University of Minnesota Duluth researchers mimic the seven grandfather teachings of what children need to learn to live a good life. They are: wisdom, love, respect, bravery, honesty, humility, and truth. Children raised in this way will have a good opportunity to grow up healthy in spite of environmental challenges. They will be more likely to make good decisions and avoid high-risk behaviors. They will understand and apply positive cultural values and feel comfortable with themselves. They will seek their spiritual purpose in life and engage with a larger cultural family and community. These are all the things the elders said describe a healthy American Indian/Alaska Native child.

These teachings are learned in many ways over the course of a lifetime. Cultural structures exist that position children for learning. They include naming ceremonies, fasting, sweat lodges, sun dances, coming of age, and many other tribally specific ceremonies. As tribal people we are rich in traditions. They are always there for us to learn so we may live as we were intended—a good life. This is why it is imperative for children to be raised within their culture.

If someone has been raised outside of their culture, there are many opportunities to learn. It is never too late to learn about your relatives and your tribal ways.

Learning about culture is not a destination, but a lifelong journey. As the elders say, if you make a mistake, learn from it and keep trying. If you are a provider working with someone raised outside of their culture, you can support them in finding cultural connections, but you need to remember that the choice is always theirs to make.

The Search Institute domains provide examples of how American Indian/ Alaska Native parents can raise children in a healthy manner. Three important areas for all parents to be aware of are the importance of teaching strong values, making sure children are raised in a cultural milieu that includes tribal language and cultural traditions, and that children have strong family, extended, and cultural family connections. Culture and tradition are more than raising healthy American Indian/Alaska Native children; they are about insuring the cultural survival of Indigenous Peoples across the world.

> Children are taught to respect everything and everyone, and they are to be encouraged to connect with mother earth. Children are to be raised with respect because they will become their parents' caretakers someday. (Simard and Blight 2011, 28)

References

Adams, A.K., Harvey, H.E., and Prince, R.J. 2005. Association of maternal smoking with overweight at age 3 in American Indian children. *American Journal of Clinical Nutrition*, 82(2), 393–8.

Association of Alaska School Boards (nd). *Alaska Initiative for Community Engagement (AlaskaICE)*. Retrieved September 12, 2013, from http://alaska ice.org/developmental-assets/what-are-assets/.

Brave Heart, M.Y.H. 2004. The historical trauma response among Natives and its relationship to substance abuse: A Lakota illustration. In *Healing and Mental Health for Native Americans: Speaking in Red*, E. Nebelkopf and M. Phillips (eds). Walnut Creek, CA: Alta Mira Press, 7–18.

Cobb, A.J. 2006. Understanding tribal sovereignty: Definitions, conceptualizations, and interpretations. *Indigenous Studies Today*, 1, 115–32.

Cross, T. 2010. Relational worldview model. National Indian Child Welfare Association. Retrieved September 12, 2013, from http://www.nicwa.org/ Relational_Worldview/.

Day, P. 2011. The seventh generation: The future of Minnesota's American Indian youth. *Rural Minnesota Journal*, 6, 39–57.

Deloria, V. 1995. Rethinking tribal sovereignty. In *The Legal and Historical Importance of Tribal Sovereignty: A Summary Report of the Spring Forum*, May 1995. St Paul, MN: American Indian Research and Policy Institute.

Geary, E. and Day, P. 2010. Key considerations and best practices for tribal Title IV-E data collection and reporting. March 2010. Washington, DC: National

Congress of American Indians. Retrieved September 12, 2013, from http://childwelfare.ncaiprc.org.

Gundersen, C. 2006. *Measuring the Extent and Depth of Food Insecurity: An Application to American Indians in the United States* (#06-02). National Poverty Center Working Paper Series. Retrieved September 12, 2013, from http://www.npc.umich.edu/publications/working_papers/.

Little River Band of Ottawa Indians 2012. *Anishinaabemdaa: The Seven Grandfather's Teachings*. Retrieved September 12, 2013, from http://www.anishinaabemdaa.com/grandfathers.htm.

Medicine, B. 2004. Context is everything. In *Every Day is a Good Day: Reflections by Contemporary Indigenous Women*, W. Mankiller (ed.). Golden, CO: Fulcrum Publishing, 41–74.

National Center for Children in Poverty 2012. *Young Child Risk Calculator*. Retrieved September 12, 2013, from http://www.nccp.org/.

Office of Health Policy 2011. *American Indian/Alaska Native Heritage*. Retrieved September 12, 2013, from http://www.cdc.gov/Features/AIANHeritageMonth/.

Peacock, T. and Wisuri, M. 2006. *The Four Hills of Life: Ojibwe Wisdom*. Afton, MN: Afton Historical Society Press.

Poupart, J., Martinez, C., Red Horse, J., and Scharnberg, D. 2000. *To Build a Bridge: Working with American Indian Communities*. St Paul, MN: American Indian Policy Center.

Red Horse, J.G., Martinez, C., and Day, P. 2001. Family preservation: A case study of Indian tribal practice. National Indian Child Welfare Association. Retrieved May, 25, 2012 from http://www.nicwa.org/research/01.family%20pres01.rpt.pdf.

Rheault, D. 1999. *Anishinaabe Mino-Bimaadiziwin: The Way of a Good Life*. Peterborough, ON: Debwewin Press.

Search Institute 2012. *Developmental Assets*. Retrieved September 12, 2013, from http://www.search-institute.org/developmental-assets.

Simard, E. 2009. Culturally restorative child welfare practice: A special emphasis on cultural attachment theory. *First People's Child and Family Review*, 4(2), 44–61.

Simard, E. and Blight, S. 2011. Developing a culturally restorative approach to Aboriginal child and youth development: Transitions to adulthood. *First Peoples Child and Family Review*, 6(1), 28–55.

Snipp, M. 2002. *American Indian and Alaska Native Children in the 2000 Census*. Baltimore, MD: Annie E. Casey Foundation.

Story, M., Evans, M., Fabsitz, R.R., et al. 1999. The epidemic of obesity in American Indian communities and the need for childhood obesity-prevention programs. *American Journal of Clinical Nutrition*, 69(4), 7475–545.

Treuer, A. 2001. *Living our Language: Ojibwe Tales and Oral Histories*. St Paul, MN: Minnesota Historical Society Press, Native Voices.

University of Minnesota Duluth 2009. *Raising Healthy Anishinaabeg Children.* Center for Regional and Tribal Child Welfare Studies. Retrieved September 12, 2013, from http://www.d.umn.edu/sw/cw/anish_child/index.html.

Weaver, H.N. 2001. Indigenous identity: What is it and who really has it? *American Indian Quarterly*, 25(2), 240–55.

.

Chapter 7

Preserving Native Families, Preserving Native Cultures

Nancy Lucero and Marian Bussey

Native families in the United States, Canada, Australia, and New Zealand have faced centuries of government policies, legal decrees, and direct military actions intended to eradicate Indigenous cultures through processes that have included assimilation, genocide, and displacement from traditional lands. Additionally, large-scale, systematic removal of Native children from their families and communities through involuntary placement in residential or boarding schools (Adams 1995, Hoxie 1989, Union of BC Indian Chiefs 2002, Valentine and Gray 2006) and widespread adoption of Native children to non-Natives were common colonial experiences for American Indians, First Nations peoples, Maori, and Indigenous Australians (Armitage 1995, George 1997, McKenzie 1989, Miller et al. 1980). These processes were explicitly intended to weaken and eventually destroy Native cultures by shattering the cohesion of families and kinship networks, thereby making nearly impossible the intergenerational transmission of cultural knowledge, values, and practices (Cross 1986, Mannes 1995). The tragic result was that multitudes of Native children born in the nineteenth and twentieth centuries did not have the opportunity learn about and embrace their cultures and take their places within the kinship systems and tribal communities to which they belonged.

Today, many Native groups are responding to this colonial history by stressing the importance of their young people having strong ties to family, clan, tribe, community, and cultural values and practices—what will be referred to in this chapter as *cultural connections*. These groups recognize that healthy families and young people with strong cultural connections are essential to building strong Native nations, to tribal and urban communities that are flourishing, and to the exercise of sovereignty and self-determination through continued observance of cultural traditions and practices. In this way, cultural preservation is directly linked to children's cultural connectedness, which in turn is dependent upon the preservation of Native families. Cultural preservation and family preservation go hand in hand and are interdependent.

The child welfare system in the US, as well as Canada, Australia, and New Zealand has, both historically and in many cases, in the present, been a principal agent responsible for severing or weakening Native children's community, kinship, clan, identity, and spiritual bonds. Both official policies and practices and the discriminatory and racist attitudes of individual administrators and workers have resulted in disproportionate numbers of Native children growing up in non-Native homes. While this impact has been felt acutely by the families of these children, the loss of member children has been deeply felt by their tribes and Native communities, as well. Recently, a number of tribal and urban Native communities have begun to develop community-based family preservation programs, such as those discussed later in this chapter, that incorporate cultural knowledge, traditions, and practices as a means of addressing the impact of decades of large-scale child removals, and to help children and young adults maintain their cultural connectedness.

What is involved in preserving Native families so that they are cohesive, nurturing, and able to play their role in transmitting and strengthening culture? As this chapter will explore, *what* constitutes family preservation and *why* family preservation is so important may be seen by Native groups as quite different from how the public child welfare system sees it—as an *intervention* used to remediate family *deficiencies*. To build a foundation for this exploration, the chapter opens with an American Indian perspective on family preservation, then shares some examples of family preservation in tribal and urban communities. It will then go on to provide a short history of public child welfare family preservation and reunification policies and practices, including a brief discussion of the link between these elements and the disproportionate representation of American Indian children in this system. Finally, approaches to community-based family preservation practice in tribal and urban communities in the United States are highlighted.

This chapter is grounded in the American Indian experience; however, readers may find information and ideas also relevant to Aboriginal/Indigenous Peoples in Canada, Australia, and New Zealand. Groups in these countries share with American Indians histories of colonialism, as well as engagement in ongoing efforts to resist assimilation and cultural destruction and to exercise sovereignty and self-determination. Each group exhibits pride in its culture, and recognizes the value and relevancy of traditional cultural knowledge and practices. Throughout the article, we use the terms "American Indian" and "Native" when we refer collectively to the peoples of the tribal groups in the United States, including Alaska. We are aware that certain groups and individuals feel strongly about what constitutes the correct terminology and we apologize for any unintended discomfort or offense our choice of terminology may cause.

American Indian Perspectives on Family Preservation

The traditional Anglo-American or dominant culture nuclear family structure typically consists of spouses, biological children, and, in cases of remarriage, some stepchildren. In this model of family structure, extended family members tend to play a minimal role in day-to-day functioning, decision-making, and child rearing

(McGill and Pearce 1996). In contrast, families in most American Indian cultures are seen as kinship networks (Red Horse et al. 1978) or relational systems (Cross 1986, Halverson et al. 2002). These systems often encompass a large network of members that may include not only parents, but aunts, uncles, grandparents, cousins, and other kin, as well as "customary" or non-blood relatives, clan relations, and individuals with ceremonial or other traditional relationships to the family or an individual member (Goodluck 1980, Lucero 2007). Typically, members of these family networks interact frequently and make decisions across generational and other relational boundaries, and share child-rearing and other family tasks (Red Horse 1980). Interdependence within the family network is stressed (Brave Heart 2002, Red Horse 1980), in contrast to the independence of the nuclear family often sought in Eurocentric or dominant culture nuclear families (McGill and Pearce 1996). Even in urban Indian communities, American Indian families often exhibit traditional attitudes toward family composition (Lucero 2007). Traditional tribal conceptualizations of family may also include non-Native members as parts of the family system. Whatever their unique composition, families are seen as the foundation of Native cultures, whether in the United States, Canada, Australia, or New Zealand.

Typically, great value is placed on children in Native families and cultures (Goodluck and Short 1980, Public Law 95-608 1978). One vital function of American Indian kinship systems, as well as family systems in other Aboriginal/Indigenous cultures, is to transmit cultural knowledge, values, and practices from older generations to younger ones (Cheshire 2001, Lucero 2009, Wagner 1976). Children represent the future of the tribal group (Union of BC Indian Chiefs 2002), thus, keeping children connected to kinship networks and communities, and passing on cultural knowledge, values, and practices to young people are vital to ensuring the group's integrity and continuity. Growing up in their Native families also allows children to more naturally assume their roles as members of the kinship network and to take their places in tribal or urban Native communities.

When social workers and other helping professionals use the term *family preservation*, they are most often referring to formal child welfare interventions as discussed in the next section of this chapter. These actions are intended to safely maintain a child in the family home and in the care of a birth parent(s) or other caregiver (such as a grandmother) while helping the parents to address challenges. When Native people think about family preservation, they often associate it with preservation of the tribal group and tribal culture. Thus, family preservation is more than simply a child welfare intervention intended to keep children out of the foster care system. Instead, family preservation is a vital part of cultural preservation, community preservation, and ensuring the future well-being of the tribal group. As such, current Native family preservation efforts (such as those described below) that maintain children's cultural and community connections play a critical role in cultural preservation for American Indians and other Native peoples.

Although preservation of American Indian culture has been supported since the 1970s by several official US policies, family preservation services have not typically been the first choice intervention when American Indian families become involved in the child welfare system (Coleman et al. 2001). There have been charges that child welfare systems in many parts of the US have at best been reluctant to acknowledge the need to maintain children's cultural connections, and at worst have been overtly hostile toward these aims (Red Horse et al. 2001). In many Child Protective Services (CPS) departments, fundamental and unexamined institutional and individual racism has driven child welfare decision-making in cases involving American Indian families. Departments in some areas with large Native populations continue to treat American Indian children and families in discriminatory ways that may indicate deep-seated and ongoing racism (Sullivan and Walters 2011).

In the United States, currently, Native children and families may become involved with one of several child welfare systems, depending upon factors such as where they are domiciled, where the child welfare concern took place, and whether they are enrolled members (or eligible for membership) of a federally recognized American Indian tribe. Children who are both tribal members and domiciled within the tribe's boundaries typically fall under the jurisdiction of the tribal court and tribal child welfare department. Tribally based children who become involved with their tribe's child welfare program and are able to continue living in their tribal community are often able to retain their family, kinship, clan, community, and cultural bonds.

In contrast, Native children living outside the boundaries of a tribal nation, such as the large numbers now living in urban areas, initially come under the jurisdiction of the state or county CPS department where they live and/or where the child welfare concern has taken place. If these children are enrolled tribal members, or eligible for membership, they are covered under the Indian Child Welfare Act of 1978 (ICWA) and their tribe may choose to take jurisdiction of the case. However, an increasing number of American Indian children are no longer eligible for tribal enrollment for various reasons. In cases involving these children, the state or county CPS department continues to have sole jurisdiction, and the unique cultural needs of these young people may not be addressed because they fail to meet the legal definition of an Indian child under the ICWA. A lack of understanding of the history and current complexity of tribal enrollment often results in their mistakenly being considered to no longer be *culturally* Indian. Unless their families are preserved, these children are often at great risk of losing not only family connections, but connections to their communities and culture, as well.

In the United States, and in Canada, Australia, and New Zealand as well, Native children have been placed in out-of-home, non-relative care at disproportionally high rates (Hill 2006, Valentine and Gray 2006, Union of BC Chiefs 2002, Walmsley 2005), despite both group efforts and laws calling for alternatives to removals (Plantz et al. 1989, Mannes 1993). The initial discussions and debates that took place when the United States' Indian Child Welfare Act (ICWA) legislation was initially proposed in the late 1970s appeared as if those pointing out the need for the Act conceived of it as legislation to not only stem the removal of Native children but to preserve families as well. The Act is well known for wording that calls for preventing the breakup of the Indian family, and includes a provision calling for active efforts that provide remedial and rehabilitative services to either prevent removal or support reunification (Native American Rights Fund 2007, Public Law 95-608 1978). Preventing the breakup of the family and providing remedial and rehabilitative services to prevent child removal sound remarkably similar to the basic goals of family preservation interventions. However, due to the high numbers of Native children who continue to be removed from home, it appears that while American Indians may see the ICWA as calling for family preservation efforts on the part of state/county CPS departments, many of these departments do not. The contrasting perspectives on family preservation held by CPS are outlined in the next section.

**History and Perspectives on Family Preservation
in Child Protective Services**

White children were originally served by local child rescue societies, who would place children that were determined to be maltreated with foster families or in group homes (Anderson 1989). Anderson notes that this began to change during the Progressive Era, when in 1906 the Massachusetts Society for the Prevention of Cruelty to Children took steps to look into why families had reached a point where rescue was needed and to provide social services that would support these families. In the same era, the passage of the federal Mother's Pension Law (1910) allowed poor women who would have otherwise lost their children solely by reason of poverty to provide a home for their children. Aside from the Mother's Pension and the establishment of a federal Children's Bureau in 1912, child welfare services were handled at the state and local levels; these departments were often assisted by guidance from private organizations such as the Child Welfare League of America (CWLA) and the American Humane Association (AHA). It was not until the early 1970s, after national attention was drawn to the problem of the "battered child," that the US Congress passed federal legislation to deal with child abuse and neglect (Anderson 1989). This first law, the Child Abuse Prevention and Treatment Act of 1974 (CAPTA), created national standards for responding to child abuse and neglect, created federal funding for states, and provided federal support for data collection and research.

Supportive services were called for in the cases of families where caseworkers determined that with further education, resources, support, and case management, parents could solve the issues that had led to a child maltreatment report. In contrast, out-of-home care (foster care or group homes) was indicated in cases where workers felt a child was at imminent risk of harm or where there was a real risk that maltreatment would continue in the home unless the children were removed. When children were removed, CPS workers could work with the courts to terminate parents' rights and free children for adoption, but were supposed to work toward reunification of the children with their parents whenever possible. However, this ideal was not always met, particularly for children of color, and many children stayed in foster care for years (often called foster care drift) only to "age out" of the system at age 18 (Roberts 2002).

This reality of foster care drift led to increased calls for more supportive services to preserve families. Family preservation cases are defined by the child welfare system as those where CPS, often with the blessing of the courts, has determined that children can remain safely in their own home. In most family preservation intervention models used by CPS, an intensive level of services is provided to the parents/caregivers to assist them to remedy the conditions that brought the child and family to the attention of the child welfare department. Family preservation, in the sense of preventing removal of children by providing social services, has been a goal of American child welfare since the era of the settlement houses. However, the practice of intensive family preservation was formally introduced in the 1970s as a Tacoma, Washington-based program called Homebuilders (Kinney et al. 1991), and encouraged as an example of "reasonable efforts" to keep a family intact, as called for by the Adoption Assistance and Child Welfare Act of 1980 (AACW). This Act increased funding for family support services while still authorizing out-of-home placement for serious cases.

As a result of the AACW, Intensive Family Preservation Services (IFPS), as a more focused and intense form of family support services, were implemented on a large scale during the 1980s and 1990s; at this time, CPS was operating under the policies and requirements of both CAPTA and AACW. Near the end of this period, controversy arose around the Homebuilders model, and later, after evaluation and further study, its use and that of other IFPS models was abandoned by many CPS departments.

The reasons for the controversy surrounding IFPS, and specifically the Homebuilders model, are beyond the scope of this chapter. However, they impact the funding, availability, and CPS attitudes toward family preservation as a philosophy, and so require some brief exploration. First, the Homebuilders model called for work with families with children at "imminent risk of placement" and this proved to be a concept that was hard to define. Services would last only 90 days, would require that a caseworker have a very low caseload (2 to 5 families at a time rather than the hundreds some caseworkers normally carried), spend several hours with the family each week, and be available 24/7 by phone.

The measure of successful preservation was initially defined as avoiding the out-of-home placement of any children in the family. Early program evaluations of just IFPS families, without a control group, showed that the great majority of them were preserved. However, later program evaluations found that when these results were compared with families who were either given services as usual, or put on a wait list, many of these families avoided out-of-home placement as well, suggesting that the treatment and control groups were not at equal risk (Berry 2005). This called into question the value of this type of resource-intensive model.

Additionally, when reports of children being hurt, or even killed, while receiving services (even if technically not intensive family preservation services) surfaced, the media and several children's legal advocacy groups called for a return to stricter rules for families (Gelles 1996).

It was in this atmosphere that the current legislation directing child welfare policy and practice in the US, the Adoption and Safe Families Act of 1997 (ASFA), was passed. ASFA calls for short timelines in which to effect major changes in a family system, and focuses on moving children quickly through the system by either returning them home or placing them in an adoptive home. Often, reunification cases utilize a process referred to as "concurrent planning," in which adoption is seriously explored, alongside reunification services, in case parents do not satisfactorily complete the requirements to have children returned home. The shortened timeline to work with families, along with budgetary constraints, are additional factors that have reduced the use of family preservation services, although they continue to be offered by some CPS departments. However, Pelton (1997) argued that family preservation was a myth. He maintained that in the era of ASFA, the offer of supportive services to a family was often just a guise used to expand child welfare involvement in the family's life, which brings with it further scrutiny and the risk of additional punitive measures.

White children and Native children have been treated differently over the entire course of US child welfare provision. American Indian families were neither the recipients of Mother's Pensions nor of progressive social services designed to support families and avoid their breakup. Instead, Native children were the subjects of systematic federal efforts to assimilate them into the dominant culture by forced removal to boarding schools. Along with boarding schools, thousands of Native children were adopted into White families, a practice that accelerated in the 1950s and 1960s, under policies supported by the Bureau of Indian Affairs (BIA) and implemented by state child welfare agencies and the CWLA. By the 1970s, one third of all American Indian children born after 1900 had been adopted by non-Indian families (Mannes 1995). It was this two-pronged destruction of Native families that led to the passage of the ICWA in 1978.

Despite the passage of the ICWA, family preservation services appear to have never been the intervention of choice when American Indian families become involved with CPS (Coleman et al. 2001). There is an extensive body of literature about the differential treatment of minority families in the child welfare system, particularly American Indian and African American, compared to White families facing similar challenges (Fluke et al. 2010, Hill 2006). National data from 2009 revealed that American Indian/Alaska Native children were the highest proportion of children in foster care; placement rates were 13 per 1,000 for Native children, 12 per 1,000 for African American children, and 4 per 1,000 for White children, creating a disparity ratio for American Indian children of 3.17 compared to White children (Farrow et al. 2010).

Data from a number of states further illustrate this disparity. In 2008, data from Washington State showed that American Indian children were almost three times more likely to be referred to CPS, and once in foster care, were less likely to be reunified within two years than children of other groups (Fluke et al. 2010). Longitudinal data from California showed significantly higher rates of both substantiation of maltreatment and placement of American Indian and African American children (Magruder and Shaw 2008). Furthermore, researchers in Minnesota found that even controlling for variables thought to influence child maltreatment rates (factors such as poverty, substance abuse, and domestic violence), American Indian children were still 1.7 times more likely to be removed from their families than White children (Johnson et al. 2007). Finally, data from Colorado covering 1995–2000 showed that once American Indian children were removed, they were less likely to have reunification listed as a goal, and they remained in foster care significantly longer than all other children (Bussey and Potter 2002).

Out-of-home placement and long lengths of time away from the home for Native children have been found to be intimately tied to the socioeconomic context of many Native families and communities. National data from *Child Maltreatment 2007* (US Department of Health and Human Services 2008) document that it is not physical or sexual abuse that is leading to long out-of-home stays for American Indian children. Instead, it is the finding of neglect which was the most frequent type of maltreatment among American Indian families (67 percent of all cases), higher than the neglect rate for any other group and higher than the overall average rate of neglect (59 percent). Analysis of reported child abuse and neglect in Canada confirmed a similar pattern for Native families in Ontario, where rates of physical and sexual abuse were actually the lowest of any racial/ethnic group (Trocme et al. 1995). While neglect is a serious problem for children, and judged so by American Indian parents as well (Evans-Campbell 2008), there is the danger that child welfare workers, in determining the level of risk they perceive in a family and thus the need for out-of-home placement versus the provision of family preservation services, will overemphasize a parent's presumed pathology and fail to consider the influence of years of racism, economic discrimination, forced relocation, and lost opportunities for creating a living. Dettlaff et al. (2011) suggest that this tendency is due to a "fundamental attribution error" (1635), and that it is one of the causes of racial disparity in child protection case substantiation rates. It is the error of attributing problems to personal traits rather than to contextual or situational factors such as poverty that has impacted, and continues to detrimentally impact, many American Indian families who come into contact with the child welfare system.

Family preservation services continue to be offered by some CPS departments, and the practice of differential response is another, newer, method of helping families before the child welfare concerns become serious (DePanfilis 2005). There is some research on how these CPS programs impact Native families. One county in Iowa, for example, hired an American Indian liaison to work with Native families, resulting in reduced disproportionality and higher satisfaction on the part of the families (Richardson 2008). A specific family preservation intervention offered in Oklahoma in the homes of Native families had significantly better outcomes, and increased satisfaction, compared to treatment as usual (Chaffin et al. nd). Additionally, Kirk and Griffith (2008) found that intensive family preservation services in North Carolina reduced out-of-home placement for all children of color, including American Indians.

If family preservation were to be fully funded and implemented, these examples illustrate its promise for improving family functioning and keeping children within their families and cultures. But, as Hutchinson and Sudia (2002) have noted, "families exist only on the margins of United States child welfare policies—never achieving much prominence and with only a shadow presence in the minds of those whose focus is on service to children" (81). These authors go on to charge that "the dominant discourse of child welfare is child saving ... Debate among professionals and child welfare advocates is remarkable for its constancy: the core system remains essentially the same while around it swirls controversy over which grand new plan will solve its problems" (138). Family preservation has been caught up in this process, and thus the efforts of both tribes and urban Native programs to do the work necessary to preserve Native families takes on critical importance.

American Indian Family Preservation Practice in Tribal and Urban Communities

Tribal Child Welfare

Reservation-based child welfare programs run and administered by tribes often face significant resource and workforce challenges as compared to state/country-administered programs. Few tribal programs have specific family preservation programs and most efforts by workers are focused on addressing family crises, handling emergency removals and placements, and working to reunite children (Butler Institute for Families 2012). Despite these challenges, The National Child Welfare Resource Center for Tribes (NRC4Tribes) 2010 national needs assessment of tribal child welfare programs in the United States (Leake et al. 2011) revealed that these programs incorporated an overall approach to practice and service provision that was deeply focused and committed to keeping children with their families and kinship networks and living as part of their tribal community, while also focusing on maintaining and strengthening children's cultural connections—in other words, preserving families, communities, and tribal cultures.

> A sense of obligation to make sure that everything possible was done to prevent the severing of children's connections to their extended families and the tribal communities of which they were a part drove programs and individual workers. Programs and workers sustained their commitment despite serious challenges that included a lack of adequate funding and insufficient staff. Commonly, many

tribal child welfare workers saw their work as an investment in the future of their tribes. (23)

Tribal child welfare programs' embedded position within tribal communities (which are frequently small and close-knit), and workers' membership in these same communities, supported regular contact with children and family members, and permitted a working relationship based on shared history, worldview, and culture that is not typically present when Native families are involved with state/county CPS. By working with families within the relational context that forms the basis of many tribal cultures, tribal child welfare workers are able to conceptualize many of the contextual challenges that tribal families face, such as poverty or housing inadequacy, as shared community challenges rather than individual deficiencies. Further, it allows workers to team with families as "tribal members helping other tribal members" (Leake et al. 2011, 27). This role allows workers to help strengthen the family system based on a mutual acknowledgement of needs, and may be contrasted with the common CPS approach in which the worker identifies inherent family inadequacies that must be remediated by family members and exercises authority-based oversight of case-plan compliance.

While tribal child welfare programs may not call their approach "family preservation," the two elements identified here—understanding and addressing contextual challenges and teaming with families—are both hallmarks of a number of mainstream family preservation interventions. Thus, Native family preservation in tribal child welfare practice can be summarized as community member workers who believe their work entails: (a) doing whatever it takes to keep children with their families and in their tribal communities; (b) helping parents and extended family systems access needed (yet frequently scarce) resources and services; (c) strengthening families so they may successfully nurture and support children and all family members; and (d) strengthening and building the tribal community as well (Leake et al. 2011).

Urban Indian Child Welfare

In some cities, community-based agencies, such as the Denver (Colorado) Indian Family Resource Center, the Minneapolis (Minnesota) American Indian Center, the United Indians of All Tribes Foundation in Seattle, Washington, and the American Indian Families Partnership in Los Angeles, California, provide culturally responsive services to assist Native families as they negotiate non-tribal child welfare systems. The Denver Indian Family Resource Center (DIFRC) was formed in 2000 to provide comprehensive and culturally based services to American Indian families at risk of, or currently involved with, the child welfare system. DIFRC has collaboration agreements with each county child welfare department in the Denver metro area; one aspect of these agreements allows CPS departments to refer families, when it is determined that children can remain safely in their homes, to DIFRC for services rather than opening a formal child welfare case. DIFRC also works collaboratively with tribes and CPS departments on ICWA reunification cases, and in cases involving the adoption of Native children (which have been few due to DIFRC's intensive family reunification and preservation efforts).

DIFRC provides family preservation services to urban-based American Indian families guided by a practice model developed by the agency and evaluated in two separate studies (Leake 2007, Lucero and Bussey 2013). Similar to the underlying philosophy in many tribal child welfare programs, the DIFRC family preservation model recognizes that American Indian children are part of family and kinship networks and are members of Native communities, both in the city and on the reservation. The model defines family broadly, and sees families as being preserved not only when children remain with their biological parent(s), but when this is not possible, in cases where children remain with extended family, kin, or other tribal members (Bussey 2011).

It is believed that in order to flourish, children must develop and maintain connections to their Native cultures, extended family and kinship systems, communities, and tribes. Active and ongoing efforts are thus directed toward helping children maintain these connections, should they become involved in the child welfare system. Working directly with the child's tribe, or through members of the tribe, is an essential part of the work. In cases where families have lost, or have only tentative connections to the tribe, efforts focus on helping children reestablish these connections. The model works from an understanding that children, and their families, are integral parts of the urban Indian and tribal communities of which they are a part. While the disruptions and struggles families face impact these Native communities, so too does the healing of families. Finally, the model is guided by the practice principle that stresses that, when it is safe to do so, urban American Indian children and their family members involved with the child welfare system are best served in their homes and communities by providers who are knowledgeable about American Indian history, culture, and contemporary Native contexts, and who provide services that incorporate and are responsive to families' cultures.

The following quotes exemplify the feelings of family members who received family preservation services at DIFRC, and emphasize the family preservation model's focus on being connected to Native culture (Bussey 2011):

I'm glad that they're there and able to help Native families. It's hard to be an Indian in society today. It's difficult to maintain your identity and to also blend and cope with the rest of society. So it's very good services ... (Native mother who sought help for her teenage child)

It feels comfortable because you feel the culture there. You see it all around, and then you feel it come through the teachers as well. And then there are certain topics and issues that we talk about that we all can relate to because we're the same culture … Our lives are probably way better than they were before … (Native mother who attended the Nurturing Parenting program)

DIFRC is extremely awesome, especially since our heritage is so lost. So to bring it back like that, and to show that we still have it, that we have the support that we need, it makes it all worth it … (Native mother referred by CPS)

My kids loved [the cultural presentation] … They said, 'Daddy, I'm 100% Indian now.' My oldest, he said, he feels good. And I liked that part because before, he knew his grandma was an Indian but he never saw what being an Indian meant … But after he saw the things, he felt proud, he liked it. (A father, who identifies as Mexican American, and who is raising his American Indian children)

Conclusion

Native perspectives on why family preservation services should be provided contrast markedly with those of child protective services. While CPS considers family preservation to be a short-term intervention aimed at addressing family deficiencies, Native perspectives understand that family preservation is an investment in the future of American Indian and other Indigenous/Aboriginal peoples. Tribal and urban child welfare programs share two common goals: preserving families *and* maintaining children's cultural, kinship, community, and tribal connections. The urban/reservation divide, that so often exists in the United States, falls away as the two programs acknowledge that, regardless of whether American Indian children live in tribal or urban areas, of utmost concern is ensuring that they have opportunities to remain a member of their family network and a part of their tribal community, and maintain connections to their tribal culture. Thus, family preservation services become a means of supporting the inherent strengths of the family system to help young people develop the strong cultural connections vital to the preservation of Native cultures and the future viability of both tribal and urban Native communities. While CPS priorities shift with new regulations and budget policies, Native programs continue to see family preservation as the foundation upon which their work is built. Hope for the continued use and development of family preservation services lies with tribes and Native community-based organizations who understand that by preserving Native families, Native cultures are preserved as well.

References

Adams, D.W. 1995. *Education for Extinction: American Indians and the Boarding School Experience, 1875–1928*. Lawrence, KS: University Press of Kansas.

Anderson, P. 1989. The origin, emergence, and professional recognition of child protection. *Social Service Review*, 63(2), 222–44.

Armitage, A. 1995. *Comparing the Policy of Aboriginal Assimilation: Australia, Canada, and New Zealand*. Vancouver: University of British Columbia Press.

Berry, M. 2005. Overview of family preservation. In *Child Welfare for the 21st Century*, G. Mallon and P. Hess (eds). New York, NY: Columbia University Press, 319–34.

Brave Heart, M.Y.H. 2002. Culturally and historically congruent clinical social work interventions with Native clients. In *Culturally Competent Practice: Skills, Interventions, and Evaluations*, R. Fong and S. Furuto (eds). Boston, MA: Allyn and Bacon, 285–98.

Bussey, M.C. 2011. *Honoring the Tradition of Strong Indian Families: Evaluation of Process and Outcomes*. Denver, CO: Denver Indian Family Resource Center.

Bussey, M. and Potter, C. 2002. *Minority Over-representation in Child Welfare Services*. Denver, CO: Colorado Department of Human Services.

Butler Institute for Families 2012. *The Bureau of Indian Affairs ICWA Evaluation: A Secondary Analysis*. Denver, CO: Author.

Chaffin, M., Bard, D., Bigfoot, D., and Maher, E. (nd). A comparative outcome study of home-based services for American Indian parents in child welfare. Unpublished manuscript.

Cheshire, T.C. 2001. Cultural transmission in urban American Indian families. *American Behavioral Scientist*, 44(9), 1528–35.

Coleman, H., Unrau, Y., and Manyfingers, B. 2001. Revamping family preservation services for Native families. *Journal of Ethnic & Cultural Diversity in Social Work*, 10(1), 49–68.

Cross, T.L. 1986. Drawing on cultural tradition in Indian child welfare practice. *Social Casework*, 67(5), 283–9.

DePanfilis, D. 2005. Child protective services. In *Child Welfare for the 21st Century*, G. Mallon and P. Hess (eds). New York, NY: Columbia University Press, 290–301.

Dettlaff, A., Rivaux, S., Baumann, D., et al. 2011. Disentangling substantiation: The influence of race, income, and risk on the substantiation decision in child welfare. *Children and Youth Services Review*, 33, 1630–37.

Evans-Campbell, T. 2008. Perceptions of child neglect among urban American Indian/Alaska Native parents. *Child Welfare*, 87(3), 115–42.

Farrow, F., Notkin, S., Derezotes, D., and Miller, O. 2010. Racial equity in child welfare: Key themes, findings and perspectives. In *Disparities and Disproportionality in Child Welfare: Analysis of the Research*, 127–50. Retrieved September 12, 2013, from http://www.cssp.org/publications/child-welfare/alliance/Disparities-and-Disproportionality-in-Child-Welfare_An-Analysis-of-the-Research-December-2011.pdf.

Fluke, J., Harden, B., Jenkins, M., and Ruehrdanz, A. 2010. Research synthesis on child welfare disproportionality and disparities. In *Disparities and Disproportionality in Child Welfare: Analysis of the Research*, 1–126.

Retrieved September 12, 2013, from http://www.cssp.org/publications/child-welfare/alliance/Disparities-and-Disproportionality-in-Child-Welfare_An-Analysis-of-the-Research-December-2011.pdf.

Gelles, R. 1996. *The Book of David: How Preserving Families Can Cost Children's Lives*. New York: Basic Books.

George, L.J. 1997. Why the need for the Indian Child Welfare Act? *Journal of Multicultural Social Work*, 5(3/4), 165–75.

Goodluck, C.T. 1980. Strength of caring. *Social Casework*, 61(8), 519–21.

Goodluck, C.T. and Short, D. 1980. Working with American Indian parents: A cultural approach. *Social Casework*, 61(8), 472–5.

Halverson, K., Puig, M.E., and Byers, S.R. 2002. Culture loss: American Indian family disruption, urbanization, and the Indian Child Welfare Act. *Child Welfare*, 81(2), 319–36.

Hill, R.B. 2006. Synthesis of research on disproportionality in child welfare: An update. Casey-CSSP alliance for racial equity in the child welfare system. Retrieved from http://www.aecf.org/KnowledgeCenter/Publications. aspx?pubguid=%7BBAF150AB-6C9C-4004-B0F1-48B7B001BA42%7D.

Hoxie, F.E. 1989. *A Final Promise: The Campaign to Assimilate the Indians, 1880–1920*. Cambridge, MA: University Press.

Hutchinson, J. and Sudia, C. 2002. *Failed Child Welfare Policy: Family Preservation and the Orphaning of Child Welfare*. Blue Ridge Summit, PA: University Press of America.

Johnson, E., Clark, S., Donald, M., et al. 2007. Racial disparity in Minnesota's child protection system. *Child Welfare*, 86(4), 5–20.

Kinney, J., Haapala, D., and Booth, C. 1991. *Keeping Family Together: The Homebuilders Model*. New York: Aldine de Gruyter.

Kirk, R. and Griffith, D. 2008. Impact of intensive family preservation services on disproportionality of out-of-home placement of children of color in one state's child welfare system. *Child Welfare*, 87(5), 87–105.

Leake, R. 2007. *Denver Indian Family Resource Center Research Report: Rocky Mountain Quality Improvement Center Project*. Englewood, CO: American Humane Association.

Leake, R., Lucero, N.M., Walker, J., and McCrae, J. 2011. *Findings from the NRC4Tribes Technical Assistance Needs Assessment: Guidance for the Children's Bureau T/TA Network*. West Hollywood, CA: National Resource Center for Tribal Child Welfare. Retrieved September 12, 2013, from http://www.americanhumane.org/assets/pdfs/children/pc-rmqic-dif-report.pdf.

Lucero, N.M. 2007. *Resource Guide: Working with Urban American Indian Families with Child Protection and Substance Abuse Challenges*. Englewood, CO: American Humane Association. Retrieved September 12, 2013, from http://www.americanhumane.org/assets/pdfs/children/pc-rmqic-dif-guide.pdf.

Lucero, N.M. 2009. "Creating an Indian space in the city": Development, maintenance, and evolution of cultural identity and cultural connectedness among multiple generations of urban American Indians. Doctoral Dissertation,

University of Denver. Retrieved from http://0-proquest.umi.com.bianca.penlib. du.edu/pqdweb?did=1878966081&sid=1&Fmt=2&clientId=48347&RQT=30 9&VName=PQD.

Lucero, N.M. and Bussey, M.B. 2013. Effective child welfare interventions with urban American Indian families: A collaborative and trauma-informed model. *Child Welfare*, 91(3), 89–112.

Magruder, J. and Shaw, T. 2008. Children ever in care: An examination of cumulative disproportionality. *Child Welfare*, 88(2), 169–88.

Mannes, M. 1993. Seeking the balance between child protection and family preservation in Indian child welfare. *Child Welfare*, 72(2), 141–52.

Mannes, M. 1995. Factors and events leading to the passage of the Indian Child Welfare Act. *Child Welfare*, 74(1), 264–82.

McGill, D. and Pearce, J. 1996. American families with English ancestors from the Colonial era: Anglo Americans. In *Ethnicity and Family Therapy*, M. McGoldrick, J. Giordano, and J. Pearce (eds). New York, NY: Guilford, 451–66.

McKenzie, B. 1989. Child welfare: New models of service delivery in Canada's Native communities. *Human Services in the Rural Environment*, 12(3), 6–11.

Miller, D.L., Hoffman, F., and Turner, D. 1980. A perspective on the Indian Child Welfare Act. *Social Casework*, 61(8), 468–71.

Native American Rights Fund 2007. *A Practical Guide to the Indian Child Welfare Act*. Boulder, CO: Author.

Pelton, L. 1997. Child welfare policy and practice: The myth of family preservation. *American Journal of Orthopsychiatry*, 67(4), 545–53.

Plantz, M., Hubbel, R., Barrett, B., and Dobrec, A. 1989. Indian child welfare: A status report. *Children Today*, 18(1), 24–9.

Public Law 95-608 1978. *The Indian Child Welfare Act of 1978*. Washington, DC: Federal Register, November 8, 1978.

Red Horse, J.G. 1980. American Indian elders: Unifiers of Indian families. *Social Casework*, 61(8), 490–93.

Red Horse, J.G., Lewis, R., Feit, M., and Decker, J. 1978. Family behavior of urban American Indians. *Social Casework*, 59, 67–72.

Red Horse, J.G., Martinez, C., and Day, P. 2001. *Family Preservation: A Case Study of Indian Tribal Practice*. National Indian Child Welfare Association. Retrieved September 12, 2013, from http://www.nicwa.org/research/01.fami ly%20pres01.rpt.pdf.

Richardson, B. 2008. Comparative analysis of two community-based efforts designed to impact disproportionality. *Child Welfare*, 87(2), 297–317.

Roberts, D. 2002. *Shattered Bonds: The Color of Child Welfare*. New York: Basic Civitas Books.

Sullivan, L. and Walters, A. 2011. Native foster care: Lost children, shattered families—Part 1: Incentives and cultural bias fuel foster system. National Public Radio, October 27. Retrieved September 12, 2013, from http://www. npr.org/2011/10/25/141672992/native-foster-care-lost-children-shattered-fam ilies.

Trocme, N., McPhee, D., and Tam, K. 1995. Child abuse and neglect in Ontario: Incidence and characteristics. *Child Welfare*, 75, 563–86.

Union of BC Indian Chiefs 2002. *Calling Forth our Future: Options for the Exercise of Indigenous Peoples' Authority in Child Welfare*. Retrieved September 12, 2013 from http://www.ubcic.bc.ca/files/PDF/UBCIC_OurFuture.pdf.

US Department of Health and Human Services 2008. *Child Maltreatment 2007*. Washington, DC: DHHS.

Valentine, B. and Gray, M. 2006. Keeping them home: Aboriginal out-of-home care in Australia. *Families in Society*, 87(4), 537–45.

Walmsley, C. 2005. *Protecting Aboriginal Children*. Vancouver: UBC Press.

Wagner, J.K. 1976. The role of intermarriage in the acculturation of selected urban American Indian women. *Anthropologica*, 18(2), 215–29.

Chapter 8

ICWA: Legal Mandate for Social Justice and Preservation of American Indian/Alaska Native Heritage

Thalia González and Edwin González-Santin

Then I was standing on the highest mountain of them all, and round about beneath me was the whole hoop of the world. And while I stood there I saw more than I can tell and I understood more than I saw; for I was seeing in a sacred manner the shapes of all things in the spirit, and the shape of all shapes as they must live together like one being. And I saw that the sacred hoop of my people was one of many hoops that made one circle, wide as daylight and as starlight, and in the center grew one mighty flowering tree to shelter all the children of one mother and one father. And I saw that it was holy—Black Elk, Oglala Sioux. (Neihardt and Black Elk 2000, 33)

Black Elk, great seer of the Oglala Sioux, received his sacred vision at the age of nine in which he described the interrelationships of all beings as many interconnected hoops that form one circle under one protective tree in an expansive universe. This vision has been at the center of many of the conflicts between tribes and the federal government throughout history, as tribes have fought to exercise their sovereignty, as independent nations, over issues related to American Indian/Alaska Native children. It is in the context of Black Elk's vision and the historical struggle of American Indians/Alaskan Natives against the destruction of families and tribal culture that this chapter considers the evolving legal protections for tribes, children, and families under the Indian Child Welfare Act.

The Struggle for Tribal Sovereignty

For contemporary tribal American communities, no aspect of sovereignty is more important than protecting the well-being of children. In 1819, the Indian Civilization Fund Act was passed to civilize American Indians by funding missionary groups willing to provide for the moral education of American Indian children (Graham 1998). Teachers in the mission schools used curricula "devoid of any indigenous cultural knowledge … [and] strove to keep the children away from the influences of family by denying or limiting parental and familial visitation" (Graham 1998, 14–15). Children were punished for communicating in their tribal language, using religious ceremonial symbols or clothing, or engaging in any vestige of the tribal cultural life the child had known before his or her removal to the boarding school (Lacey 1986). During the mid-twentieth century, federal policies emphasized assimilation (Cohen 2005). Beginning with relocation programs to move American Indian populations from reservations to urban areas (Graham 1998), and followed by initiatives to remove American Indian children from their families and cultures by placing them in educational institutions, foster care, and non-Indian adoptive homes (Administration on Children Youth and Families, Children's Bureau 2006). Conservative estimates compiled by the Association of American Indian Affairs in the 1970s indicated that one-third of all American Indian children were being separated from their families (Graham 1998).

The experience of American Indians in the United States was not isolated. First Nations tribes in Canada also suffered similar child welfare atrocities. First Nations children were removed from their homes in numbers of tens of thousands to boarding schools and under the child welfare system policies known as the "Sixties Scoop" (Sinha et al. 2011). During the "Sixties Scoop," Canadian laws allowed the enforcement of child welfare practices by provinces on First Nation reserves, which increased the rate of out-of-home placement from virtually zero in 1951 to 12 percent of children in care (Sinha et al. 2011). In the British Columbia community of Spallumcheen First Nation, approximately 67 percent of the child population was apprehended by provincial child welfare communities between 1951 and 1979 (Sinha et al. 2011). According to the Canadian Incidence Study of Reported Child Abuse and Neglect, investigations involving child maltreatment of First Nations are 4.2 times the rate of non-Indigenous children (Trocmé et al. 2010). The rate of First Nations investigations involving informal kinship care during the investigation period was 11.4 times the rate for non-Indigenous investigations, and the rate for investigations involving formal child welfare placement was 12.4 times the rate for non-Indigenous investigations (Trocmé et al. 2010).

Passage of the Indian Child Welfare Act

For decades, American Indian families suffered from federal and state child welfare practices that resulted in removals of American Indian children at extremely high rates compared to removal of other children. Collectively, such actions often led to the loss of individual tribal languages and customs, disruptions of American Indian families, and serious challenges for children attempting to reintegrate into their tribal settings. In addition to the disproportionately high number of American Indian children placed in foster or adoptive homes, testimony established that American Indian family breakups frequently occurred as a "result of conditions which [were] temporary or remedial and where the American Indian people involved [did] not understand the nature of the legal actions involved" (S. Rep. No. 95-597 1977, 11).

From 1974 to 1978 Congress held hearings on the topic of American Indian child welfare to investigate the extent to which current child welfare policies undermined tribal survival through unwarranted removal of children. As the 1974 testimony of William Byler, executive director of the Association on American Indian Affairs, concluded, "[t]he wholesale removal of children from their homes, we believe, is perhaps the most tragic and destructive aspect of American Indian life today" (American Indian Child Welfare Program 1974, 3–4). Byler's testimony was echoed by Calvin Isaac, chief of the Mississippi Band of Choctaw and representative of the National Tribal Chairmen's Association, who emphasized the destructive impact of governmental policies on tribal sovereignty and survival: "Culturally the chances of American Indian survival are significantly reduced if our children, our only real means of transmission of cultural heritage, are to be raised in non-American Indian homes and denied exposure to the ways of their People" (Jones 2009, 30).

Passed in 1978, the Indian Child Welfare Act (ICWA) is considered to be the most significant federal law governing American Indian children, as it established protections for these youth and their tribes and ensured that "Congress through statutes, treaties, and the general course of dealings with American Indian tribes, has assumed the responsibility for the protection and preservation of American Indian tribes and their resources" (25 U.S.C. §1901 1978). ICWA clearly states that preserving American Indian families by ensuring that American Indian children remain in homes reflective of their unique Native cultures and values is in their best interest and the best interest of the tribe.

The purpose of ICWA can be viewed as twofold: the prevention of the wholesale removal of American Indian children from their homes, and promotion of tribal stability. ICWA sets forth the basic principle that the best interest of an American Indian child is analogous to the best interest of the tribe. As Professor Barbara Atwood has argued, American law should respect the distinct worldviews held by American Indian tribes and their richly diverse approaches to community, family, parenting, child welfare, and adoption (Atwood 2010). Such respect should guide the recognition of tribal decrees, tribal agreements, tribal courts, inform questions of jurisdiction, and resolve disputes that involve child well-being. Given that the majority of American Indian children now live on non-reservation lands, state courts and tribal courts often share concurrent jurisdiction and face conflicts when questions arise involving American Indian children welfare, raising larger questions regarding the cultural and political identities of American Indian tribes within larger pluralistic communities.

Protections under the Indian Child Welfare Act

Under ICWA, self-determination includes the right to oversee how families experiencing problems are treated and, if necessary, to ensure the protection of American Indian children. The jurisdictional provisions of ICWA implement the congressional view that tribes must maintain the power to decide matters that involve the removal of American Indian children from their homes. In placing limits on the power of state courts to maintain exclusive jurisdictional control over American Indian children was recognition of the key role that courts historically, and arguably contemporaneously, play in removing American Indian children from their homes. ICWA provides for exclusive tribal jurisdiction over child welfare and adoption proceedings involving American Indian children domiciled or residing on their tribal reservation or who are wards of tribal court (25 U.S.C. §1911(a) 1978). Given that a majority of American Indians no longer reside on reservation or trust lands, ICWA's provision for transfer and concurrent state jurisdiction in cases involving American Indian children must be given significant attention. The concurrent tribal-state authority creates what has been termed "presumptive tribal jurisdiction" (*Mississippi Band of Choctaw American Indians v. Holyfield* 1989, 36). Section 1911(b) requires state courts to transfer child custody proceedings to tribal court upon petition of a parent of the child's tribe, unless either parent objects or the court finds good cause to the contrary (25 U.S.C. §1911(b) 1978). Despite this "presumptive" tribal jurisdiction, state courts continue to exercise jurisdiction in high numbers (Atwood 2002, Graham 1998). If a state court does not transfer jurisdiction to a tribal court, ICWA places a heightened duty on the state to avoid removal of the child from the home by ensuring that active efforts (25 U.S.C. §1912(d) 1978) are made to reunify the family and that preference for out-of-home placements is given first to the extended family, then to tribal and other American Indian homes (25 U.S.C. §1915 1978).

ICWA establishes minimum standards of evidence, including testimony of expert witnesses with knowledge of tribal culture, before a state court may remove an American Indian child from his or her home (25 U.S.C. §1912(e) 1978). States must maintain records of each state court placement of an American Indian child (25 U.S.C. §1915(e) 1978), as well as evidence of efforts made to comply with the ICWA placement preferences (25 U.S.C. §1915 1978). ICWA also provides notice requirements for the parents and any person who has legal or temporary custody: 1) if the court has reason to know the proceedings involve an American Indian child (25 U.S.C. §1912(a) 1978); and 2) if the tribe or American Indian custodian has a right to intervene in such proceedings (25 U.S.C. §1911(c) 1978) or a right to court-appointed counsel (25 U.S.C. §1912(b) 1978). One of the purposes of the notice requirement is to enable an American Indian tribe to participate in determining whether the child involved in the proceeding is an "American Indian child" under ICWA. The notice requirement recognizes that American Indian tribes have an interest in American Indian child welfare proceedings apart from the parties. Indigent parents or custodians are also entitled to court-appointed counsel (25 U.S.C. §1912(b) 1978) and to rehabilitative services designed to preserve the family (25 U.S.C. §1912(d) 1978). ICWA imposes heightened burdens of proof before state courts can order the removal of American Indian children from their homes. For example, foster care placements must be based on "clear and convincing evidence, including testimony of qualified expert witnesses, that the continued custody of the child by the parent or custodian is likely to result in serious emotional or physical damage to the child" (25 U.S.C. §1912(e) 1978). For parental rights terminations, ICWA requires the same showing of serious harm to the child, through a showing of proof beyond a reasonable doubt (25 U.S.C. §1912(f) 1978). With the passage of ICWA there has been a diversity of viewpoints regarding the nature of American Indian child identity, the rights of tribes, the role of tribal courts, and evolving relationship between American Indian tribes and the government.

State Adoption of Indian Child Welfare Act Legislation

Some states have chosen to enact their own American Indian child welfare laws or develop policies that clarify requirements of the federal ICWA and specify what state action is necessary for compliance. For example, in 1985, the Minnesota Indian Family Preservation Act was enacted. The Minnesota American Indian Family Preservation Act "emphasiz[ed] the State's interest in supporting the preservation of the tribal identity of an American Indian child and recogniz[ed] tribes as the appropriate entities to provide direction to the State as to the best interests of tribal children" (Minnesota Department of Human Services 2007). In 2003, the Iowa legislature enacted SF 354, codified in chapter 232B of the Iowa Code, to clarify state policies and procedures regarding implementation of the Act (Iowa Indian Child Welfare Act 2003). The Iowa Act provides that both the federal ICWA and the Iowa Act apply to any child custody proceeding involving an American Indian child. The law requires full state cooperation with American Indian tribes and tribal citizens to ensure the intent and provisions of the Indian Child Welfare Act are enforced.

Similarly, the Colorado legislature passed HB 1064, which created an American Indian child welfare law for Colorado and amended relevant sections of the Colorado Children's Code to ensure compliance with the federal Act, during the 2002 legislative session (Colorado Revised Statutes Annotated, Compliance with the Federal Indian Child Welfare Act, 2002). The legislature recognized that, in order to achieve the goals of the federal ICWA, it is necessary for the state to determine whether children who are the subject of child welfare proceedings in the state court system are American Indian children. In addition, the state has formed an American Indian Child Welfare Act Team, comprised of officials from around the state who monitor efforts made in relation to the Colorado Indian Child Welfare Act.

In 2011, Washington enacted the Washington State Indian Child Welfare Act. Washington's law codifies the federal ICWA to strengthen enforcement in state courts and clarify implementation. The Department of Social and Health Services also created Local Indian Child Welfare Advisory Committees throughout the state to review state child custody cases involving American Indian children

(Administration on Children Youth and Families, Children's Bureau 2006). Each committee reviews cases individually to ensure compliance with ICWA.

While Alaska has not passed specific state legislation, it has taken several innovative steps to improve state court compliance with the ICWA. The state's Office of Children's Services has established an American Indian Child Welfare Act Help Desk, which "functions as a comprehensive information resource for case workers searching for available American Indian placements for American Indian children" (van Straaten and Buchbinder 2011, 9). In addition, the Office of Children's Services has developed a Tribal State Collaboration Group to discuss a wide range of issues faced by Alaska Native children, in addition to a Native Rural Recruitment Team for Foster Care and several other cooperative initiatives.

**The Need for a More Comprehensive Approach to
the Indian Child Welfare Act**

Understanding ICWA as protecting American Indian children in state court proceedings is not a radical idea. ICWA has achieved success on many levels, for example by establishing respect for tribal authority and the expansion of tribal preservation policies and programs. While the overall rate of removal of American Indian children from their homes in child welfare proceedings has decreased, American Indian children are still being removed from their homes in disproportionate numbers (Atwood 2010). The fact that the majority of American Indian children and their families do not reside on tribal lands is of core significance when considering the history and purpose of ICWA. While the state of crisis present in the 1970s leading to the passage of ICWA is not present in today's court systems, there is serious concern regarding the impact of a lack of systemic adoption and enforcement of ICWA's protections.

The question of American Indian identity is at the center of all ICWA proceedings as protections are triggered by tribal membership, eligibility for tribal membership, or tribal affiliation. Even with this central placement, the construction of American Indian identity or status continues to raise controversial legal, political, and social questions. The controversies become more complex when legal rules, federal or state, define a child's status as American Indian or non-American Indian for purposes of determining applicable substantive and jurisdictional rights. Adding to this complexity, in certain state proceedings, even when a child meets the legal definition of American Indian child under ICWA, the jurisdictional and substantive protections are not automatically extended to these children, their families, and tribes. For example, American Indian children involved with the child welfare and juvenile justice systems are subject to a multi-jurisdictional framework complicated by where the activity occurs and the nature of activity, potentially subjecting them to state, federal, or tribal law.

Within this context the legal protections provided by ICWA are not equally applied across the states. Consider that fewer than half the states have passed laws that automatically trigger ICWA's protections for status offenders, parents, and tribes (González 2012). In these states American Indian status offenders find themselves in a jurisdictional gray area without clear guidance as to whether the ICWA's protections apply, leaving them subject to potential ad hoc decision-making by judges, court officials, officers, lawyers, or state agencies, which places severe limits on compliance. While Arizona is the only state to affirmatively state that the Indian Child Welfare Act does not apply in status offense cases, when read in totality, the Rhode Island and New Hampshire statutes have also removed the ICWA from applying in status offense proceedings (González 2012). In states that have not adopted laws, court rules, or policies incorporating the Act's protections in status offense proceedings involving American Indians/Alaskan Natives, this has led to increased contact of these children with the juvenile justice system, a failure to provide culturally competent services to American Indian/Alaskan Native children and families, increased separation of American Indian/Alaskan Native children from their families and tribes, and a lack of coordinated action by state courts, state child welfare agencies, advocates, and practitioners.

Essential to understanding the increasingly significant harm of inconsistent application of ICWA's jurisdictional, procedural, and substantive protections in juvenile justice and child welfare cases is an understanding that at many stages of their lives, American Indian children represent a disproportionately high population within state systems. In 2010, American Indians were overrepresented among the national population of youth in foster care by a factor of 2.1 (Summers et al. 2012). From 1994 through 2001, American Indian youth accounted for 10 percent of federal arrestees aged 18 and younger, around 70 percent of all youth committed to the Federal Bureau of Prisons as delinquents, and around 31 percent of those committed as adults (Snyder and Sickmund 2006). While American Indian youth disproportionately account for cases at many different stages of the juvenile justice system, overrepresentation is at its highest when involving the harshest sanctions, out-of-home placement after adjudication and waiver to the adult criminal justice system (Hartney and Silva 2007). American Indian youth also represent the highest case rate of petitioned status offenses among all racial groups in the United States between 1995 and 2008 (Puzzanchera et al. 2011). Their case rate at 10.1 is twice that of White children, four times that of Asian children and nearly double the overall national rate of 5.1 per 1,000 children. While this is true across all status offenses, American Indian children have the highest representation in cases specifically regarding curfew, liquor law, and truancy violations (Puzzanchera et al. 2011). These three categories increased by 28 percent, 32 percent, and 54 percent, respectively, between 1995 and 2008 (Puzzanchera et al. 2011). In this way, the disproportionate representation of American Indian youth in status offense cases is compounded by the significant increase in the number of petitioned cases precisely for offenses most characteristic of this population.

Nationally, 12,900 or 8.25 percent of the 156,300 petitioned status offense cases in 2008 involved detention for the offenders (Puzzanchera et al. 2011). However, the comparable statistic for cases involving American Indian youth was 13.32

percent (Puzzanchera et al. 2011). These numbers, however, do not represent the full extent to which status offenders are incarcerated. In 1980, Congress amended the Juvenile Justice and Delinquency Prevention Act to allow juvenile courts to incarcerate children "charged with or who have committed a violation of a valid court order" (42 U.S.C. §5633(a)(11)(A)(ii) 1974). This expanded authority means many of the 11,604 children incarcerated in secure facilities in 2010 for "technical violations" may be status offenders (Sickmund et al. 2011). Without application of the legal requirements of the ICWA, such as notice, standards of proof, or jurisdictional preferences, American Indian youth involved in status offense proceedings will continue to be removed from their homes and sent to residential facilities, such as detention centers, shelters, reception/diagnostic centers, long-term secure facilities, ranch/wilderness camps, group homes, boot camps, or other out-of-home facilities, at alarming rates.

Questions at the intersection of child welfare and juvenile justice are not the only controversial issues more than 30 years after the passage of ICWA. Consider the varying interpretations of the heightened duty ICWA places on state agencies when removing an American Indian child from their home. ICWA provides that any party seeking foster care placement or termination of parental rights must show that "active efforts" have been made to prevent the breakup of the American Indian family (25 U.S.C. §1912(d) 1978). When interpreting the active efforts requirement, states also struggle with determining the correct burden of proof. Some courts have applied the burden of proof of the underlying proceeding based on federal law, while others have applied a lesser burden of proof based on state law (*E.A. v. State* 2002, *In re A.M.* 2001, *In re Cari B.* 2002, *In re Enrique P.* 2006, *In re G.S.* 2002, *In re Adoption of Hannah S.* 2006). Adding to this confusion, Section 1912(d) of ICWA does not include a clear statement of the required burden of proof. This allows some courts to apply the clear and convincing burden as required in foster care placement under Section 1912(e) or in a termination of parental rights, courts apply a reasonable doubt burden under Section 1912(f). The definition of "active efforts" fluctuates depending on the jurisdiction. States like California and Colorado treat active efforts the same as "reasonable efforts," the standard used in proceedings that do not involve ICWA (*In re Adoption of Hannah S.* 2006, 612, *People ex rel. K.D.* 2007, 636–38). Other states, like Utah and Oklahoma, assert that the "active efforts" language in Section 1912(d) requires more than just "reasonable efforts" (*In re J.S.* 2008, 592–3, *State ex rel. C.D.* 2008, 205). Yet even the states holding that active efforts require something more do not agree on what those efforts might entail, nor does a consensus exist regarding when or how that term should be applied in ICWA cases. To further complicate the matter, the Nevada Supreme Court held in 2009 that an inquiry regarding "active efforts" is unnecessary if the "existing Indian family" exception applies (*In re N.J.* 2009, 1264).

The use of the "existing Indian family" exception represents another critical area in which the question of American Indian identity is at the center of the proceedings and is inextricably linked to a larger understanding of tribal sovereignty. The "existing Indian family" exception is a judicially created rule that allows courts to preclude application of ICWA when neither the child nor the child's parents have maintained a significant social, cultural, or political relationship with his or her tribe. The exception emerged in the case of *Matter of Baby Boy L.* (1982), a case before the Kansas state court, which involved a child of mixed heritage. In the case, a non-American Indian mother sought to voluntarily relinquish her child for adoption to a non-American Indian couple. The American Indian father and tribe objected to the placement and argued that the tribe had the legal right to intervene in the proceeding under ICWA and the trial court should comply with the placement priorities prescribed by ICWA. The Kansas Supreme Court rejected the applicability of ICWA to the proceeding and reasoned that since the child was not being removed from an "existing Indian family," no legislative purpose of ICWA would be served by allowing intervention by the tribe. While the Kansas Supreme Court ultimately abandoned the "existing Indian family" doctrine in 2009 (*In re A.J.S.* 2009), more than half a dozen states have continued to apply the exception in proceedings where a child is of mixed American Indian heritage (Atwood 2010).

In cases that apply the exception there remain many unanswered questions about a child's future social identity. Consider the ruling in *S.A. v. E.V.P.* (1990), which involved a child of a non-American Indian mother and an American Indian father. While the court accepted the tribal determination of the child's legal eligibility for membership, it applied the "existing Indian family" doctrine and rejected the applicability of the Act in the proceeding. The court specifically stated,

> The child may be an American Indian child as defined by the act, by virtue of her biological father. However, since birth, she has either resided with her non-American Indian mother or her non-American Indian great-uncle except for a period of four weeks when she lived with her father and paternal grandmother … The child has had minimal contact with her father. She has had no involvement in tribal activities or any participation in tribal culture. (*S.A. v. E.V.P* 1990, 1189)

Scholars have argued that this exception adds requirements to this simple definition of "Indian child," making it unnecessarily complex (Jaffke 2006, 739). Others have argued that it places too much discretion in the hands of state court judges and allows them to make decisions that undermine the effectiveness of ICWA (Graham 2001, Jaffke 2011, Metter 1998). Furthermore, other courts have determined that the exception denies tribes the sovereign right to determine tribal membership. As the Arizona Court of Appeals stated, "[f]irst among our reasons [to reject the exception] is to support the ICWA's goal not only of preserving its American Indian families, but also of protecting the tribe's interests in the welfare of its American Indian children and the maintenance of its culture" (*Michael J. v. Michael J.* 2000, 963).

Since its passage, many courts have used state law to guide their decision-making in American Indian child welfare cases. In the absence of a federal statutory definition under ICWA, state courts have borrowed and applied state-law concepts to construe individual terms of the federal statute. The extent to which state law influences interpretation of ICWA remains unresolved. For example, *In re Custody of S.E.G.* (1993) and *In re Welfare of Child of T.T.B* (1994) consider the issue of the "good cause" exception in the context of adoptive placement. In *S.E.G.* (1993), the struggle arose from the Indian Child Welfare Act's permissive, but ambiguous, "good cause" exception, and the extent to which state courts could deviate from ICWA's placement preferences via state-law principles (*In re Welfare of Child of T.T.B* 1994). Initially, the Minnesota Supreme Court set aside the adoption petition of the trial court, finding that the state's "best interests of the child" standard for determining placement tended to subvert the intent of the Indian Child Welfare Act (*In re Welfare of Child of T.T.B.* 2006). The standard involved a subjective evaluation generally grounded in "values of majority culture." Instead, the court utilized factors listed in the Guidelines in conjunction with a *de novo* standard of review as to whether the factors were properly weighed and considered (*In re Welfare of Child of T.T.B* 1994). In *In re Welfare of Child of T.T.B.* (2006), the Minnesota Supreme Court held that state rules may be applied in the interpretation of ICWA's "good cause" exception in considering the timeliness of a request to remove an American Indian child welfare proceeding to tribal court (*Mississippi Band of Choctaw American Indians v. Holyfield* 1989, 47). In *T.T.B.* (2006) the court asked the question: When does a mid-proceeding transfer from state court to tribal court do greater harm through the inevitable procedural delay than continuing to adjudicate the matter in state court, risking the historical bias of state law? The Minnesota Supreme Court concluded the flexible nature of the "good cause" provision permitted state rules to determine whether the proceedings had reached an advanced stage (*T.T.B.* 2006). On further review, the Minnesota Supreme Court, in *In re Welfare of Child of: T.T.B. & G.W.*, determined that there is nothing in the record to suggest that resort to the good-cause exception was done for purposes of undermining ICWA (2006). Instead, the record reflected significant effort on the part of the district court and the county to comply with the Act's directives (*In re Welfare of Child of: T.T.B. & G.W.* 2006).

ICWA is a remedial statute. Its passage signaled a strong move by Congress to begin addressing the cultural erosion and abuse by multiple state systems that were fundamentally incongruent with and ignorant of the social and cultural context of American Indian tribes. As such, it is imperative to ensure the intent and clear language of ICWA is being interpreted to protect American Indian children, families, and tribes. As the discussion above suggests, there are still many areas in which states cannot be left to their own devices to interpret, and in essence amend, the critical protections of ICWA.

Conclusion

> *And I, to whom so great a vision was given in my youth—you see me now a pitiful old man who has done nothing, for the nation's hoop is broken and scattered. There is no center any longer, and the sacred tree is dead*—Black Elk, Oglala Sioux. (Neihardt and Black Elk 2000, 207)

An understanding of the historical development of the relationship between the federal government and the Indian tribes is fundamental to the understanding, application, and enforcement of the Indian Child Welfare Act. Children are not only the life force of tribal societies, but also a protected national resource under federal law. As the 2013 decision by the United States Supreme Court in *Adoptive Couple v. Baby Girl* highlights, continued narrow interpretations by the courts of the Act not only ignore its primary purpose to ensure that children are not separated from their families, but threatens the future of tribal communities. It is imperative that knowledge of this law be taught and shared among many disciplines such as social work, health care, and public safety sectors, to name a few. Tribal culture and values are passed from one generation to the next through the extended family system. These families need to be strengthened to ensure success in life and put an end to the intergenerational transmission of historical trauma. Compliance with the Indian Child Welfare Act will ensure that Black Elk's vision is restored, regenerating the sacred tree and restoring the sacred hoops of Indian people. ICWA is the legal framework upon which rests the sovereignty and survival of America's varied and unique Indigenous cultures.

References

Adoptive Couple v. Baby Girl, 133 S. Ct. 2552 (2013).

Administration on Children, Youth and Families, Children's Bureau 2006. *Tribal-State Relations*. Washington, DC: US Department of Health and Human Services.

American Indian Child Welfare Program 1974. *American Indian Child Welfare Program, Problems that American Indian Families Face in Raising Their Children and How These Problems Are Affected by Federal Action or Inaction: Hearing before the Subcommittee on American Indian Affairs of the Senate Committee on Interior and Insular Affairs*, 99th Cong., 2nd sess. 3 1974 (testimony of William Byler, Executive Director, Association on American Indian Affairs).

Atwood, B.A. 2002. Flashpoints Under the American Indian Child Welfare Act: Toward a New Understanding of State Court Resistance. *Emory Law Journal*, 51, 587–676.

Atwood, B.A. 2010. *Children, Tribes, and States: Adoption and Custody Conflicts Over American Indian Children*. Durham, NC: Carolina Academic Press.

Cohen, F.S. 2005. *Cohen's Handbook of Federal Indian Law 2005 Edition*. Irvine, CA: LexisNexis.

Colorado Revised Statutes Annotated, Compliance with the Federal Indian Child Welfare Act, 2002.

E.A. v. State, 46 P.3d 986 Alaska 2002.

González, T. 2012. Reclaiming the Promise of the Indian Child Welfare Act: A Study of State Incorporation and Adoption of Legal Protections for Indian Status Offenders. *New Mexico Law Review*, 42, 131–55.

Graham, L.M. 1998. "The Past Never Vanishes": A Contextual Critique of the Existing Indian Family Doctrine. *American Indian Law Review*, 23, 1–54.

Graham, L.M. 2001. Reparations and the Indian Child Welfare Act. *25 Legal Studies Forum*, 619, 619–40.

Hartney, C. and Silva, F. 2007, January. *And Justice for Some, Differential Treatment of Youth of Color in the Justice System.* Retrieved May 9, 2012, from National Council on Crime and Delinquency: http://www.nccdglobal.org/sites/default/files/publication_pdf/justice-for-some.pdf.

In re A.J.S., 204 P.3d 543 Kan. 2009.

In re A.M., 22 P.3d 828 Wash. Ct. App. 2001.

In re Adoption of Hannah S., 48 Cal. Rptr. 3d 605 (Cal. Ct. App. 2006).

In re Cari B., 763 N.E.2d 917 (Ill. App. Ct. 2002).

In re Custody of S.E.G., 507 N.W.2d 872 (Minn. Ct. App. 1993).

In re Enrique P., 709 N.W.2d 676 (Neb. Ct. App. 2006).

In re G.S., 59 P.3d 1063 (Mont. 2002).

In re J.S., 177 P.3d 590 (Okla. Civ. App. 2008).

In re N.J., 221 P.3d 1255 (Nev. 2009).

In re Welfare of Child of T.T.B, 521 N.W.2d 357 (Minn. 1994).

In re Welfare of Child of T.T.B, 710 N.W. 2d 799 (Minn. App. 2006).

In re Welfare of Child of: T.T.B. & G.W., 724 N.W.2d 300 (Minn. App. 2006).

Indian Child Welfare Act, 25 U.S.C. §1901–1963 1978.

Iowa Indian Child Welfare Act, 2003.

Jaffke, C.L. 2006. The "Existing Indian Family" Exception to the American Indian Child Welfare Act: The States' Attempt to Slaughter Tribal Interests in American Indian Children. *Louisiana Law Review*, 66, 733–61.

Jaffke, C.L. 2011. Judicial Indifference: Why Does the "Existing Indian family" Exception to the American Indian Child Welfare Act Continue to Endure? *Washington State University Law Review*, 38, 127–50.

Jones, B. 2009. Differing Concepts of "Permanency": The Adoption and Safe Families Act and the Indian Child Welfare Act. In *Facing the Future: The Indian Child Welfare Act at 30*, M.L. Fletcher, W.T. Singel, and K.E. Fort (eds). East Lansing: Michigan State University Press, 127–47.

Lacey, L.J. 1986. The White Man's Law and the American Indian Family in the Assimilation Era. *Arkansas Law Review*, 40(2), 327–79.

Matter of Baby Boy L., 643 P.2d 168 (Kan. 1982).

Metter, C. 1998. Hard Cases Making Bad Law: The Need for Revision of the American Indian Child Welfare Act. *Santa Clara Law Review*, 38, 419–72.

Michael J. Jr. v. Michael J. Sr., 7 P.3rd 960 (Ariz. Ct. App. 2000).

Minnesota Department of Human Services 2007, February 22. *2007 Tribal State Agreement*. Retrieved May 17, 2012, from https://edocs.dhs.state.mn.us/lf server/Legacy/DHS-5022-ENG.

Minnesota Indian Family Preservation Act 1985.

Mississippi Band of Choctaw American Indians v. Holyfield, 490 US 30 1989.

Neihardt, J.G. and Black Elk, N. 2000. *Black Elk Speaks: Being the Life Story of a Holy Man of the Oglala Sioux*. Lincoln, NE: University of Nebraska Press.

People ex rel. K.D., 155 P.3d 634 (Colo. App. 2007).

Puzzanchera, C., Adams, B., and Sickmund, M. 2011, July. *Juvenile Court Statistics 2008*. Retrieved April 25, 2012, from National Center for Juvenile Justice: http://www.ncjj.org/pdf/jcsreports/jcs2008.pdf.

S. Rep. No. 95-597 1977.

S.A. v. E.V.P., 571 So. 2d 1187 (Ala. Ct. App. 1990).

Sickmund, M., Sladky, T., Kang, W., and Puzzanchera, C. 2011. *Easy Access to the Census of Juveniles in Residential Placement 1997–2010, US & State Profiles*. Retrieved April 23, 2012, from Office of Juvenile Justice and Delinquency Prevention, US Department of Justice: http://www.ojjdp.gov/ojstatbb/ezacjrp/.

Sinha, V., Trocmé, N., Fallon, B., et al. 2011. *Kiskisik Awasisak: Remember the Children. Understanding the Overrepresentation of First Nations Children in the Child Welfare System*. Ontario: Assembly of First Nations.

Snyder, H.N. and Sickmund, M. 2006, March. *Juvenile Offenders and Victims: 2006 National Report*. Retrieved May 16, 2012, from Office of Juvenile Justice and Delinquency Prevention, US Department of Justice: http://www. ojjdp.gov/ojstatbb/nr2006/downloads/NR2006.pdf.

State ex rel. C.D., 200 P.3d 194 (Utah Ct. App. 2008).

Summers, A., Wood, S., and Russell, J. 2012, May. *Disproportionality Rates for Children of Color in Foster Care*. Retrieved June 3, 2012, from National Council of Juvenile and Family Court judges: http://www.ncjfcj.org/sites/ default/files/Disproportionality%20Rates%20for%20Children%20of%20Col or%202010.pdf.

Trocmé, N., MacLaurin, B., Fallon, B., et al. 2010. *Canadian Incidence Study of Reported Child Abuse and Neglect, Final Report*. Ontario: National Clearinghouse on Family Violence.

Van Straaten, J. and Buchbinder, P.G. 2011. *The American Indian Child Welfare Act: Improving Compliance through State-Tribal Coordination*. Retrieved May 9, 2012 from Center Court Innovation: http://www.courtinnovation.org/ sites/default/files/documents/ICWA.pdf.

Washington State Indian Child Welfare Act, 2011.

Chapter 9
Tradition Keepers:
American Indian/Alaska Native Elders

Priscilla A. Day

I am now considered an elder on my reservation ... it seems just a season ago that I was a little boy who spent my summer days running and playing in the woods. And it seems only one winter has passed since I was sledding with my brothers and cousins. In my dreams I still help my grandmother haul water from the spring. The seasons have passed so quickly. My heart still sings the songs of my childhood. I still feel but a child. (Peacock and Wisuri 2006, 8)

The quote above illustrates the transition between roles based on age and the close connections often found between American Indian youth and elders. Elders play an important and esteemed role in Indigenous communities. This chapter examines issues related to providing services to American Indian/Alaska Native elders. The first is to understand the role of elders in their communities; the second is how historical trauma and intergenerational trauma have impacted elders; the third issue is a brief overview of medical issues prevalent in the elder population; and lastly, what role social workers can take in supporting American Indian/Alaska Native elders to live a quality life that embraces their role as elder.

American Indian/Alaska Native elders play important roles in Indigenous families and communities (Day 2007, Red Horse et al. 2000). Those who are not part of these communities often do not understand these roles. Traditionally, American Indian/Alaska Native elders are the keepers of knowledge, wisdom, and teachings. Their role in Indigenous communities is to pass this information to the next generations in order to keep our communities strong and connected to the ones that went before (Day 2007, Rheault 1999).

According to the US Census Bureau, American Community Survey (2011), 17.8 percent of the American Indian/Alaska Native population is over 55 years old. This percentage has grown since the days when American Indian/Alaska Native life expectancy was less than 50 years old. American Indian/Alaska Native elders, defined as those who are age 55 and over, are a growing population (UCLA Center for Health Policy Research 2010). Approximately 43 percent of American Indian/Alaska Natives live on reservations or trust lands, and 53 percent reside in urban areas (Indian Health Service 2012, paragraph 3). While many receive health care from the Indian Health Service, others do not. This is problematic because 27.6 percent of American Indian/Alaska Natives have no health insurance (US Census Bureau 2011, 6). It has been well documented that American Indian/

Alaska Natives have higher poverty rates than others, but poverty goes down for elders from 29.5 percent for all American Indian/Alaska Natives to 19.7 percent for elders 65 and over (US Census Bureau 2011, 6). Even though the poverty rate declines as elders age, it still means that 1 in 5 (20 percent) American Indian/ Alaska Native elders live in poverty.

The Path of Life

Different tribes have different stories and teachings about the path of life. For Anishinaabe Peoples this path is called "*mino-bimaadiziwin*," which roughly translated means living the life that the Creator wants you to live. Our beliefs are that as humans, we all have free will to choose which path we take. Some people choose not to take the path that the Creator wants them to take. This choice can result in a life filled with challenges. According to Rheault (1999) who interviewed Anishinaabe elders, there are seven stages of life. Each stage has tasks that someone on their life journey should learn and master, and each stage is developmental. Mastering the tasks in one stage before going on to the next stage is important (157). In each stage there are teachings and responsibilities that must be learned.

When a child is born, their spirit enters what is called the "good life" because babies and young children are considered sacred. They are taken care of in every way by their family and community. The next stage, approximately ages 7–13, are the years in which the child/adolescent is learning more about their world and often acts impulsively without giving his or her actions much thought or reflection. Up until approximately age 20, young people develop a stronger sense of who they are and what their life purpose may be. They enter early adulthood in their 20s. During these years, the person assumes adult responsibilities and starts to fulfill their purpose that has become clearer. If one is following the good path, they become and are seen as a "good person." As they move into their late 20s and 30s, life is filled with raising a family and assuming community responsibilities. Gradually people transition into the "doing" stage in their mid-30s to early 40s. In these years, adults generally have more time to further expand on personal and community interests as their children become more independent. Each stage is preparation for becoming an elder, so as one ages, one begins to assume greater responsibility and understanding of the teachings. Over time, one starts to be a teacher, gradually moving into the role of an elder. In this stage, one is treated with great respect. However, the role of elder is more about how one carries oneself in the world than about age. There are some people who are elders by age but not looked to as teachers or role models because they were not able to master all the tasks of each stage of life. The final stage on the path of life is passing into the next world (Rheault 1999).

Peacock and Wisuri (2006) have written about the stages of life for Anishinaabe people in a slightly different way. They describe the "four hills of life," so called because each stage has challenges similar to climbing a hill. The journey follows the seasons of the year starting with springtime, which is birth and infanthood. This is similar to Rheault's description of the "good life." The second hill of life is summer, which is when the baby becomes a youth and adolescent. In this part of life, children learn proper ways of behaving and life skills to be successful. They also begin to take on greater responsibilities for self and others such as how to hunt, garden, and take care of younger children and elders. The third hill of life is adulthood, the autumn of life, which starts with the early fall and gradually leads to late fall and winter. This hill is filled with the business of having and raising children, working to support families, and taking care of elders. Some adults assume the role of community leader. It is also a time of moving from participant in ceremonies to one who is responsible for them. The final hill of life is winter, a time when things begin to slow down, eventually leading to death. For Anishinaabe, this is the hill of wisdom, acquired over a lifetime of watching, learning, and trying. On this hill, one should have the knowledge and skills to pass on to others. Both Peacock and Rheault would agree that becoming an elder, in the true sense, literally takes a lifetime of preparation. This is why elders are so revered in American Indian/Alaska Native communities.

As keepers of tradition and knowledge, elders learn and retain knowledge about many things. In Anishinaabe culture, the path of knowledge has four stages that build upon one another. These stages are: feeling, watching, reflection, and doing (Rheault 1999). The first path, feeling, is about learning to have balance with one's emotions. "The Elders teach that emotional balance—through trusting one's intuition and one's reason—allows one to hear and see with open ears, clear eyes and a good heart" (Rheault 1999, 124).

The second path, watching and learning, teaches us that we need to be silent in order to learn what is going on, what is behind words and actions, and the proper course of action. "At times, asking too many questions obscures the obvious knowledge available in the physical-spiritual world. Observation without questioning also teaches patience and humility since one is forced to quiet one's natural inclination to want to know everything all at once" (Rheault 1999, 124). By watching and learning, one learns to find their own tempo and the tempo of the world around them in a gradual way. Because of this way of knowing, elders have experienced this process many times and therefore are able to teach and role model patience.

The third path, reflection, reminds us that we need to take time to integrate what we have observed in order to use it in the correct way in our behavior. "It is here that one uses the power of one's mind and spirit to reflect upon the knowledge that one has gained, understanding it for what it means, and for what it can do in one's life" (Rheault 1999, 127). Reflection is part of learning to think in a critical manner and an important task to develop in order to gain wisdom. Lastly, the fourth path is about doing. In Anishinaabe culture, only after one has felt, watched, and learned, and reflected, is one ready to take action (Rheault 1999). Elders have gone through and developed mastery in each of these stages and only then become the transmitters of this knowledge across generations and time. This way of being has sustained American Indian families and communities across time.

Anishinaabe elders believe that when a child comes into this world, they are complete. The task in life is to come to know your role in life; in other words, to become fully actualized as a person as you become an elder. Elders play a critical role as teachers on this path of life. They help children learn proper behavior and what it means to live a good life. "Without these Teachers, how else can a person know how to be good? They are oral reference libraries that account for stories, legends, prophecies, ceremonies, songs, dances, language and the philosophy of the people" (Rheault 1999, 138). Because of their central role, elders were cherished in traditional families and communities. Unfortunately, the impact of boarding schools, child welfare disparities, and years of family and cultural disintegration has led some American Indian/Alaska Native elders to lack knowledge about their roles. It has also led some tribal members to treat elders in disrespectful ways. The impact of these policies and practices on individuals, families, and communities is referred to as historic and intergenerational trauma.

Intergenerational Trauma

American Indian/Alaska Natives share a similar history of oppression across the Americas. Much of this legacy continues to resonate in tribal communities. This phenomenon, known as historic trauma, has even greater consequences for the elders (Day 2007, Wasserman 2005, Weaver and Yellow Horse Brave Heart 1999). The Office of the US Surgeon General reports that American Indian/Alaska Natives have experienced Post Traumatic Stress Disorder (PTSD) at almost three times the rate of the general population—22 percent prevalence rate for American Indian/Alaska Natives versus 8 percent for the general population (Wasserman 2005, 5).

> We do not know how the experiences of American Indian and Alaska Native people throughout the past generations may have permanently impacted physiological development. If the experience of childhood abuse and neglect can change the structure of the brain, what impact did colonization, massacres, and forced confinement have on the physiological and psychological development of the indigenous people of the past? (Wasserman 2005, 21)

This is a frightening question and it has only recently started to be discussed in tribal communities, but one doesn't have to look far to see disparities across the board for American Indian/Alaska Native elders and their families. No one really knows how much this can be attributed to actual changes in the brains of millions of American Indian/Alaska Native children who were severely traumatized by boarding school and other oppressive policies. No one knows how much these traumas have forever changed American Indian/Alaska Native families and communities, but the impact has surely occurred.

It is, therefore, important that social workers and other health and human service providers know some basic information in order to understand and address these influences. Historical loss can result in many factors which impact American Indian/Alaska Natives across the lifespan but is perhaps most evident on elders, many of whom lived through first-hand traumatic events like boarding schools, other out-of-home placements, and trauma. Many elders were sent to boarding schools as children and remain traumatized by the experience. Those elders are now 70 years old and older. It is estimated that during the 1930s and 1940s, half of all American Indians attended boarding schools (Ziibiwing Center of Anishinaabe Culture and Life Ways 2011). Some elders have shared their boarding school stories so that others can understand what happened, and the impact it continues to have in our communities (Red Horse et al. 2000, Ziibiwing Center of Anishinaabe Culture and Life Ways 2011). Results from researchers who have attempted to measure the impact of historic trauma seem to indicate that American Indian/ Alaska Natives have high levels of emotional distress including "anger, avoidance, anxiety, and depression" (Whitbeck et al. 2004, 127).

Researchers have found that there are lasting impacts not only on the person who has experienced the trauma, but also on their parents, their children, and their communities. This impact continues across generations in many different ways. Besides the trauma itself, which might have been physical, sexual, emotional abuse, or neglect, the children and adolescents who experienced trauma often had a hard time re-entering their family systems or communities. Often they lost their language and cultural traditions. Many lost the ability to learn how to be a good parent who is able to look out for and protect their children. Many lost their cultural identity or were taught a negative view of their culture. All of these impacts were passed on to a new generation of children who continued to be traumatized by additional events. Many American Indian/Alaska Native elders carry the wounds of these traumas. They weren't able to learn the important tasks that elders need to learn, which resulted in many not being able to carry on the traditions and values of their communities. This is the legacy of boarding schools and other traumatic practices (Day 2007, Ziibiwing Center of Anishinaabe Culture and Life Ways 2011).

What are some of the other ways that this intergenerational trauma impacts American Indian/Alaska Native elders? These kinds of traumas create distrust of government and others in authority, including social workers. Chronic stress from historic trauma impacts the health and well-being of tribal peoples (Struthers and Lowe 2003, Weaver and Yellow Horse Brave Heart 1999, Ziibiwing Center of Anishinaabe Culture and Life Ways 2011). Recent research has concluded that early childhood trauma can have lasting impacts and may impact developmental growth (Wasserman 2005). These impacts are seen in the dismal health, mental health, child welfare, and other poor outcomes present in American Indian/Alaska

Native communities. Knowing about this history and understanding how it might impact elders is important.

We have only recently come to understand the impact these policies and practices have on not only individuals and families but on tribes as a whole. "Collective trauma unfolds as an omnipresent, community wide phenomenon, while individual trauma unfolds as a personal psychological phenomenon unrelated to a collective common experience" (Red Horse et al. 2000, 14). This connection between historical trauma and contemporary individual and community health is critical for understanding what is happening today with American Indians (Peacock and Wisuri 2002, Ziibiwing Center of Anishinaabe Culture and Life Ways 2011).

As mentioned earlier, some American Indian/Alaska Native elders are vulnerable to abuse. While few studies have been done on the extent of elder abuse, the National Center on Elder Abuse did fund the National Indian Council on Aging (NICOA) to conduct research on elder abuse specific to American Indian/Alaska Native elders. They found that some things contribute to the greater vulnerability of tribal elders, including poverty and isolation of rural tribal members (NICOA 2004). Not surprisingly, they found that families that: 1) believe in traditional values and hold elders in high regard; 2) continue to engage in strong extended family networks; and 3) engage in cultural practices tend to have less elder abuse (NICOA 2004).

The Role of Elders

The role and status of American Indian/Alaska Native elders within their families and communities is well documented (Day 2007, Henderson 2002, Red Horse et al. 2000). Unlike most non-Indian elders, American Indian/Alaska Native elders, as they age, are expected to assume "increased kinship responsibilities" (Red Horse 1997, 245). From an early age, American Indian/Alaska Native children are taught to respect and care for the elders (Day 2007, Dubray and Sanders 1999).

As work ends or slows, elders have time to spend with grandchildren and great grandchildren. They sing, garden, hunt, fish, play, and tell stories. They are more patient. At ceremonies and feasts, elders are treated respectfully and are often served food or allowed to go first in line. I've observed at ceremonies that those who cook the meals often make special efforts to cook "old time" foods that are comforting to elders. At these events, when elders speak they are listened to without interruption as they have earned the right to be heard.

Understanding culture can assist us in making culturally appropriate practice decisions when working with members of another culture (Day 2007). Just like any other ethnic group, American Indian/Alaska Native elders identify culturally and practice traditional culture to varying degrees. This is dependent on many things, including the level of acculturation. Elders may engage in behaviors that appear acculturated, for example in dress and appearance, but they might actively practice cultural teachings, such as sweat lodges. In contrast, some American Indian/Alaska

Native elders may appear to be traditional but they may be Christian or know little about cultural ways. Most elders are likely bi-cultural, meaning they have some experience and varying degrees of comfort in both white and tribal settings. Even though past social work policies and practices were designed to acculturate tribal peoples, it is very difficult to totally replace one's cultural worldview. Elders who may not practice traditional ways tend to respect traditional practices and may see the world through an Indigenous lens in terms of values and norms of behavior, although this is not always true. Internalized oppression was taught in boarding schools and passed on through the generations, resulting in negative cultural self-image. The cultural continuum that American Indian/Alaska Native elders fall within ranges from those who could be called "primarily traditional" to those who do not have knowledge or practice any traditional ways. Most probably fall somewhere in between as "bi-cultural" (Day 2007, Lum 1996, Dubray and Sanders 1999).

Health

One of the rights guaranteed to American Indian/Alaska Native people by treaty, and clarified through the years of court rulings and Acts of Congress, are tribes' right to health care. According to their website, the Indian Health Service was established to provide health care to federally recognized tribal members. "The mission of the Indian Health Service, in partnership with American Indians and Alaska Natives, is to raise their physical, mental, social, and spiritual health to the highest possible level" (Indian Health Service 2012, paragraph 1). This is done through the provision of public health services to "promote healthy American Indians and Alaska Natives, communities, and cultures and to honor and protect the inherent sovereign rights of tribes" (Indian Health Service 2012, paragraph 1).

Thirty-five percent of American Indian/Alaska Natives who are 150–200 percent below the poverty line rely solely on the Indian Health Service for their health care. About 50 percent living in poverty are eligible for Medicaid (James et al. 2009). American Indian/Alaska Natives over 65 are eligible for Medicare. The Indian Health Service spends $2,741 per person annually on health expenditures, while the US average per-person health expenditure is $7,239 annually (Indian Health Service 2012, paragraph 1). Most American Indian elders who live on tribal lands still receive their health care from the Indian Health Service.

Not surprisingly, American Indians have high rates of health disparities and mortality in comparison to the general population, often leading to debilitating conditions and greater levels of chronic disability. Health conditions earlier in life often catch up with elders in their 50s. These include rates of alcoholism, which is 514 percent higher; tuberculosis, which is 500 percent higher; diabetes, which is 177 percent higher; and unintentional injuries, 140 percent higher (Indian Health Service 2012, paragraph 5). Diabetes often leads to other serious health conditions such as hypertension, heart disease, and stroke. Chronic diseases significantly affect elders, with the largest disparity gap between American Indian/Alaska Native and non-Natives in the 55 to 64-year-old group (Satter et al. 2010, 2).

American Indian/Alaska Native elders also have serious lack of access to important medical screenings. For example, cancer screening rates are low. Twenty-nine percent of American Indian/Alaska Native women age 55–64 have not had a cervical cancer screening in the last three or more years, compared to 12 percent for whites. Almost one-quarter (23 percent) have not had a mammogram in over two years, compared to 17 percent of whites. Twenty-nine percent of American Indian/Alaska Natives have never had a colon cancer screening, compared to 16 percent of whites (Satter et al. 2010, 2). When elders don't receive early access to medical care they find that when they do go to the doctor their illness has progressed farther than it would have if they had gone earlier.

American Indian/Alaska Native elderly health risk factors are strongly influenced by social/economic conditions and are related to the following health disparities: Almost one in five American Indian/Alaska Natives currently smoke tobacco regularly (17 percent), twice the rate of whites. American Indian/Alaska Native males age 55–64 report heavy alcohol use at twice the rate of whites (41 percent compared to 20 percent). More than one in five (22 percent) American Indian/Alaska Natives report being sedentary, compared to 12 percent of whites. Because of sedentary lifestyles and poor diets, one-third of American Indian/ Alaska Natives are obese, compared to one-fifth of whites (Satter et al. 2010, 2).

American Indians elders are at risk of falling more than any racial or ethnic group. One in five (22 percent) elders aged 65 years and older have had multiple falls in the past year, the highest prevalence of any racial group (all races, 14 percent). This risk goes up considerably if the elder is among the poorest; nearly twice as many American Indian/Alaska Native elders who live below 200 percent of the federal poverty level (FPL) had multiple falls, compared to all other races who live below 200 percent of the FPL (Satter et al. 2010, 2). This may be because American Indian/Alaska Native elders may live in more isolated areas and, if they are poor, they have less access to medical care and may live in poorer housing.

Access-to-care barriers exist at high levels for American Indian/Alaska Natives. For example, one study looked at American Indian/Alaska Native elders in California. They found that one-half (52 percent) aged 55 to 64 years utilized employment-based insurance compared to three-quarters (73 percent) of whites. American Indian/Alaska Natives aged 55 to 64 are nearly twice as likely to be uninsured compared to whites (12 percent versus 7 percent). Contrary to public opinion, only one in 20 (5 percent) American Indian/Alaska Native elders use, or are eligible for, the Indian Health Service (IHS) coverage in California (Satter et al. 2010, 2). Those in rural areas often have to travel long distances to health clinics. Even when the Indian Health Service is available to elders, it is grossly underfunded and understaffed to meet the needs of this population.

Research has consistently found that American Indian/Alaska Native elders expect to be cared for within their families (Day 2007, Henderson 2002, Redford 2002). Because of the strong role of elders in the family and community fabric, most American Indian elders are taken care of within the context of their families. While tribes recognize the need for long-term care, only a few have the resources to develop tribal nursing homes (Day 2007). As a result, elders in need of nursing home care are either cared for at home or reside in non-Indian nursing homes. Most reservations are in rural areas, some quite remote, and many physicians and other skilled nursing home staff are reluctant to reside in those locations. As the population of American Indian/Alaska Native elders continues to grow there is a need to address long-term care (Day 2007).

The Wisdom of Elders

What is wisdom? According the Merriam-Webster dictionary (2012), wisdom is a noun that means

1. a) accumulated philosophic or scientific learning: knowledge; b) Ability to discern inner qualities and relationships: insight; c) Good sense: judgment; d) Generally accepted belief;
2. A wise attitude, belief, or course of action;
3. The teachings of ancient men. (Paragraph 1)

Just like the dictionary definition, most people would agree that there are different kinds of wisdom. For some it is about the knowledge you have acquired; for others, it is more about one's intuition, gained from a life of experience. For most Native people, wisdom is about embracing traditional values and living a life consistent with those values and cultural norms. This often embodies spiritual beliefs, knowledge, and respect for the physical world, plants, and animals. For Anishinaabe elders, it is also about living the seven grandfather teachings. Those teachings embody Anishinaabe teaching. They are: wisdom—to value knowledge and learning; love—to embrace peace and have unconditional regard for others; respect—to treat others in a caring manner; bravery—to act with integrity even in the face of fear; honesty—to keep one's word and behave in an honorable way; humility—to know your place in the larger picture and not put yourself above the Great Spirit, animals, plants, or other life; and truth—to be honest with yourself and others (Ontario Native Literacy Coalition 2012, paragraph 3). These Anishinaabe values are expected from someone who is an elder. An elder should live these values and be able to teach them to others and to demonstrate them in their behavior. "It is the wisdom of everyday things—of humor when it is most needed, of an encouraging hug when something is done right, of singing to children when they have bad dreams" (Peacock and Wisuri 2006, 102).

Social workers must know the history of their American Indian/Alaska Native elder clients and understand how that history has impacted the community and elder. They need to understand the role elders have played in their family and communities. Above all, they need to know about and practice culturally competent social work. There are some national resources that can provide information, such as NICOA that was established in 1976. Its mission is "to advocate for improved comprehensive health, social services and economic well being for American Indian and Alaska Native elders" (NICOA 2012, paragraph 1). Its website includes information on diabetes education, elder abuse, long-term care, Medicare and Medicaid, and links to resources and other information.

The role of elder has prevailed despite efforts to diminish it. In my own life, my grandmother played a very significant role. My grandmother's spirit name was Shawonosakwe—Lady Going South. She was given this name by her uncle who named her after the headwaters of the Mississippi River in northern Minnesota. Even at the very end of her life she was still teaching me. She lay in a hospice room, three months shy of being 100 years old, surrounded by her grandchildren. She had been unconscious and we somberly gathered for the inevitable passing of our family matriarch. She suddenly awoke from her unconscious state and began talking to us. She was smiling and telling stories about each of us. We went from being somber to laughing and joking with one another. She began to talk about places she had been in her life as though she were flying over different parts of the country. Finally after about 45 minutes, she got a peaceful look on her face. "I see the lake [the place she was born and lived her whole life]. I am home. Thank you." She closed her eyes and never regained consciousness. As she had done throughout my life, at the end of her life she was teaching me about death—about leaving the physical world and entering the spiritual one—with joy and grace.

References

Day, P.A. 2007. American Indian Elders. In *Social Work Practice with Ethnically and Racially Diverse Nursing Home Residents and Their Families*, P.J. Kolb (ed.). New York, NY: Columbia University Press, 41–71.

Dubray, W. and Sanders, A. 1999. Interactions between American Indian ethnicity and health care. In *Health and the American Indian*, P.A. Day and H.N. Weaver (eds). Co-published simultaneously as *Journal of Health and Social Policy*, 10(4), 67–84.

Henderson, J.N. 2002. *How do we understand and incorporate elder's teaching and Tribal values in planning a long term care system?* American Indian and Alaska Native Roundtable on Long Term Care: Final Report 2002. Albuquerque, NM: National Indian Council on Aging.

Indian Health Service 2012. Retrieved December 8, 2012, from http://www.ihs.gov.

James, C., Schwartz, K., and Berndt, J. 2009. Race, Ethnicity and Health Care-Issue Brief. "A profile of American Indian/Alaska Natives and their healthcare coverage." The Kaiser Family Foundation.

Lum, D. 1996. *Social Work Practice and People of Color: A Process-stage Approach*. Pacific Grove, GA: Brooks/Cole Publishing Company.

Merriam-Webster Online Dictionary. 2012. Retrieved December 8, 2012, from http://www.merriam-webster.com/dictionary/wisdom.

NICOA (National Indian Council on Aging) 2004. *A Review of the Literature: Elder Abuse in Indian Country: Research, Policy, and Practice.* Washington, DC: National Center on Elder Abuse, 1–29.

NICOA (National Indian Council on Aging) 2012. Advocates for American Indian and Alaska Native Elders. Retrieved September 13, 2013, from www.nicoa. org.

Ontario Native Literacy Coalition Social Community Enterprise 2012. Seven grandfather teachings. Retrieved September 13, 2013, from http://www.7grand fatherteachings.ca/teachings.html.

Peacock, T. and Wisuri, M. 2002. *Ojibwe waasa inaabidaa: We look in all directions.* Afton, MN: Afton Historical Society Press.

Peacock, T. and Wisuri, M. 2006. *The Four Hills of Life: Ojibwe Wisdom.* Afton, MN: Afton Historical Society Press.

Red Horse, J. 1997. Traditional American Indian family systems. *Families, Systems, & Health*, 15(3), 243–50.

Red Horse, J., Martinez, C., Day, P., et al. 2000. *Family Preservation Concepts in American Indian Communities.* National Indian Child Welfare Association. Retrieved May 25, 2012, from http://www.nicwa.org/research/01.family%20 pres01.rpt.pdf.

Redford, L. 2002. *Long Term Care in Indian Country: Important Considerations in Developing Long Term Care Services.* American Indian and Alaska Native Roundtable on Long Term Care: Final Report 2002. Albuquerque, NM: National Indian Council on Aging.

Rheault, D. 1999. *Anishinaabe Mino-Bimaadiziwin: The Way of a Good Life.* Peterborough, ON: Debwewin Press.

Satter, D.E., Wallace, S.P., Garcia, A.N. and Smith, L.M. 2010. Health of American Indian and Alaska Native Elders in California. Recent Work, UCLA Center for Health Policy Research, UC Los Angeles. Retrieved December 8, 2012, from http://128.48.120.176/uc/item/1108k4mc.

Struthers, R. and Lowe, J. 2003. Nursing in the Native American culture and historical trauma. *Issues in Mental Health Nursing*, 24, 257–72.

UCLA Center for Health Policy Research 2010. American Indian Elder Health Care: Critical Information for Researchers and Policymakers. Los Angeles, CA.

US Census Bureau, American Community Survey 2011. Retrieved December 8, 2012, from http://www.census.gov/newsroom/releases/archives/facts_for_feat ures_special_editions/cb11-ff22.html.

Wasserman, E. 2005. *Understanding the Effects of Childhood Trauma on Brain Development in Native Children.* West Hollywood, CA: Tribal Law and Policy Institute.

Weaver, H.N. and Yellow Horse Brave Heart, M. 1999. Examining two facets of American Indian identity: Exposure to other cultures and the influence of historic trauma. *Journal of Human Behavior in the Social Environment*, 2(1/2), 19–33.

Whitbeck, L.B., Adams, G.W., Hoyt, D.R., and Chen, X. 2004. Conceptualizing and measuring historical trauma among American Indian people. *American Journal of Community Psychology*, 33(3/4), 127.

Ziibiwing Center of Anishinaabe Culture and Life Ways 2011. *American Indian Boarding Schools: An Exploration of Global Ethnic and Cultural Cleansing.* Mount Pleasant, MI, 1–28.

PART IV
Well-Being and
the Community Context

Social and health disparities are often seen as the defining factor of contemporary Indigenous existence. While, indeed, Native Americans are often at the bottom of statistics reflecting social and health issues, resilience and survival are also critical components of Indigenous lives. Additionally, understanding contemporary social and health disparities requires an understanding of the influence of the larger social environment; a context of colonization that perpetuates a power imbalance and associated inequities.

The larger societal context presents both challenges and opportunities for change. While Indigenous nations retain some aspects of sovereignty, clearly, in today's world they exist within a larger context of surrounding settler societies. Indigenous Peoples, while remaining distinct, are typically interdependent with their non-Indigenous surroundings. Individuals concerned about the well-being of Indigenous Peoples need to recognize this larger context.

This section of the book includes an examination of large-scale or community-level issues. Weaver reflects on violence in the lives of Native Americans and how this is perpetuated by the larger societal context. She highlights how the dominance inherent in colonization is not just an historical artifact or a thing of the past but continues to shape contemporary social issues. The Bubar chapter gives insight into the issues of domestic violence and sexual assault for Indigenous women. In particular, she examines how different aspects of Indigenous women's identity intersect in ways that influence responses to these social problems. Mehl-Madrona and Mainguy review various health statistics, thus painting a portrait of significant disparities, but go beyond a deficit perspective to discuss Indigenous conceptualizations of well-being. The chapter includes an overview of therapeutic approaches aligned with Indigenous belief systems and provides an example of an agency providing holistic, culturally grounded services for Native people.

Hertle, Wagner, and Black examine how assets are defined and can be enhanced in Indigenous communities. Their chapter highlights specific, successful asset-building strategies that have been implemented in Indigenous communities. Finally, Blackstock gives concrete examples of how advocacy can be used to promote change on behalf of Indigenous Peoples and communities. Indeed, her mosquito advocacy approach gives both hope and specific techniques for addressing the concerns of Indigenous communities within the context of much larger and more powerful settler societies.

Chapter 10

Violence in the Lives of Native Americans

Hilary N. Weaver

While stereotypes of Native Americans abound, they typically focus on Native people as romantic, suffering, spiritual remnants of a distant past or images of brave warriors caricatured as mascots for sports teams. In reality, Native people are diverse and multifaceted. There are, however, some common themes that permeate the Native American experience and are reflected in many social and health statistics such as high rates of poverty, diabetes, and suicide.

Another dismal but seldom acknowledged reality is the ongoing presence of violence in the lives of many Native people. While recent scholarship has begun to examine violence against Native women and children, such as the groundbreaking report *Maze of Injustice* (Amnesty International 2007), there is significantly less attention to other expressions of violence in Native communities such as assaults, gang violence, and homicide. This chapter explores the historical antecedents of violence in Native communities and makes connections between historical and contemporary violence. Multiple manifestations of violence are examined including homicide, suicide, hate crimes, police brutality, domestic violence, and violence against youth.

Antecedents of Contemporary Violence

When Europeans first ventured to what would later become known as the United States, although many of them espoused racist attitudes, generally they recognized the inherent sovereignty of Indigenous Peoples and dealt with them on a government-to-government basis. Recognition of sovereignty began to erode as the balance of power shifted and Europeans gained the ability to dominate interactions with Indigenous Peoples and pursue their own interests with little incentive to compromise.

As colonization efforts expanded, so did attacks on Indigenous sovereignty. Native Americans came to be defined as "deviant others," not worthy of possessing land or due any respect or basic human rights. It was this mindset (i.e., Native people as subhuman savages) that set the stage for, and legitimated violence against, Native people. This philosophy both undergirds the creation of Native people as vulnerable targets of violence and legitimizes their targeting (Perry 2002).

In the United States, the nineteenth century can be characterized as the era of extermination (Jacoby 2008). The United States undertook campaigns of deliberate and violent annihilation of Native Americans. These official government efforts were supplemented by the efforts of private citizens such as homesteaders and miners, who often massacred Native people in their quest to seize land still in Indigenous hands.

Today it is clear that historical attacks on Native Americans were nothing less than genocide. As Native Americans became no longer able to muster the military might necessary to effectively defend themselves, victimization shifted from genocide to ethnocide.

> Genocide refers to the explicit and frequently brutal physical violence perpetrated against Native Americans in an effort to eliminate them as a people while ethnocide refers to the much more 'subtle' efforts to deculturate Native Americans, sometimes through physical violence but more often through the social violence or 'resocializing' or 'civilizing' the natives. Whether through direct violence or assimilationist policies, whites have consistently sought to physically and culturally annihilate Native peoples. The origins of the 'anti-Indian movement' might be seen as embedded in the combined doctrines of Manifest Destiny and European superiority, providing as they did a clear rationale for genocide. (Perry 2002, 234)

Violence against Native women was a key element of colonization because of the important roles that women played in tribal communities (Halldin 2008). As per the Cheyenne saying, a nation is not conquered until the hearts of its women are on the ground. Armed with this knowledge, colonizers attacked the egalitarian gender roles that characterized most Indigenous societies, thus undermining the role and status of Indigenous women.

Connecting Historical and Contemporary Violence

The massive and comprehensive campaigns of violence conducted against Native Americans throughout American history set the stage for continued, multiple manifestations of violence in the lives of many contemporary Native Americans. For example, the violence inherent in patriarchally grounded colonization efforts such as the boarding schools has left a legacy of trauma illustrated by high rates of child abuse and Native youth in foster care (Willmon-Haque and BigFoot 2008). Likewise, colonization and historical trauma are often cited as the foundation for a myriad of social problems that provide the context for suicide (Alcantara and Gone 2007).

Indeed, there are significant parallels between the nature of macro-level colonization efforts and contemporary expressions of violence on the micro level. The dynamics of abuse tend to be the same regardless of scale. Domestic violence typically involves intimidation, subjugation, isolation, and maintenance of control through threats of violence. These are the same dynamics at work through colonization (Hukill 2006). Minimizing, denying, and blaming others are common defense mechanisms that perpetuate both individualized and societal violence.

Building on theories of learned behavior, some scholars propose that centuries of colonization, violence, and unprocessed trauma have led Native Americans to internalize violence as a norm (Berg and DeLisi 2006, de Ravello et al. 2008). As supporting evidence they cite high rates of Native Americans who commit violent crimes and high rates of incarceration. Colonization and dispossession are often cited as key factors in leading Native people to become violent. It is important to note, however, that while all Indigenous Peoples experienced colonization, most are not involved in crime (Weatherburn 2010). Rather than resorting to a simplistic explanation that colonization and dispossession have led to higher rates of violence among Native Americans, we would do well to look to the broader literature on victimization that has closely examined theories of risk and resilience and their relationship to victims becoming perpetrators.

While officially the United States government no longer espouses campaigns of violence against Native Americans, some believe that the mentality that supported the use of violence and oppression lingers. As an example, some scholars believe that state power is still used to suppress Native dissidents and activists (Perry 2002).

Likewise, prominent elected officials are often blatant in their negative attitudes toward Native Americans. In 2010, Mayor Michael Bloomberg of New York City urged the governor of New York to "Get yourself a cowboy hat and a shotgun" to deal with the Seneca Nation of Indians around a controversial issue regarding state taxation of gasoline and cigarettes sold on reservations (Williams 2010). The fact that a prominent elected official sees nothing wrong with using this type of hate speech speaks to a continuing social climate in which some people find vigilantism and advocating for violence against Native Americans to be acceptable.

Indeed, significant violence continues to occur in the context of Native rights claims (Perry 2002).

> The only good Indian is a quiet Indian or better yet a dead Indian. Once Indians step outside the boundaries that define 'good Indian,' they become vulnerable to retaliatory violence. Hate crimes are little more than reactionary measures for the reassertion of whiteness over color … Racially motivated violence then becomes a legitimate response to the Other who is out of control, who has overstepped his or her social, political, and on occasion geographical boundaries. (Perry 2002, 241)

Contemporary hate crimes against Native Americans are rooted in historical persecution (Perry 2002). "Ethnoviolence [is] nested within a matrix of social processes which have long produced and reproduced the subordinate status of Native Americans in the United States" (Perry 2002, 231). Clearly, any thoughtful, comprehensive examination of violence in the lives of Native Americans must fully consider the role of the social environment or macro-level context in allowing and/or facilitating disproportionate levels of violence.

The Grim Picture of Violence in Native Communities

There are multiple manifestations of violence in the lives of many Native Americans. The common links among these various expressions of violence are that Native Americans are typically over-represented, regardless of type of violence, and that violence exists within a societal context that tolerates and at times facilitates its expression.

Native American crime victimization is twice that of non-Native people, with 57 percent of crimes being perpetrated by Whites. That number rises to 80 percent for sexual assaults (Death Penalty Information Center 2012). Native Americans have the highest rates of intimate partner homicide at 2.1 per 100,000 (Department of Health and Human Services 2010). Native women are almost three times more likely to be killed by a partner than Whites or Hispanics, and twice as likely to be raped. While precise statistics are lacking, elder abuse is rising among Native Americans (Smyer and Clark 2011). The determinants of interpersonal violence exist at multiple levels including individual, family, organizational, community (i.e., colonization), and policy. Consequently, prevention and intervention efforts to address violence must occur at all levels.

From 1979 to 1992, 4,718 Native Americans living on or near reservations died violent deaths; 2,324 of these were from homicide and 2,394 were from suicide. These rates are approximately two times higher for homicide and 1.5 times higher for suicide than the national average for those years (National Center for Injury Prevention and Control 2012). During this time, 63 percent of males and 75 percent of females were killed by family members or acquaintances. Native Americans have the second highest homicide rate; 10.5 per 100,000 behind non-Hispanic Blacks at 19.3 and followed by Hispanics at 7.2 (Department of Health and Human Services 2010).

Other forms of violent death are also common in some Native American communities. While deaths in motor vehicle accidents are declining in the US in general, deaths in motor vehicles are highest among Native Americans (Public Health News Center 2012). Death by unintentional injury is 140 percent higher than for the general population (Indian Health Service 2012). Native Americans have the highest rate of deaths of undetermined intent at 6.1 per 100,000 (Department of Health and Human Services 2010).

Native Americans have the highest rates of suicide of any population: 18.2 per 100,000, with the next highest being non-Hispanic Whites at 14.0 (Department of Health and Human Services 2010). Suicide is the second leading cause of death for Native Americans aged 15–24 and the third leading cause for those aged 5–14 and 25–44 (Alcantara and Gone 2007). While the suicide rate for Native

Americans is approximately twice as high as the US average, there are significant regional variations. For example, the suicide rates found in Indian Health Service catchment areas for Tucson, AZ, Aberdeen, SD, and Alaska are five to seven times the national average. Lower than average rates are found in California, Nashville, and Oklahoma. The most common methods of suicide are death by firearms and hanging. There is a high prevalence of suicidal behaviors (not just completed) among adolescents and young adults, with higher prevalence for females.

Violence and threats of violence are prominent in the lives of many Native youth. Data collected from 1997–2003 using the Youth Risk Behavioral Survey (YRBS) contains information on 513 urban Native youth in grades 9–12. This data reveals that suicidal behaviors, feeling unsafe at school (and therefore not attending school), and needing medical attention after a fight were all at least threefold higher for Native youth than their White peers. Being physically hurt by a boy/girlfriend, being physically forced to have unwanted sex, carrying a gun in the last month, and being threatened or injured with a weapon at school in the last year were over twofold higher than their White peers. Since the YRBS only surveys youth in school, actual rates of these violent behaviors may well be higher (Rutman et al. 2008).

The Navajo Nation experiences cataclysmic levels of violence (Snell 2007). The violent crime rate far exceeds the national average. This can be attributed to a shift from traditional clan culture to gang culture that has led to an epidemic of lethal beatings, stabbings, and execution-style shootings. Under these current conditions, virtually everyone on the reservation has had a family member murdered. Community-wide trauma has become the norm (Snell 2007).

Extensive police brutality has been documented across tribal groups in United States and Canada (Perry 2002). Likewise, the incarceration rate of Native Americans is 38 percent higher than the national rate. The US Commission on Civil Rights attributes this disparity to racial profiling, differential treatment in the criminal justice system, and lack of access to adequate legal counsel (Death Penalty Information Center 2012). As of January 1, 2010, 37 Native people are on death row (Death Penalty Information Center 2012). While in prison, Native people are often subject to abuse for attempting to maintain cultural practices including maintaining long, braided hair, wearing headbands, listening to Indigenous music, and speaking their languages (Death Penalty Information Center 2012).

Hate crime is an institutionalized mechanism for establishing and maintaining physical and social boundaries. Violence and threats of violence remind Native people that there are places where they are not welcome, and they need to stay in their place (Perry 2009). "Bigots are informed by broader patterns of a EuroAmerican cultural imperialism that continues to inform Native/non-Native interactions" (Perry 2002, 244).

Racially based violence against Native people is more than the acts of bigoted individuals. Rather, this violence is part of "a network of norms, assumptions, behaviors, and policies that are structurally connected in such a way as to reproduce the racialized and gendered hierarchies that characterize the society in question"

(Perry and Robyn 2005, 594). Examining such societal hierarchies followed by systematic efforts at deconstructing these power structures are necessary components of decreasing violence.

Another reflection of the status of Native people in United States society is the continued use of Native images as mascots. While stereotypical images of other groups (i.e., the Frito Bandito, Little Black Sambo) are generally no longer considered socially acceptable and have largely disappeared from sight, Native American caricatures are still commonly used. Sports nicknames like the "Fighting Sioux" perpetuate stereotypical images of Native Americans as warlike (Williams 2006). Visceral violence is encouraged by sports along with promotion of masculine, aggressive attitudes toward opponents. The use of Native American mascots both reflects and perpetuates a social environment that tolerates violence in the lives of Native people.

The Impact of Violence

The extensive and multiple manifestations of violence discussed above have a significant and lasting impact on Native people and communities. Violence is a learned behavior that is often self-perpetuating. Those who have experienced violence may behave in ways that are violent themselves, thus carrying on a dysfunctional cycle. Additionally, violence is intimately connected with trauma. Violence leads to trauma and many trauma-related symptoms (i.e., mental health issues, substance abuse) which themselves increase the risk for future expressions of violence. It is important to remember, however, that violence is not simply a micro-level issue perpetrated by one individual against another. Rather, violence exists within and is facilitated by a societal context or social environment that supports its existence. One of the results of violence is a reinforcing or maintenance of a social climate that facilitates violence.

Children exposed to violence often replicate the violence they have seen and end up in the juvenile justice system (Bryan 2012). A study of incarcerated Native women found that as children 72 percent had witnessed violence in their home, 53 percent were sexually abused and 42 percent were physically abused (de Ravello et al. 2008). These women who experienced victimization during childhood went on to manifest a variety of anti-social and high-risk behaviors, including violent interactions with others.

Exposure to violence has also been linked with other types of violent expression. Native Americans have higher rates of gang involvement than African Americans and Latinos (Bryan 2012). Additionally, Native Americans are among the most violent prison inmates. This is likely a reflection and outgrowth of the disproportionate amount of violent criminal victimization experienced by Native Americans in society (Berg and DeLisi 2006).

Damaging social conditions, multiple marginalizations, poverty, historical trauma, cultural hegemony, and multiple forms of violence have left Native

Americans vulnerable to trauma (Willmon-Haque and BigFoot 2008). Frequent, recurrent traumas with insufficient time to recovery between traumatic events have a cumulative effect on many Native Americans (Smyer and Clark 2011).

Women's drug use is often linked to histories of physical and sexual assault. Drug use, in turn, increases vulnerability for repeated physical and sexual assault (de Ravello et al. 2008). Other risky behaviors are also used as coping mechanisms to deal with the inherent stresses that accompany abuse. Unprocessed childhood trauma can lead to further expressions of violence (de Ravello et al. 2008).

A study of incarcerated Native women found that 83 percent had attempted suicide at least once (de Ravello et al. 2008). Forty-three percent of Native women in prison had been arrested for a violent offense. Adverse childhood events (ACE) increase the likelihood of a variety of social and health problems during adulthood (Felitti et al. 1998). Native women with a high incidence of adverse childhood events as measured by ACE scores were more likely to attempt suicide and be arrested for violent offenses than other Native women in prison (de Ravello et al. 2008).

The well-being of women is an essential element of community well-being. Harmonious relationships are the foundation of traditional Indigenous communities. The high rates of violence and sexual assault of Native women must not be viewed solely as an individual matter but as a threat to Native communities (Halldin 2008). Just as colonization deliberately undermined egalitarian gender roles, contemporary devaluing of Indigenous women fosters a climate that facilitates violence. Conversely, efforts to rectify this power imbalance and empower Indigenous women can help stabilize and promote wellness in Native communities.

Contemporary oppression fosters a climate of blatant stigmatization, disempowerment, and violence. For the Chippewas of northern Wisconsin this racist climate was illustrated by the spearfishing controversy of the 1980s and 1990s (Perry and Robyn 2005). When tribal members asserted their right to traditional fishing practices they were met with protests and threats. Bumper stickers and posters promoted violence and racism through slogans such as "Spear an Indian, Save a Fish."

Indigenous traditions offer some recognition of the importance of breaking the self-perpetuating cycle of violence begetting violence. Instances of violence in the community must be handled in thoughtful, non-violent ways. Navajo culture views violence as a sickness to be treated, and instructs against the taking of human life in vengeance. This cultural belief provides the foundation for a tribal resistance to the death penalty (Snell 2007).

Similarities and Differences across Indigenous Groups

Within the United States there are some differences among Indigenous populations in terms of violence. For example, suicide rates, while typically higher for Native

Americans than other US populations, vary substantially across regions, with Alaskans and Native people of the Great Plains and Southwest having some of the highest rates. Differences in violence between urban and reservation populations are less clear, as this has received little attention from researchers or demographers; however, it is known that people experiencing violence in rural or reservation areas are likely to have significantly less access to services than those in urban areas. The isolation of many tribal communities complicates accessing help for those who are experiencing violence (Bryan 2012).

Indigenous groups across the world have very different cultures, beliefs, and forms of social organization; however, the common experience of colonization has led to the development of substantial commonalities such as health, social, and economic disparities. Indigenous Peoples are typically the most vulnerable populations across the globe. The collective history of genocide, dispossession, and dislocation has implications for contemporary violence in the lives of Indigenous Peoples (United Nations 2009).

Disproportionate violent victimization of Indigenous Peoples is an international phenomenon. In Australia, Aboriginal people and Torres Strait Islanders experience double the victimization rate of non-Indigenous Australians. In Canada, Indigenous Peoples are three times more likely than non-Indigenous Canadians to experience a violent assault. Likewise, in New Zealand, Maori people experience nearly double the violent crime rate as non-Indigenous New Zealanders (Weatherburn 2010). The domestic violence data is similar with Aboriginal Australians suffering much higher rates of intimate partner violence and homicide than non-Indigenous Australians (Marchetti 2010). Interpersonal violence is the leading cause of injury hospitalization for Aboriginal Australians, with disproportionate rates clearly linked to the historical and political context of disadvantage and oppression associated with colonization (Berry et al. 2009).

High rates of contemporary Indigenous youth suicide are directly linked to colonization, historical trauma, and discrimination (United Nations 2009). Colonization has cast a dark shadow over the lives of contemporary Maori youth in New Zealand, leading to a disproportionately high suicide rate (Aho and Liu 2010). Native people in the US and Canada both have dramatically higher suicide rates, as do many other Indigenous populations within settler societies (United Nations 2009). Indeed, it appears that disproportionate experiences with violence are remarkably similar for Indigenous populations, regardless of country.

Indigenous Peoples around the world continue to be targets of violence when others seek to possess the mineral wealth or other resources in their possession. Related to this, Indigenous Peoples continue to be displaced and severely impacted by violence and militarism in their territories (United Nations 2009). Indigenous women continue to be exposed to sexual violence. The violence against Indigenous women "is inextricably linked to violations of the collective rights of Indigenous Peoples and colonization" (United Nations 2009, 172).

Implications

In synthesizing the data on violence and Native people, several things become clear. Violence has a disproportionate impact on Native Peoples. Expressions of violence are cyclical, self-perpetuating, and require deliberate and specific efforts designed to interrupt these cycles in order to achieve change. Manifestations of violence occur on micro and macro levels, thus necessitating multilevel intervention strategies. Efforts at addressing violence require prevention, intervention, and societal change strategies.

Recognition of the nature and extent of the problem is a prerequisite to change. We must first begin to talk about it. Native Americans are largely an invisible population in the United States and there is little public discourse on the disproportionate impact of violence on this population. US Attorney General, Eric Holder, emphasized the need to publicly discuss the epidemic of children exposed to violence as a prerequisite to ending the cycle of violence (Bryan 2012). The National Task Force on Children Exposed to Violence held a public meeting in Albuquerque to gather information from victims and experts on violence in rural and Native American communities. This is an important foundation for developing violence prevention initiatives.

It is clearly documented that violence begets violence. Stopping ACE, and provision of early interventions where ACE occur, are key steps in reducing and preventing violence (de Ravello et al. 2008). Specific strategies may vary to reflect the nature of different communities. Violence prevention strategies must mirror the fact that each Native community is unique, and violence, including homicide and suicide, has multiple, complex causes (National Center for Injury Prevention and Control 2012).

Interventions are needed to address a variety of social and health problems in Native communities. In the past these pressing needs have led us to ignore the root causes of violence and subsequent trauma. Social and economic disparities must be addressed as a prerequisite to reducing violence in Indigenous communities (Berry et al. 2009). We must find ways to simultaneously promote the healing of individuals and interrupt the violence that intensifies the risk of trauma for other generations.

Gil Vigil, former governor of Tesuque Pueblo, lamented that while we often look at symptoms such as drug and alcohol abuse and domestic violence, we typically fail to look at the impacts on children (Bryan 2012). A national taskforce has been convened that hopes to develop a blueprint and policy recommendations for preventing and reducing the negative effects of exposure to violence on children.

Perhaps most importantly, we must recognize the larger societal context that supports disproportionate violence in the lives of many Native Americans. The history of colonization lingers in the United States, as well as in other settler societies. Devaluing and dehumanizing Indigenous Peoples was a psychological prerequisite to massive genocidal practices. While such large-scale genocidal policies and practices no longer exist in the United States and Canada, elements of the attitudes that accompanied them persist, as illustrated by police brutality, caricatured sports mascots, and public authorities such as the mayor of New York City who feel free to express blatantly racist attitudes.

Extensive erosions of sovereignty reflect a severe power imbalance between Indigenous groups and colonizing powers. Violence is allowed to fester in the context of domination and subordination. Dominance is structured into the relationship between the federal government and Indian tribes, as is clearly demonstrated by their legal designation as domestic dependent nations. While efforts to prevent violence in the home and community, as well as efforts to treat subsequent trauma and interrupt the transmission of violent behavior to future generations, are important and necessary, it is unlikely that such efforts can fully succeed in a societal context that maintains such an extensive power imbalance.

Conclusion

Balance is a key element in Indigenous conceptualizations of well-being. Indeed, talking things through to restore social balance is the traditional problem-solving strategy for the Navajo (Snell 2007) as well as many other Indigenous groups. Punitive justice, such as calls for the death penalty, are contradictory to Indigenous understandings of healing and erode the traditional values and practices that are the community's best hope for stemming the rising tide of violence (Snell 2007). Incarceration and the death penalty for violent offenders do nothing to interrupt the cycle of violence. Other solutions must be sought.

Restoration of balance offers hope for reducing violence at all levels. Stereotypes and racism that dehumanize Indigenous Peoples perpetuate a climate in which Native Americans are devalued and violence can flourish. A change in societal attitudes to promote the value and inherent dignity of all human beings will reduce the power imbalance so prevalent in today's society. In turn, this more balanced societal context will reduce racism and oppression and make violence prevention and treatment efforts more productive.

References

Aho, K.L. and Liu, J.H. 2010. Indigenous suicide and colonization: The legacy of violence and the necessity of self-determination. *International Journal of Conflict and Violence*, 4(1), 124–33.

Alcantara, C. and Gone, J.P. 2007. Reviewing suicide in Native American communities: Situating risk and protective factors within a transactional-ecological framework. *Death Studies*, 31, 457–77.

Amnesty International 2007. *Maze of Injustice: The Failure to Protect Indigenous Women from Sexual Violence in the USA*.

Berg, M.T. and DeLisi, M. 2006. The correctional melting pot: Race, ethnicity, citizenship, and prison violence. *Journal of Criminal Justice*, 43, 631–42.

Berry, J.B., Harrison, J.E., and Ryan, P. 2009. Hospital admissions of Indigenous and non-Indigenous Australians due to interpersonal violence, July 1999 to June 2004. *Australian and New Zealand Journal of Public Health*, 33(3), 215–22.

Bryan, S.M. 2012. Taskforce eyes rural, tribal exposure to violence. *Reznet News*. http://www.reznetnews.org/article/task-force-eyes-rural-tribal-exposure-violence. Accessed 2/8/12.

De Ravello, L., Abeita, J., and Brown, P. 2008. Breaking the cycle/Mending the hoop: Adverse childhood experiences among incarcerated American Indian/ Alaska Native women in New Mexico. *Health Care for Women International*, 29, 300–15.

Death Penalty Information Center 2012. Native Americans and the Death Penalty. http://www.deathpenaltyinfo.org/native-americans-and-death-penalty. Accessed 2/8/2012.

Department of Health and Human Services 2010. Surveillance for violent deaths: National violent death reporting system, 16 states, 2007. *Morbidity and Mortality Weekly Report*, 59(SS-4), 1–50.

Felitti, J.F., Anda, R.F., Nordenberg, D., et al. 1998. Relationship of childhood abuse and household dysfunction to many of the leading causes of death in adults: The Adverse Childhood Experiences (ACE) study. *American Journal of Preventive Medicine*, 14(4), 245–58.

Halldin, A. 2008. Restoring the victim and the community: A look at the tribal response to sexual violence committed by non-Indians in Indian Country through non-criminal approaches. *North Dakota Law Review*, 84(1), 1–21.

Hukill, S.L. 2006. Violence in Native America: A historical perspective. *Journal of Transcultural Nursing*, 17(3), 246–50.

Indian Health Service 2012. IHS Fact Sheets: Indian Health Disparities. http://www.ihs.gov.

Jacoby, K. 2008. "The broad platform of extermination": Nature and violence in the nineteenth century North American borderlands. *Journal of Genocide Research*, 10(2), 249–67.

Marchetti, E. 2010. Indigenous sentencing courts and partner violence: Perspectives of court practitioners and elders on gender power imbalances during the sentencing hearing. *The Australian and New Zealand Journal of Criminology*, 43(2), 263–81.

National Center for Injury Prevention and Control 2012. *Homicide and suicide among Native Americans, 1979–1992*. Violence Surveillance Summary Series, No. 2. http://www.cdc.gov/ncipc/pub-res/natam.htm. Accessed 2/8/2012.

Perry, B. 2002. From ethnocide to ethnoviolence: Layers of Native American victimization. *Contemporary Justice Review*, 5(3), 231–47.

Perry, B. 2009. "There's just places ya don't wanna go": The segregating impact of hate crime against Native Americans. *Contemporary Justice Review*, 12(4), 401–18.

Perry, B. and Robyn, L. 2005. Putting anti-Indian violence in context: The case of the Great Lakes Chippewas of Wisconsin. *American Indian Quarterly*, 29(3/4), 590–625.

Public Health News Center 2012. More efforts needed to address motor vehicle deaths among American Indians and Alaska Natives. http://www.jhsph.edu/publichealthnews/press_releases/2012/pollack_vehicledeaths.html. Accessed 2/8/12.

Rutman, S., Park, A., Castor, M., et al. 2008. Urban American Indian and Alaska Native youth: Youth Risk Behavior Survey 1997–2003. *Maternal and Child Health Journal*, 12, S76-S81.

Smyer, T. and Clark, M.C. 2011. A cultural paradox: Elder abuse in the Native American community. *Home Health Care Management & Practice*, 23(3), 201–206.

Snell, M.B. 2007. The talking way. *Mother Jones*, 32(1), 30–35.

United Nations 2009. *State of the World's Indigenous Peoples*. New York: United Nations.

Weatherburn, D. 2010. Indigenous violence. *The Australian and New Zealand Journal of Criminology*, 43(2), 197–8.

Williams, D.M. 2006. Patriarchy and the "Fighting Sioux": A gendered look at racial college sports nicknames. *Race, Ethnicity, and Education*, 9(4), 325–40.

Williams, J.K. 2010. New York's Native Americans outraged over Bloomberg's "cowboys and Indians" remark. *The New York Amsterdam News*, August 26–September 1, p. 3, continued on p. 40.

Willmon-Haque, S. and BigFoot, S.D. 2008. Violence and the effects of trauma on American Indian and Alaska Native populations. *Journal of Emotional Abuse*, 8(1/2), 51–66.

Chapter 11

Indigenous Women and Sexual Assault: Implications for Intersectionality

Roe Bubar

I've been thinking about the buffalo and how they're our relatives, and we are supposed to mirror each other's lifeway. This guy told me a story about raising buffalo: the mom broke her leg, and she tried to get up, and she couldn't. There was her baby and there were others in the herd trying to encourage her and her baby started crying. Pretty soon the herd started to get going, the baby was frantic, and then the baby started after the herd. Soon the men came back and they were trying to lift her with their horns, but she couldn't get up, so the men paid their last respect, took her baby and left. How do we decide who gets left behind ... because we don't want to leave anyone behind? Who will lay there broken? So we are really talking about dealing with systems that are broken.
(Participant, National Pilot Study of Native Women)

The context in which violence against Indigenous women and children occurs is aptly described by the story of the wounded female buffalo. The story provides a metaphor for Western tribes in the United States and Canada trying to respond and find solutions for violence within a broken system. Historically, the killing off of buffalo herds on the plains functioned as a form of colonization aimed at decreasing the food source of Indigenous populations, and western tribes in particular. Without this primary food source western tribes were pressured to stay on reservations, otherwise they would starve or leave valuable range lands (Moulton 1995). The same pattern occurred in Canada; thus, by the mid 1870s decimation of buffalo herds on First Nations prairies caused starvation and poverty of Aboriginal populations. Currently, the prevalence of sexual assault, stalking, and violent victimization of Indigenous women is such that participants ask if there is an effort to leave them behind wounded, much like federal and local Western policies to kill off buffalo in the nineteenth century. These policies weakened plains and prairies tribes since their economies and lifeways centered on the buffalo. Interdependence between women and men among western tribes, which arguably provided a level of respect and potential protection of women, was also impacted. Traditional ways were based on Indigenous cosmology and on the plains; for example, White Buffalo Calf woman brought the pipe to the Lakota people. She represents the unity and respect for all people.

Indigenous Peoples[1] in Canada and Australia are struggling with similar challenges of violence against Indigenous women (Lucashenko 1997, Kelm 1998, Culhane 2003, Amnesty International 2004, Keel 2004, Brzozowski et al. 2006, Andrews 1997). Many Indigenous women that survive violence find themselves alone within a system where women and their children are left behind, often times without adequate means to assist them or provide an adequate community response (Levan 2003, Hamby 2004, McGlade 2006, Thorpe et al. 2004, Weaver 2009). Although there is considerable diversity of peoples, Indigenous women are united by race as a social identity and tribal political status as Indigenous citizens or members within their homeland or Aboriginal communities. At the same time, these interrelated social and political identities unique to Indigenous Peoples significantly marginalize them within colonial settler states. The very presence of Indigenous bodies within colonial settler states serves as a constant reminder of the legal maneuvering embedded in law to support land dispossession and subordination of Indigenous Peoples that underlies a colonial history. In the colonial imagination of North Americans, the narrative that the land wasn't fully occupied, and that Natives didn't really know how to properly use the land and harvest its resources, further justifies land dispossession. That Indigenous Peoples are currently challenges socially and politically, with an overrepresentation of crime, violence, poverty, and drug/alcohol problems in their communities, only further serves to support the narrative that Indigenous Peoples are not able to manage the land or its people.

For Indigenous women, this social and political positioning can create reluctance to report men in their communities who are offenders since tribal communities as a whole become implicated in the violence. Providers and advocates are hard pressed to know how they can be effective given the gravity, prevalence, and inadequate systems responding to this critical public health issue.

Focusing on sexual violence on the micro or individual level presents rape and sexual assault as interpersonal phenomena. This approach promotes the perspective, particularly among outside agency professionals, that implicates Indigenous Peoples and tribal communities as deficient and simply seeks to pathologize individual offenders. Clearly, offenders must be held accountable. However, when funding and criminal justice efforts function to myopically focus on the offender at hand without consideration of more distal and proximate factors structurally and politically, Indigenous women remain at significant risk for disparate impact from sexual violence.

Violence against Indigenous women is complex and remains underresearched. Indigenous scholars, among others, consider the importance of examining this issue within the larger context of factors associated with this health and social

---

1   In general, "Aboriginal" refers to the diversity of Indigenous populations within Canada (First Nations, Métis, and Inuit) and Australia. Indigenous is used here to include Aboriginal people residing within the US, Canada, and Australia. The term Native is used to designate Aboriginal people in the US.

issue. Andrea Smith (2004) and Rayna Green (1992) argue that colonization and a history of rape of Native women by settler populations contributed to the construction of Native women as inherently rapable. Duran and Duran (1995), Yellow Horse Brave Heart and DeBruyn (1998), and Yellow Horse Brave Heart (2003) argue that federal laws and policies aimed at ethnic cleansing and cultural genocide are associated with historical trauma, resulting in an overrepresentation of contemporary mental health as well as drug and alcohol issues plaguing Indigenous populations. Several scholars add heteropatriarchy as a colonial invention naturalizing heterosexuality and gender dominance. Today, we can see the impacts of colonial logics at work in current day homophobia, violence against Indigenous women, lateral oppression, and violence against queer/Two Spirit people in tribal communities (Finley 2011, Smith 2004, Roscoe 2000, Deer 2005). Historic accumulation of social harms that include "extreme poverty, homelessness and chronic health problems in Native communities creates a vulnerability for prostitution and trafficking" (Farley et al. 2011, 15). Local tribal community context is discussed as important in understanding how Indigenous women are empowered, protected, and/or oppressed and marginalized (Hamby 2000, Bubar and Thurman 2004). The invisibility of Indigenous issues in general, and sexual assault of Indigenous women in particular, remains a critical concern.

Intersectionality provides one potential framework to explore the complexities of how Indigenous women and children are positioned to experience violence. The historical impact of federal law, policies, and particular ways in which colonization is an ongoing project in North America have a cumulative effect on Indigenous populations (Yellow Horse Brave Heart and DeBruyn 1998, Whitbeck et al. 2004, Deer 2005).

This chapter argues that intersectionality theory can assist in deconstructing violence against Indigenous women, thus illuminating ways in which Indigenous women are positioned by the state and the greater society for violence. I also argue that sexual assault of Indigenous women is invisible to most Americans, while those who are well aware of the sexual assault crisis and work with tribal communities are systemically underfunded. This level of invisibility coupled with inadequate resources seeks to encourage a lack of empathy in the system response and a lack of empathy towards Indigenous women. Alone, a criminal justice response is focused on tribal offenders and tribal communities, thereby ignoring the larger structural role and response of the state. Indigenous Peoples of North America, Australia and Canada all live within former British settler states where impacts of law and policy are intimately connected to historical trauma and where Indigenous women today continue to experience extreme levels of sexual assault and violence.

Examining Violence against Indigenous Women

In 1999 the American Indian and Crime Report made national news when it came to light that Indigenous Peoples experience more than three times the violent victimization of the general population in the United States (Greenfield and Smith 1999). Crime statistics and a national study also exposed the violent victimizations of Native women specifically claiming they are battered, raped, and stalked at far greater rates than any other group of women in the US (Greenfield and Smith 1999, Tjaden and Thoennes 2000, Perry 2004). SDespite the initial outcry of violent victimizations, continued reports of sexual assaults, and claims of human rights issues, Indigenous women continue to experience high rates of rape, sexual assault, stalking, domestic violence, child sexual abuse, and trafficking (Malcoe et al. 2004, Amnesty International 2006, Evans-Campbell et al. 2006, Bachman et al. 2010, Farley et al. 2011, Chenault 2011). The Department of Justice estimates that 34.1 percent or more than 1 in 3 Native women will be raped in their lifetimes (Tjaden and Thoennes 2000). Native women are 2.5 times more likely to be raped than other women and are more likely to be physically brutalized during sexual assault than non-Native women (Perry 2004, Bachman et al. 2010). Native women are also stalked at a rate at least twice that of any other population (Perry 2004).

Current data indicates that non-Native men represent the most significant risk of violence against Native women. Sixty-seven percent of Native women describe the offender of rape or sexual assault as non-Native, and 71 percent of the offenders were reported to be under the influence of alcohol and/or drugs (Bachman et al. 2010, Perry 2004). Today in the US, 46 percent of the people living in tribal communities are non-Natives and 55 percent of Native women are in relationships with non-Native people (US Census Bureau 2010). Complicating matters, the US Attorney's office declined almost 52 percent of the violent crimes, with 67 percent of these declined cases being sexual abuse occurring in tribal communities (US Government Accountability Office 2010).

A more recent study of 90 Native advocates/providers indicates women were sexually assaulted by Native and non-Native men, raising additional considerations around reporting (Bubar 2010). Indigenous women in Canada also report higher rates of rape, sexual assault, prostitution, and trafficking than their non-Indigenous counterparts (Culhane 2003, Brzozowski et al 2006, Farley et al. 2011).

Canada and the United States are former British colonial settler states in which Indigenous Peoples are impacted in similar ways by colonization and historical trauma. Each of these countries has tribal homeland areas in which Indigenous populations coexist within provinces or states surrounded by non-Indigenous populations. The status of Indigenous Peoples in each of these countries differs with respect to specific laws and policies, constitutions, case law, and sovereignty. Tribal nations in Canada and the US exercise sovereignty in different ways. The health status of Indigenous women and their children remains critical. First Nations women and First American women are the most at-risk group for violence in the United States and in Canada (Ontario Native Women's Association 2007).

Intersectionality

Intersectionality has its origins conceptually in the 1983 edited works of Cherrie Moraga and Gloria Anzaldua in *This Bridge Called My Back: Writings by Radical Women of Color* (Moraga and Anzaldua 1983). Feminists at the time considered gender issues a representation of "women's experiences," thereby obscuring any differences for queer women and women of color. Moraga and Anzaldua explore the ways queer/women of color experience oppression and the intersectionality of their identities as gendered, raced, classed, and queer. bell hooks is credited with "one of the starting points of an analytical and political move by Black and other feminists and social scientists to deconstruct the categories of both 'women' and 'Blacks' and to develop an analysis of the intersectionality of various social divisions, most often—but not exclusively—focusing on gender, race and class" (Yural-Davis 2006, 193).

In the late 1980s and early 1990s, Crenshaw furthered developed intersectionality and coined the term "intersectionality" as a more formal theory when she wrote about African American women suing their employers for discrimination. As African American women they were unable to use race and gender to describe the intersectional manner in which their discrimination occurred as women, and more specifically as African American women. The legal system was unprepared to consider the intersectional way in which African American women experienced discrimination, which was distinct from non-African American women and different than the experiences of African American men (Crenshaw 1989). Crenshaw later established a framework for the theory as well as a description of the multidimensional ways in which "race and gender intersect in shaping structural and political aspects of violence against women of color"(Crenshaw 1994, 1242). In "Mapping the Margins," Crenshaw defines political and structural intersectionality. Political intersectionality emphasizes how women of color are located within two or more marginalized groups with conflicting political agendas. Crenshaw suggests that identity politics functions in political intersectionality to erase intra-group difference—such that in the discourses of either feminism or antiracism the experiences of women of color tend to be marginalized in both discourses. Women of color are positioned for solidarity within one group in one instance and in opposition in the same instance (Crenshaw 1991). Structural intersectionality occurs where women of color are positioned within intersecting systems of subordination. In the context of violence for example poor women of color who present in a shelter program seeking assistance experience classed based oppression yet violence for many poor women of color may simply represent the most immediate site of their oppression (Crenshaw 1991, 1242)

Patricia Hill Collins also considers ideologies that justify oppression, rules, and practices that seek to manage oppression, and large-scale structures that reproduce oppression (Collins 2000). Thus the framework for intersectionality emerged from the "study of the production and reproduction of inequalities, dominance and oppression" (Shields 2008, 303).

Intersectionality theory considers the multiple ways in which oppression is exerted upon the "other" and acknowledges that dynamics of racism, sexism, classism, heterosexism, etc. interact in particular ways to problematize the experience of being oppressed. Identities based on race, gender, class, and gender identities are viewed as socially constructed. Thus, notions of power, privilege, and oppression are not characteristics of people but of society (Johnson 2005). Intersectionality uncovers how privilege and oppression intersect and the complicated ways in which those intersections situate social identities, thereby exposing the diversity of experiences within groups (Baca Zinn and Thorton Dill 1996). Therefore, intersectionality renders social identities mutually constitutive as Shields (2008) describes: "one category of identity such as gender, takes its meaning as a category in relation to another category such that one social identity necessitates another. The formation and maintenance of identity categories is a dynamic process in which the individual herself or himself is actively engaged" (302).

Native women in this study discuss the ways in which sexual violence is complicated by their political identities as tribal members and the difficulties they encounter within the tribal context when Native men are identified as offenders. At the same time, Native women must negotiate embedded "forms of domination hindering their ability" (Crenshaw 1991 1242) to address or seek services for sexual violence all of which is further complicated by structural systems and the government's responsibility to provide adequate health care and protect Indigenous women. Thus, political and structural intersectionality becomes an important way to explore sexual violence.

Methods

This qualitative study is guided by critical and feminist theories in which intersectionality is used as a framework to understand and deconstruct the data. Feminist and critical theorists seek to understand issues of power, power relations, privilege, and oppression within larger structural institutions (Crotty 2010, Hesse-Biber and Leavy 2007). The research questions guiding this study consider how professional Native women understand the prevalence of sexual violence and how prevalence relates to the intersectional ways in which they identify.

Sample

Professional Indigenous women who work to address violence against Native women were recruited to participate in this study. There were 10 participants in the focus group representative of tribal communities throughout Native America from urban, suburban, rural, and geographically isolated Indigenous communities. Participants reported between 7 and 20 years of experience working as professionals in the field of domestic violence with Indigenous women. Participants traveled from diverse locations to attend the focus group, travel costs were covered, and each participant received an incentive from a national Native organization collaborating on the project to cover mileage and meal per diem.

Data Collection

Recruitment procedures involved collaboration with a national Native organization specializing in Indigenous women's issues. The national organization recruited participants for the focus group from its membership. There are approximately 30 shelters or domestic violence programs in tribal communities and participants were largely representative of this group of providers, with one participant representing an urban Indigenous perspective. The focus group was held in a central location and lasted for over 4 hours. Contemporaneous laptop notes were taken throughout the focus group and the session was also recorded on audiotape.

Data Analysis

Inductive qualitative methods were used to analyze focus group data. This study incorporated aspects of grounded theory to create categories, uncover emergent themes, conduct constant comparisons, and engage an iterative process (Charmaz, 2010). Constructivism is the epistemological stance in Charmaz's grounded theory approach and is often used where issues of power, social justice, and oppression are under study (2010). Women of color feminist methodologies fit within the narrative and reflexive aspects of the constructivist paradigm.

The researcher in this study read through the focus group transcript and conducted a line-by-line analysis to create initial codes. Next, more focused coding occurred as categories began to emerge, which involves a decision-making analytical process (Charmaz 2010). Constant comparative methods help to develop mutually exclusive categories where an iterative process was engaged to accomplish this stage of the analysis (Lincoln and Guba 1985). Categories were then collapsed into themes. Themes emerging from this study included: Indigenous nation status, the role of race, poverty as Indian Country, and gender as raced. Given the categories that emerged, intersectionality represents the overarching theme in this study.

Limitations

The findings in this study should be interpreted with caution. First, this research focuses on the experience of sexual assault for Native women, yet participants in this study are more representative of professional advocates or program providers. Generalizability is not the primary purpose of qualitative research These results are more appropriately considered for transferability and fittingness, particularly with the population under consideration (Lincoln and Guba 1985). Most of the participants in this study work with tribal communities, while only two participants were experienced in working with urban Indigenous sexual assault issues and only one person was currently working in that capacity. Moreover, this study didn't explore differences of sexual assault experienced by Indigenous women living in urban versus rural communities specifically, as this study focused on perceptions of prevalence.

Findings

Indigenous women considered how Native people experience more violence than non-Natives. Participants were well informed on the data surrounding the prevalence of sexual assault for Indigenous women. The focus group was primarily a discussion of participants perceptions on prevalence of sexual assault and how Indigenous women made sense of this phenomenon.

As discussed above intersectionality describes how one category of identity, such as race, takes its meaning as a category in relationship to another category, such as gender. Here intersectionality uncovers how privilege and oppression intersect in complicated ways, thereby exposing the diversity of experiences within a group of Indigenous women. Indigenous providers in this study acknowledge their own class and education status as a source of potential privilege relative to other Native women without those same privileges who may be more likely to be the ones wounded and left behind like the female buffalo in the opening passage above. At the same time, how race, gender, class, citizenship , and sexuality intersect for Indigenous women is believed to set up a complicated maze of subordination that places Indigenous women at much greater risk for sexual assault and increases the likelihood that resources will not be adequate or readily available.

Intersectionality, while the overarching theme in this study, must be contextualized within a history of ethnic cleansing and genocidal policies promulgated by settler states and embedded in policies like forced boarding schools, the termination of tribes, relocation of Native Peoples, and removal of tribes from traditional homeland areas. Providers in this study make reference to the historic treatment of Natives within the context of discussing intersectional ways Indigenous women are positioned for violence and victimization.

Prevalence related to nation status, race, gender and class
Participants discussed the connections, particularly of risk and the relationship between domestic violence and sexual assault. In the programs they administered, some program providers did not ask individual women about sexual assault because the shelter programs they administered or worked in did not provide substantial services for sexual assault survivors. Providers felt the women they were serving were already in a vulnerable state and eliciting disclosures of sexual assault without appropriate resources might position the women for additional harm. Race, class, gender, and tribal membership status were identified as social and political identities that place Indigenous women at greater risk and potentially shapes the nature of how the intersections of Native women's identities complicates their

sexual assault. Two Spirit and LGBTQ people were not mentioned or discussed by participants, yet these identities place individuals at additional risk for sexual assault.

Indigenous nation status

The political status of Native women as citizens of Indigenous nations and the US may contribute to the ways Native women are set apart and targeted via policy, attitudes, and lack of adequate funding for appropriate services; lack of prosecution and funding making them even more vulnerable and potential targets of sexual assault. The membership status of Indigenous people as citizens of tribal nations is considered a political status not based on race (*Morton v. Mancari*, 1974), creating another way sexual assault is potentially different for Native versus non-Native women. Participants believed that tribal women were treated differently than non-Natives in investigations of sexual assault. Perceptions of alcohol use by tribal people were believed to shape how investigators approached investigations in tribal communities. Program providers situate their role as advocates in a political atmosphere as shared here: "I do think we have to go to a place for work that can be personal and political. The blessing of my life is to get through the tough period and do the analysis. I started at an advocacy program that had a shelter, and tried to deal with the gang rapes. I was being told by the CI [Criminal Investigator] and was asked, 'Was she drinking?' and I said, 'Yes.' And then they said no [to the investigation]." The ways in which tribal communities are thought about is also implicated in how tribal identity is perceived by outsiders. Consider how participants discussed the system's response to sexual assault in their tribal community: "We have ignorant sexist, racist, criminal justice systems," and "People [agency professionals] have no investment in our community, they're here and then they're gone. A few years ago we had outsiders who came here to build roads. And I talked to this guy doing work on my driveway. He said, 'People are so nice and feeding me ... we've been trained that you guys are scary and your people are drunks.'"

Participants discussed unique political and social aspects of tribal communities which help support or detract from tribal advocates' efforts when working with survivors: "I think that is why we've been more successful on a tribal level because we have credibility, we know our people, we've had people fired over the years because of poor domestic response, but in our community we don't get FBI agents." Challenging tribal leadership can add to the difficulty victims face: "In tribes, there's no separation of powers, so the tribal council has a lot they're telling tribal courts what to do. If there's a prominent community figure, a lot of times cases will get dropped or evidence will get lost. One of our CIs [Criminal Investigators] has a brother who is a known perp in the community and he gets away with things." Federal and state system responses presented serious challenges central in how participants talked about and considered the prevalence and severity of sexual assault for Native women. Participants discussed how they were failed by the United States despite a duty owed them by the trust responsibility.[2] Providers asked, "Why do Native men and non-Native men feel it is ok to target Native women? You could say that Native men and non-Native men know they won't be held accountable so women become more rapable." Health and mental health issues for survivors are also a concern given health care is part of the trust responsibility of the United States. Providers comment on how mental health issues are well known yet little is done to address the issue: "The church was doing a lot of work on the reservation on alcoholism and found that sexual assault was high in alcohol use. People came back with intense suicide attempts. This is the biggest risk because there is a lack of treatment in our communities."

The role of race

Race and tribal membership status, while closely connected, are different; as discussed earlier, tribal status is political such that jurisdiction over crimes and provision of health and criminal justice services is different for tribal women in homeland areas, while race remains more of a socially constructed identity not necessarily dictating jurisdiction, health care, and service provision. Participants considered sexual assault prevalence related to race as part of their Indigenous experience in the world. Participants noted that confidentiality was provided more in a research context than for actual victims of sexual assault: "All the women that we have worked with get more confidentiality and more protection by participation here in this focus group because it's research, than any Native women, because the federal law protects research confidentiality." Sexual assault prevalence based on race is noted across the experiences of Native women: "Whether Native women are providers, or Native professionals, the histories of rape connects us all." The idea that Indigenous women are associated with victimization by outsiders was noted as well:

> I went to a national sexual assault and violence conference in L.A. This Black woman had talked about Native women being raped and said, 'I always thought that was part of your culture, Native women were objectified in the family unit and men could do whatever they wanted.' We were all talking about our tribes and she didn't realize we had our own traditional values. She worked in a rural southern community and that was an interpretation she had, but it was interesting, she talked about her family as slaves as well and she knew Native people had been slaves too and that's where she was given this history.

---

2   The *federal Indian trust responsibility* is a legal obligation under which the United States "has charged itself with moral obligations of the highest responsibility and trust" toward Indian tribes (*Seminole Nation v. United States*, 1942). This obligation was first discussed by Chief Justice John Marshall in *Cherokee Nation v. Georgia* (1831). Over the years, the trust doctrine has been at the center of numerous other Supreme Court cases, thus making it one of the most important principles in federal Indian law (Bureau of Indian Affairs, 2012).

Gender as raced

Participants discussed how gender coupled with race was related to increased victimization for sexual violence: "There isn't any type of safety for sexual assault issues with women in Indian Country." The changing status and roles of Native women historically is argued to be one of comparable worth and interdependence with men, women and Two Spirit people (Green 1992, Perdue 2001), with the change to a more contemporary heteropatriarchal role in which Native women, LGBTQ and Two Spirit people are viewed in a subordinate and marginalized position (Smith 2004, Driskill et al. 2011). This colonial settler perception of Native women is one in which non-Natives perceive Native women as traditionally subordinate and justified to be treated in a more primitive manner, as noted in the quote above.

Native women discussed the prevalence of sexual assault when Native women are victims of battering: "If you have been battered you have been raped. It does not get talked about, and they're not distinct things. Most women aren't going to talk about being raped by husbands, because it's not [seen as] possible to be raped by husbands." And when women are identified as being assaulted and battered the focus in the investigation will still be on the victim versus the offenders, as noted here:

My husband said in the majority of sexual assault cases, the women are all battered. It's all about women and them not protecting their children. It's never about the batterer. When women get involved with CPS they are bad mothers, not caring about their kids. Rapists aren't being held accountable.

When issues of mental health and substance abuse arose for the perpetrators, victims were viewed as expendable:

There's a major reaction when looking at Native women, they [Native men] are not going to be accountable for what they did, they're going to lose something—so they get to blame the alcohol, the drunken Indian passport, there's that dynamic that is at work with all levels of violence. Vulnerability becomes permission to be a victim and then permission to victimize.

There was a feeling among participants that outsider non-Native predators have historically come into their communities to victimize women:

I have noticed in Alaska you get IHS workers who come into rural Alaska and they're non-Native, they're violating women by giving and doing women favors, making them feel they're wanted, they're validate, then they basically abuse them. So if a person doesn't feel good about themselves, because they don't get it from a husband or men in the community then to feel validated and a non-Indian comes in as a worker in that community, showing them attention … then that person has the right to violate that individual—the man is able to violate

Native women for giving them favors. It's the same stuff going on people came in here to build things, they would bring alcohol, get women intoxicated and then abuse her. We don't talk about it, but its reality. It's a historical relationship with government agencies ... using alcohol and having access to Native women.

Victim blaming of women was understood as commonplace in tribal communities; even when White men came into the community from the outside, Native women were still to blame for their victimization, as discussed here:

Everyone talks about non-Natives, working and living here and people look up to white people. What I found out was we get hunters on the reservation. They offer a lot of money, because we're poor. This woman went with a guy (hunter) to the motel and he tried to rape her. All her Indian people said, "She asked for it, she went with him." This guy was a hunter, a stranger.

Poverty as Indian country

Indigenous populations have some of the highest poverty rates in the US, and the poorest county in the US is located in a tribal community. Poverty is heavily associated with Indigenous populations, and socioeconomic issues came up as part of the discussion, particularly since resources for victims of sexual assault are different in Native communities. One explanation by participants for the difference in service provision was expressed in this manner: "You still have to deal with the classism issue. We are still going to be seen on this level as victimizable and vulnerable." Poverty is viewed as another intersection of identity, making populations not just vulnerable but disposable: "Classism ... poverty and poor people are all disposable."

Discussion

Structural Intersectionality

The sexual assault Indigenous women experience is currently considered the primary way they are oppressed, yet it is the multilayered system response that follows the initial assault which presents an even further subordination of their personhood. Not only are women expected to deal with their assault but they are expected to traverse a system response riddled by multilayered gendered racism embedded in policy and the attitudes of professionals. This form of domination hinders reporting efforts and prevents women from seeking services after a sexual assault. Native women living in many tribal communities tend to be poor, underemployed, underskilled, and have less education than non-Native populations. These are descriptors endemic of gender, race and class oppression which can be complicated by the potential for discrimination in the ways a case is investigated, services are allocated and programs are funded. Observable class differences in allocations of resources are often correlated with race and class, such that "once in a lower economic class, race and gender structures continue to shape particular ways women of color experience poverty, relative to other groups" (Crenshaw 1991, 1244). In 2003, the US Commission on Civil Rights made it clear that Indigenous Peoples' access to criminal justice and health care, including behavioral health, was underfunded historically to a level they termed a human rights crisis. The data demonstrates how patterns of subordination for Indigenous women intersect in their experiences of sexual assault. Indigenous women are less likely to have their cases investigated and prosecuted, and less likely to have access to the necessary services provided to women who are racially privileged.

Political Intersectionality

Crenshaw discusses political intersectionality for women of color since they frequently are expected to stand in the position of representing two or more conflicting political agendas: racism as experienced by Native men or sexism as experienced by white women. As Crenshaw points out, the issue for women of color is that neither antiracism nor feminist discourses center in their analysis the intersections of subordination that women of color experience. For Indigenous women this is made even more complicated given their political identity as tribal members and that jurisdiction and services are raced for Indigenous women, as they are allocated under different laws and processes in tribal communities. Feminism and women of color feminisms need to consider the ways intersectionality places Indigenous women, LGBTQ and Two Spirit people at the very center of this inquiry. Antiracist and antisexist positions alone erase the unique ways Indigenous women, LGBTQ and Two Spirit people experience violence in a colonial settler state and risk replicating the subordination of Indigenous Peoples (Crenshaw 1991, 1250).

Conclusion

Invisibility of Indigenous women and sexual assault is compounded by the way their issues are "erased" within traditional political and structural responses that neglect to specifically address Indigenous women's unique position. Indigenous women stand in a critical position and are expected to maintain solidarity within their tribal communities even in the face of their own victimization. Indigenous women must weigh the value of speaking out in the midst of a colonial settler state where the culture reinforces the distortion of Indigenous Peoples and their communities. If we are to listen to Indigenous women providers, our focus needs to center on culturally relevant sexual assault victim services, aftercare, and holding offenders accountable in a criminal justice system. Native women make clear their identities are intersectional in particular ways and the response to sexual assault must consider the historical impact and contemporary effects of colonial settler subordination experienced and accumulated over time:

> We have all these issues and they live in one Native woman ... she is the history of child sexual abuse, of poverty, being battered, physical problems, and systemic stress of being mistreated for a lifetime.

References

Amnesty International 2004. *Stolen Sisters: Discrimination and Violence against Indigenous Women in Canada*. London: Amnesty International United Kingdom.

Amnesty International 2006. *Maze of Injustice: The Failure to Protect Indigenous Women from Justice*. New York: Amnesty International USA.

Andrews, P.E. 1997. Violence against Aboriginal women in Australia: Possibilities for redress within the international human rights framework. *60 Albany Law Review*, 917, 303–16.

Baca Zinn, M. and Thorton Dill, B. 1996. Theorizing difference from multiracial feminism. *Feminist Studies*, 22(2), 321–31.

Bachman, R., Zaykowski, H., Lanier, C., et al. 2010. Estimating the magnitude of rape and sexual assault against American Indian and Alaska Native (AIAN) women. *The Australian and New Zealand Journal of Criminology*, 43, 199–222.

Brzozowski, J., Taylor-Butts, A., and Johnson, S. 2006. *Victimization and Offending among the Aboriginal Population in Canada*. Ottawa: Canadian Centre for Justice Statistics.

Bubar, R. 2010. Listening to the voices of Native women: Personal safety and sexual violence. Paper presentation at the 12th Indian Nations Conference, Palm Springs, CA.

Bubar, R. and Thurman, P.J. 2004. Violence against Native Women [Special issue]. *Social Justice: A Journal of Crime, Conflict and World Order*, 31, 70–86.

Charmaz, K. 2010. *Constructing Grounded Theory: A Practical Guide through Qualitative Analysis*. Thousand Oaks, CA: Sage Publications.

Chenault, V.S. 2011. *Weaving Strength, Weaving Power: Violence and Abuse against Indigenous Women*. Durham, NC: Carolina Academic Press.

Collins, P.H. 2000. *Black Feminist Thought: Knowledge, Consciousness, and the Politics of Empowerment*. 2nd Edition. New York: Routledge Press.

Crenshaw, K. 1989. Demarginalizing the intersection of race and sex: A Black feminist critique of antidiscrimination doctrine, feminist theory and antiracist politics. *University of Chicago Legal Forum*, 138–67.

Crenshaw, K. 1991. Mapping the margins: Intersectionality, identity politics, and violence against women of color. *Stanford Law Review*, 43, 1241–99.

Crotty, M. 2010. *The Foundations of Social Research*. Thousand Oaks, CA: Sage.

Culhane, D. 2003. Their spirits live within us: Aboriginal women in emerging into visibility. *American Indian Quarterly*, 27 (3/4), 593–606.

Deer, S. 2005. Sovereignty of the soul: Exploring the intersection of rape law reform and federal Indian law. *Suffolk University Law Review*, 38(2), 455–66.

Driskill, Q., Finley, C., Gilley, B.J., and Morgensen, S.L. (eds). 2011. *Queer Indigenous Studies: Critical Interventions in Theory, Politics, and Literature*. Tucson, AZ: University of Arizona Press.

Duran, E. and Duran, B. 1995. *Native American Postcolonial Psychology*. Albany, NY: State University of New York Press.

Evans-Campbell, T., Lindhorst, T., Huang, B., and Walters, K.L. 2006. Interpersonal violence in the lives of urban American Indian and Alaska Native women: Implications for health, mental health, and help-seeking. *American Journal of Public Health*, 96, 1416–22.

Farley, M., Mathews, N., Deer, S., et al. 2011. *Garden of Truth: The Prostitution and Trafficking of Native Women in Minnesota*. Saint Paul, MN: William Mitchel College of Law.

Finley, C. 2011. Decolonizing the queer Native body. In *Queer Indigenous Studies: Critical Interventions in Theory, Politics, and Literature*, Q. Driskill, C. Finley, B.J. Gilly, and S.L. Morgensen (eds). Tucson, AZ: University of Arizona Press.

Green, R. 1992. *Women in American Indian Society*. New York: Chelsea Publishers.

Greenfield, L. and Smith, S. 1999. *American Indians and Crime*. US Department of Justice, Office of Justice Programs, Bureau of Justice Statistics. Washington, DC: US Government Printing, 4.

Hamby, S. 2000. The importance of community in a feminist analysis of domestic violence among American Indians. *American Journal of Community Psychology*, 28, 5, 649–99.

Hamby, S. 2004. Sexual victimization in Indian Country: Barriers and resources for Native women seeking help. Retrieved from National Online Resource Center on Violence Against Women website: http://www.vawnet.org/advanced-search/print-document.php?doc_id=420&find_type=web_desc_AR.

Hesse-Biber, S. and Leavy, P. 2007. *Feminist Research Practice*. Thousand Oaks, CA: Sage Publications.

Johnson, A. 2005. *Privilege, Power and Difference*. 2nd Edition. New York: McGraw-Hill Publishers.

Keel, M. 2004. Family violence and sexual assault in Indigenous communities: "Walking the talk." ACSSA Briefing, No. 4. Australian Institute of Family Studies.

Kelm, M. 1998. *Colonizing Bodies: Aboriginal Health and Healing in British Columbia, 1900–1950*. Vancouver: University of British Columbia Press.

Levan, M.B. 2003. *Creating a Framework for the Wisdom of the Community: Review of Victim Services in Nunavut, Northwest and Yukon Territories*. Ottawa: Department of Justice Canada.

Lincoln, Y. and Guba, E. 1985. *Naturalistic Inquiry*. Newbury Park, NJ: Sage Publications.

Lucashenko, M. 1997. Violence against Indigenous women: Public and private dimensions. In *Women's Encounters with Violence: Australian Experiences*, S. Cook and J. Bessant (eds). Thousand Oaks, CA: Sage Publications, 147–58.

Malcoe, L.K., Duran, B., and Montgomery, J.M. 2004. Socioeconomic disparities in intimate partner violence against Native American women: A cross sectional study. *Biomedical Central*, 2(1), 20–24.

McGlade, H. September 2006. Aboriginal women, girls and sexual assault: The long road. *ACSSA Newsletter*, 12. Australian Institute of Family Studies.

Moraga, C. and Anzaldua, G. 1983. *This Bridge Called my Back: Writings by Radical Women of Color*. New York: Kitchen Table, Women of Color Press.

Morton v. Mancari, 417 US 535 1974.

Moulton, M. 1995. *Wildlife Issues in a Changing World*. 2nd Edition. CRC Press.

Ontario Native Women's Association. 2007. *A Strategic Framework to End Violence Against Women*. Ontario, Canada: Ontario Federation of Indian Friendship Centers.

Perdue, T. 2001. *Sifters: Native American Women's Lives*. New York: Oxford University Press.

Perry, S.W. 2004. *American Indians and Crime*. Washington, DC: US Department of Justice, Bureau of Justice Statistics.

Roscoe, W. 2000. *Changing Ones: Third and Fourth Genders in Native North America*. New York: St Martin's Griffin.

Shields, S. 2008. Gender: An intersectionality perspective. *Sex Roles*, 59, 301–11.

Smith, A. 2004. *Conquest*. Cambridge, MA: South End Press.

Thorpe, L., Soloman, R., and Dimopoulos, M. 2004. *From Shame to Pride: Access to Sexual Assault Services for Indigenous People*. Melbourne: Elizabeth Hoffman House.

Tjaden, P. and Thoennes, N. 2000. *Extent, Nature and Consequences of Intimate Partner Violence: Findings from the National Violence against Women Survey*. Washington, DC: National Institute of Justice.

US Census Bureau 2010. Census of Population and Housing. SF1/10-4(RV). Issued September 2012. 2010 Census Summary File 1.

US Government Accountability Office 2010. US Department of Justice Declinations of Indian Country Criminal Matters. GAO-11-167R. Washington, DC: Author.

Weaver, H. 2009. The colonial context of violence: Reflections on violence in the lives of Native American women. *Journal of Interpersonal Violence*, 24, 1552–63.

Whitbeck, L., Adams, G.W., et al. 2004. Conceptualizing and measuring historical trauma among American Indian people. *American Journal of Community Psychology*, 33(3–4), 119–30.

Yellow Horse Brave Heart, M. 2003. The historical trauma response among Natives and its relationship with substance abuse: A Lakota illustration. *Journal of Psychoactive Drugs*, 35, 7–13.

Yellow Horse Brave Heart, M. and DeBruyn, L.M. 1998. The American Indian holocaust: Healing historical unresolved grief. *American Indian and Alaska Native Mental Health Research*, 8, 56–78.

Yural-Davis, Y. 2006. Intersectionality and feminist politics. *European Journal of Women's Studies*, 13(3), 193–209.

Chapter 12

Culture is Medicine that Works

Lewis Mehl-Madrona and Barbara Mainguy

The First Nations of North America have not fared well post-contact. Poverty is the rule rather than the exception. Suicide rates are high. Addictions, mental illnesses, and autoimmune disorders are rampant—the "diseases of meaninglessness" (as characterized by the World Health Organization). Indigenous Peoples continue to negotiate historical traumas while experiencing contemporary injustices. How do we even begin to address the myriad contextual factors that influence health?

Mental health, physical health, and substance abuse are integrally linked (Dell et al. 2011, Duran 2006). Health-care workers from all cultures struggle to understand the dimensions at work. The very act of dividing mental and physical health or separating substance abuse from the other extremes of life is contrary to Indigenous understandings.

Duran (2006) refers to suffering resulting from colonization as "the soul wound." To recover from this soul wound requires more than the often-resented intrusion of western medicine's quick-fix solutions. Information about health care is everywhere. No one suffers from a lack of knowledge about obesity, diabetes, lack of exercise, or the effects of alcohol on pregnancy. Still, our communities suffer.

Early Health Disparities

Disparities in health status between North America's Aboriginal people and other groups have persisted since first contact with Europeans (Jones 2006). These disparities must be understood within the context of the distinctive political relationship between Native Nations and the US government. The United States currently recognizes an obligation to provide health care for Native American communities, and does so through the branch of the US Public Health Service known as the Indian Health Service (IHS). Despite this ongoing federal obligation, such services remain chronically underfunded (US Commission on Civil Rights, 2004). Canada assumes similar treaty obligations and delivers health care through Health Canada under its First Nations and Inuit Health Care Branch (Aboriginal Affairs and Northern Development Canada 2013).

Mortality increased soon after the arrival of Christopher Columbus, and quickly reached catastrophic proportions. Every new encounter brought new epidemics. Smallpox and malaria (and possibly hepatitis, plague, chickenpox, and diphtheria) spread into Mexico and Peru during the sixteenth century, New France and New England during the seventeenth century, and throughout North America and the Pacific Islands during the eighteenth and nineteenth centuries. Populations often decreased by more than 90 percent during the first century after contact. As recently as the 1940s and 1960s, new highways and new missionaries brought pathogens to previously isolated tribes in Alaska and Amazonia (Kunitz 1994, McCaa 1995, Newson, 1993).

The combination of infection, invasion, and the disruptive effects of war on hunting, gathering, farming, and nutrition adds to a devastating combination that continues into the twenty-first century, where Native Peoples of the Americas still have excess infectious diseases (especially tuberculosis) compared to non-Hispanic white populations (2003).

To add insult to injury, beginning in the nineteenth and continuing well into the twentieth century, Aboriginal ceremonies, traditions, and activities were discouraged and at times criminalized through government legislation, policy, and practice in both the US and Canada (Frideres 2002). This response was part of a comprehensive attempt to assimilate Aboriginal Peoples into the contemporary Canadian/American mosaic, and resulted in the erosion of traditional ways of life (Dickason 2006, Morrison and Wilson 2004). Consequently, the health and well-being of First Nations and Inuit were negatively affected, demonstrated by marginalized social and economic status, poor nutrition, and high rates of violence and substance abuse (Dell and Lyons 2007).

Contemporary Health Disparities

The Social Determinants of Health indices document the foundations of health disparities. Twenty-eight percent of Native Americans live in poverty, compared with 10.6 percent of non-Hispanic whites (Department of Health and Human Services 2012a). Barriers to good health coverage include lack of insurance, education, language, and transportation. The infant death rate for Native Americans is 60 percent higher than for Caucasians (Department of Health and Human Services 2012a).

Native Americans have a strikingly higher prevalence and risk factors for mental health and suicide, obesity, substance abuse, sudden infant death syndrome (SIDS), teenage pregnancy, liver disease, and hepatitis compared to non-Hispanic Whites. For example, in 2010, American Indians/Alaska Natives were 30 percent more likely to be diagnosed with asthma (Department of Health and Human Services, 2012b), and twice as likely to have diabetes (Department of Health and Human Services 2012c). An example is the Tohono of Arizona, who have one of the highest diabetes rates in the world, approaching 60 percent of their adult population. Native Americans have disproportionately high death rates from unintentional injuries and suicide. In 2010, the tuberculosis rate was 5.8, as compared to 2.0 for the White population (Department of Health and Human Services 2012a).

In 2009, suicide was the second leading cause of death for Native Americans between the ages of 10 and 34. Violent deaths, including unintentional injuries, homicide, and suicide, accounted for 75 percent of all mortality in the second decade of life for American Indian/Alaska Natives. American Indians had 1.7 times more serious psychological distress (Centers for Disease Control 2012), reported feeling worthless 1.5 times as often, and feeling that everything is an effort twice as often (Centers for Disease Control 2011), reported feelings of nervousness all or most of the time 1.6 times more often, and restlessness all or most of the time 2.2 times more often than non-Hispanic whites. Additionally, fewer Native adults received mental health treatment (Department of Health and Human Services 2011).

The incidence and prevalence of psychiatric disorders among North America's Aboriginal Peoples is hard to determine (Gone 2003, Manson and Altschul, 2004, Department of Health and Human Services 2001). What can be said is that high levels of "frequent mental distress" are reported by Native Americans (Zahran et al. 2004). Community-based epidemiological studies (Beals et al. 2005) attest to an increased lifetime prevalence of dependence on alcohol and drugs and increased diagnosing of post traumatic stress disorder (PTSD) for people on reservations. High diagnosis rates of mood disorders, pathological reactions to violence and trauma, and rates of suicide have been found (Alcántara and Gone, 2007).

Native Americans have the highest addiction rates of any population in the United States as well as the lowest treatment success rates (French 2004). The Federal response to these problems among Native Americans has historically been incarceration, not rehabilitation. It has only been since the 1980s that health services have begun to recognize that fostering positive cultural ethnic identity is an essential predecessor to successful drug and alcohol treatment. Specific to substance-related diagnoses, Health Canada's First Nations and Inuit Health Branch, in partnership with First Nations and Inuit communities and organizations, moved toward closing this gap with the development of 56 Native-oriented alcohol and drug treatment centers (NNADAP) in the 1970s. Most of these centers were developed with an emphasis on Aboriginal understandings of healing in conjunction with conventional approaches to substance use treatment. A network of nine residential treatment centers specific to youth solvent abuse was also established, starting in 1996 (Dell et al. 2011).

Traditional Aboriginal understandings and approaches to addressing problematic substance use and mental health issues have historically been at odds with conventional biomedical approaches (Marbella et al. 1998, Morrisseau 1998). Dell et al. have described how culture-based models of resiliency are often at odds with individualized approaches to treating mental disorders (Dell et al. 2011). They reported on the gap in understanding and practice between Western psychiatric disorder–based and Aboriginal culture-based approaches to treatment and healing from substance abuse and mental disorders. They describe the difficulties encountered by front-line workers in a youth solvent abuse treatment center in applying Western responses to Aboriginal healing. "Key in [the Aboriginal] model is recognition that a person's inner spirit and community cannot be disentangled from one another, as is commonly done within a Western world view" (Dell et al. 2011, 76).

Historical Trauma

One of the profound social experiences that we have come to embrace as culturally relevant is historical trauma. Historical trauma is a much-debated, sometimes denied, crucial collective representation for the majority of Native American people (Brave Heart 2003, Duran and Duran 1995). Concepts of Native American historical trauma are modeled after long-standing clinical observations of the adverse psychological effects of the Shoah, not just for Holocaust survivors, but also for their offspring (Baranowsky et al. 1998). A biological basis exists to explain this in the science of epigenetics (Mehl-Madrona 2010). Epigenetics is the science of how experience is transmitted genetically from one generation to the next. Through modification of the structure of the DNA by actual experience, offspring receive the experiences of their parents. Thus, the child of a residential school survivor will be inclined to behave as if he or she had actually been abused in a residential school and will pass this tendency onward to his or her offspring. Corrective emotional experiences can alter this transmission, but in the absence of such healing, the transmission continues (Weaver et al. 2004). Through the science of epigenetics, historical trauma has a biological basis.

Even with limited rigorous confirmatory scientific investigations (Whitbeck et al. 2004), the historical trauma hypothesis has proliferated widely as a clinically relevant concept throughout Native American human services during the past 15 years (Evans-Campbell 2008, Lambert 2008, Waldram 2004). The concept of historical trauma is entrenched in therapeutic, behavioral health, and human services circles throughout Native North America (Gone 2009). Historical trauma is best treated through culture. Culture is medicine.

Culture Matters

Culture matters greatly in understanding and correcting health disparities Gone (2007). Culture has been defined as the public, patterned, and historically reproduced semiotic practices that both facilitate and constrain the meaningful existence of an affiliated human community (Gone 1999). Mehl-Madrona (2007) has proposed an Aboriginal definition of culture as being shared stories in a shared language for how to perform oneself in the world.

"Culture not only influences human psychology and perceptions of self, others, and reality; it also, in certain contexts influences the quality and degree of consciousness itself" (Turner and Whitehead 2008, 43). "Common sense"— the self-evident truth[s] we accept as too obvious to be subjected to critical reflection—varies among cultures, often to the extreme (Bourdieu 1972). Human perception of self, others, kin, foreigners, and the world are extremely variable (Turner and Whitehead 2008). For example, traditional belief in the New World supports instantiation—the idea that when we put on an animal mask, the spirit of that animal transforms us into that animal in actuality and not just in metaphor. This is not a common belief of mainstream society.

Mainstream American culture does not endorse spirituality to the degree that Native American culture does. Among almost 500 societies, spiritual experience is inversely correlated with structural complexity (Bourguignon 1973). In the least hierarchical, most egalitarian societies (typical of North American Aboriginal cultures), out-of-body experiences tend to be frequent, conscious, voluntary, and accessible to most people who desire them. During ceremonies, participants regularly negotiate with spiritual beings or even Creator (Katz 1982). In contrast, in the materialistic, individualistic cultures (like dominant culture North America), spiritual experiences of a life-transforming kind only occur once or twice in a lifetime, among 60 percent of the population (Hay and Morisy 1978). We can readily imagine how a rarely spiritual culture would look with suspicion and fear upon a frequently spiritual culture and how members of the frequently spiritual culture could become labeled as psychotic or mentally disturbed (Kirmayer et al., 2000).

The all-too-common practice of looking at Aboriginal Peoples through the lens of Western European-derived theory is a bias rarely overcome because it is rarely acknowledged. This is especially onerous since most studies of Aboriginal mental health have centered on cultural differences and cultural marginality (Waldram 2004). The acknowledgement that researchers are culturally biased is paramount to actually learning about the people being studied. Thus, the majority of the literature on Aboriginal mental health reflects more on the "nature of European intellectual traditions than [on] Aboriginal society" (Waldram 2004, 300).

Duran (2006) has disputed the usefulness of contemporary mainstream psychological and psychiatric models for Aboriginal people, and has urged the development of uniquely Aboriginal models for mental health. The employment of exclusively biomedical healing practices in Aboriginal communities is not an optimal solution to mental health disparities and points toward the importance of exploring healing practices that are more culture specific, or, at least, Aboriginal-friendly. Conceptualizing an Aboriginal theory of mind and mental health may help us find better solutions (Mehl-Madrona and Pennycook 2009).

Aboriginal Views of Mental Health Needs

A study of 19 traditional elders examined their beliefs about what mental health providers need to know to effectively help Aboriginal people (Mehl-Madrona

2009). Traditional elders were defined as people performing actions within communities to reduce pain and suffering, recognized by sufficient members of their community as having the skills, training, and experience necessary to do so, and embodying the traditional values and beliefs of that community (Arnault-Pelletier 2008, Waldram 1997). Discussions included their views on: 1) mind; 2) mental health; 3) the disorders they recognize of mind and mental health; 4) who should be involved in healing mental health problems; 5) what they should know; and 6) how they should be trained. Twelve points of agreement were reached:

1. Teach students the importance of listening.
2. Teach students a relational model of the self.
3. Solutions must be internally derived.
4. People are spontaneously self-healing.
5. The healer should be selfless of intent.
6. Healers need to be passionate about their work.
7. Healers have to maintain some independence from political structures.
8. Teach students the importance of faith, hope, and the power of the activated mind.
9. Empowerment is different from treatment.
10. Teach students the importance of community.
11. Only Creator can give prognoses.
12. All healing is ultimately spiritual healing.

What all this suggests is that appropriate training for working with Indigenous Peoples is different from mainstream training programs currently offered in mental health professions, which are often concerned with teaching students to be expert professionals who apply solutions to fix or treat problems and expect patients to comply with their advice. Spirituality is rarely discussed. Clinical detachment and professionalism is emphasized. Humor is rarely encouraged. Helping professionals must be more humble. They need to work hard to develop their abilities to listen and to grasp the story the person is living. They must appreciate the power of community and ground their activities in the idea of a relational self and a narrative identity. They should foster dialogue and trust in the self-healing nature of systems. We should fuel their passions, protect them from political structures, and insist that they consider the power of faith, hope, and mind. Therapy should empower more than treat and they should refrain from labeling and predicting the future based upon labels as much as possible. Educational programs should use community mentors, such as elders, from communities in which students will work. They should be equal collaborators with adjunct faculty appointments. We should include more training on methods of work that involve communities and larger groups than just the individual.

An Aboriginal Theory of Mind

Most research on Aboriginal mind and mental health has sought to apply or confirm preexisting European-derived theories to Aboriginal people (Mehl-Madrona and Pennycook 2009). The importance of culture and community has been under-appreciated. Unlike contemporary mainstream psychology, conversations with elders revealed a relational theory in which self emerges between and among people from the need to manage that relationship. Relational self is formed and shaped from what happens in that dialogue which is saturated with stories, both historical and new. Historical stories inform us about how to behave in general toward certain people, and new stories emerge from the interaction and the ensuing dialogue. Self is the point of negotiation (Mehl-Madrona and Pennycook 2009).

Mind is an elusive concept best conceptualized as the swarm of all the selves and the stories in which they are engaged. Mind is distinguished from consciousness, which is without language and exists within the individual as simple awareness. The Lakota people use the word *nagi* (Voss et al. 1999) to refer to this swarm of all the stories that have ever been told about one, by one, or have helped to form one. *Nagi* also contains the part of the person who told that story so that sharing story makes us forever interconnected. This concept is more like quantum physics than standard psychology and is initially hard to grasp for many. Since all human interaction involves the telling of stories, short or long, we are forever taking new stories (and parts of other beings) into our *nagi*. This means that what corresponds (loosely) to the self in Lakota thought is forever changing as a result of ongoing social interactions.

In Lakota thought (similar to other North American traditions), self and language are inseparable, for both emerged through social relationships in which two or more individuals told stories about their experiences so as to be understood. We have heard elders say, "without relationship there would be no emotion, no self, nothing, for everything we are emerges in relationship." The very existence of, for example, the Diagnostic and Statistical Manual (DSM) of the American Psychiatric Association runs against Aboriginal thought since our distress is not the result of "things" that we have but of relationships that are imbalanced and disharmonious. These relationships could be with other humans, the plant or the animal world, spirits, or nature, but, for the Lakota, misery is a verb and not a noun. It is a story we are enacting and not a thing that has us in its grips. In explaining this, an elder told me, "if you can't see it walk across your lawn, if you can't eat it or be eaten by it, it ain't real." This was his explanation for depression, which, he said, didn't exist. In his language, the translation was "walking on the path as if it's always raining and cloudy even though it's sunny and blue." So, he said, waving his hands to make his point, you have to actually walk the walk and talk the talk of being cloudy and rainy all the time in order to make it so.

Lakota psychology (and that of many other tribes) conceives the community to be the basic unit of study for mind and mental health, and not "mentally ill" people themselves. The Dene believe that all members of the community should contribute monetarily and energetically to the ceremony that must be done to help the sick person get well, because the sick person has shown the community that disharmony and imbalance exists. The sick person has taken the illness of the community into his or her body and should be honored, respected, and thanked by all. The person whose body displays the illness is the "canary in the social mine."

These concepts are emerging in non-Indigenous contexts as well, though often without credit being given to the Indigenous Peoples who have thought this way for many years. For example, the Social Brain hypothesis, which is showcased by the Action and Research Centre in the UK, believes that we are constituted by evolutionary biology, embedded in complex social networks, largely creatures of habit, highly sensitive to social and cultural norms, and more rationalizing than rational, based upon neurobiological research which holds that the brain is jointly constructed by biology and by the social world which its body inhabits. "Major brain pathways are specified in the genome; detailed connections are fashioned by, and consequently, reflect, socially mediated experience in the world" (Action and Research Centre 2012).

North American theories of mind are more closely related to Daoist and Shinto theories than to the logical positivism which drives most of North America's conventional psychology and psychiatry. Within European traditions, however, the thought of Mikhail Bakhtin, with his emphasis on a dialogical self, coupled with system theory comes closest to resembling North American Aboriginal theories. This model explains why ceremony and ritual, community interventions, talking circles (including AA and the Indigenous Wellbriety Movement), and family therapy are more compatible with Aboriginal thought than conventional North American biomedicine and psychology (Mehl-Madrona and Pennycook 2009).

Narrative Nature of Native American Psychology

> *This is why I tell these stories over and over again. And there are others. I tell them to myself, to friends, sometimes to strangers. Because they make me laugh. Because they are a particular kind of story. Saving stories, if you will. Stories help keep me alive. But help yourself to one if you like. It's yours. Do with it what you will. Cry over it. Get angry. Forget it. But don't say in the years to come that you would have lived your life differently if only you had heard this story. You've heard it now.* (King 2012, 3)

What King describes fits within what is being called narrative psychology (Mehl-Madrona 2008). The rise of narrative and critical psychology, along with the Indigenous Mental Health Movement, has encouraged the development of specific psychologies aimed at decolonization, empowerment, and social transformation (Dudgeon and Pickett 2000). Narrative therapy provides practical means for respectful, cross-cultural communication (Benson 2006) and is being widely applied to Aboriginal mental health problems in Australia. Narrative methods help us to appreciate others' stories which can be so different from our own for reasons of differing family background, education, religion, beliefs, and socio-political outlooks. Narrative techniques facilitate patients' feelings that their beliefs, values, and practices are understood and respected by the practitioner, which has not been the case for Aboriginal people and conventional psychology. Narrative therapists acknowledge the implicit power differentials between professionals and Aboriginal people and between non-Aboriginal and Aboriginal people as an essential hurdle to overcome before therapeutic work can take place. The narrative movement in psychotherapy also emphasizes the importance of the link between the personal and the political (Anderson 1995, White and Hales 1997).

A key feature of narrative psychology is a determination to understand that problems are constructed and experienced within culture and history, and exist in a larger field than the individual. "The person is not the problem" is an often-heard phrase. This perspective fits well with Aboriginal views of mind and mental health. Narrative psychotherapists often do what I have heard elders doing— identifying the problem as separate from the person, locating the problem in history and in a storyline, and tracing the effects of the problem on the person's life and relationships. Even the notion of psychopathology would be contested in favor of a view I heard one elder telling in a ceremony inside a Saskatchewan prison. A young man was telling him that he had "attention deficit" and "bipolar" and "antisocial" disorders and that he would be back in prison in no time. "You don't got any of those things," the elder said. "You're a good man who grew up with bad stories. Stick with us when you get out and we'll give you good stories to live by. Those good stories, they'll keep you out of jail."

Problems are always seen as being saturated in the context, broader culture, politics, and relationships of the person and not within the person per se (Russell and Carey 2003). This perspective produces a suspicion of labels and diagnoses similar to what is often expressed by Aboriginal elders. We strongly observed this in a study of Aboriginal elders in Saskatchewan working with couples in which domestic violence had occurred. The elders relocated the problem from being within the men who were violent to being the effect of a violent, colonizing culture upon them, providing them with the rationale that resisting violence against women was a means of resisting the colonizing, dominant culture and furthermore was consistent with traditional values of honoring women as being the givers of life (Puchala et al. 2010).

Narrative practitioners also acknowledge the political nature of therapeutic work and the potentially powerful position of the professional. This relates to all problems having been created and continuing to exist within relations of power and the politics of local culture. Therefore, health care and mental health care are political. Thus, we must explore, find, and acknowledge our assumptions, as they may be part of our clients' problems.

Art is Part of Culture

Native Americans tend to regard art as an element of life, not as a separate aesthetic ideal. The arts are aspects of public and spiritual life that combine dancing, poetry, singing, and the visual arts into an all-embracing expression in ritual. Throughout North American Native societies, elders and/or spiritual leaders share the power of their visions through art. For example, in the Dene culture, symbols are expressed by the healers during sand painting ceremonies (Dufrene and Coleman 1992).

Including traditional Native American healing techniques, particularly the use of art in healing, is extremely important given the disproportionate number of Native people seeking the services of psychiatric hospitals, mental health clinics, and special education in schools (Myers 1987). Art is an important cultural means of addressing the devastating social, economic, and environmental pressures of racism, poverty, alcoholism, substandard reservation housing, and hostile education systems (Dufrene and Coleman 1994). Because most contemporary Native Americans are a product of both the Western culture and their own Indigenous heritage, a blending of traditional healing techniques and counseling methods may be the best remedy for therapeutic intervention (Dufrene and Coleman 1992).

Example of a Successful Cultural Integration Project

Anishnawbe Health Centre in Toronto (AHC) maintains a hard-won vision for a truly integrative health-care facility. AHC is a vision of the late Elder, Joe Sylvester. Initial efforts began with a diabetes research project, which identified that a more comprehensive approach to health care was needed by the Aboriginal community (Anishnawbe Health Centre 2012). In response, Anishnawbe Health Resources was incorporated in 1984 in a downtown Toronto building in a lower-income urban neighborhood. One of its objectives stated, "To recover, record, and promote traditional Aboriginal practices where possible and appropriate." Today, AHC not only promotes traditional Aboriginal practices but has affirmed and placed them at its core. Its model of health care is based on an integration of western and traditional practices and approaches, and is reflected in the design of its programs and services. In 1989, having successfully secured resources from the Ministry of Health, Anishnawbe Health Centre became recognized and funded as a community health center.

AHC continues to grow to meet the needs of the community it serves. As a fully accredited community health center, AHC offers access to health-care practitioners from many disciplines including Traditional Healers, Elders, and Medicine People. Ancient ceremonies and traditions, intrinsic to an Aboriginal health-care model, are available. Their work with the homeless evolved from early directions of crisis intervention to current efforts of working with those who seek to escape homelessness. Training programs offer community members the opportunity to learn and grow in a culture-based setting. In the middle of the urban world, a purification lodge is made available to the community regularly.

A turtle, representing Turtle Island, hangs in the front room, one among many symbols that offer what the Centre refers to as "Cultural Safety," a step beyond cultural sensitivity. Their philosophy is symbolized by the medicine wheel, which comprises all four directions, each having its own meaning: north is spiritual; south is emotional; east is thinking, feeling and doing; and west is physical. The medicine wheel as a way to define health is important for Native people seeking to reclaim their culture. Within Anishnawbe and other successful programs, the medicine wheel concept is used to teach balance among the physical, mental, spiritual, and emotional aspects of one's being. This traditional approach to understanding health has been used to explore the impacts of physical activity on emotional, spiritual, and mental well-being (Lavallee 2008).

A weekly healing circle is an integral part of the center's programming. Each person in the circle gets a chance to talk uninterrupted. "'While you are talking, you are accorded respect and can say whatever is in your heart,' Morrison said. 'Sometimes there is a specific focus on a certain issue. For example, a while ago someone in the circle committed suicide, so we had a feast for her. There were people from her place of work and people who were in the circle and staff who worked with her here, so there were 40 people at this healing circle'" (Lavallee 2008).

A naturopathic clinic now exists at Anishnawbe Health Centre (Walji et al. 2010). Studies of this clinic found that naturopathic medicine was perceived to fit with health-care philosophies of Aboriginal communities in its emphasis on spiritual, mental, and emotional aspects of health. Specifically, the strengths of naturopathic medicine within the Aboriginal community related to the philosophical suitability of naturopathic medicine, its ability to meet a wide range of health needs, the lack of power imbalance in the patient–practitioner relationship, and the cultural sensitivity of the practitioners.

Through open-ended interviews with the clients, traditional healers, counselors, and biomedical practitioners of Anishnawbe Health Centre, four main themes emerged to characterize AHC (Skye 2006).

The first theme concerned the importance of establishing Aboriginal ancestry among the clients. In addition to being a requirement to access the services at the center, it serves as a starting point for the creation of an Aboriginal identity. The second theme concerned the establishment of an Aboriginal spirit name. The receiving of a spirit name serves as a spiritual foundation for an Aboriginal identity. The third theme focused on the accumulation of Indigenous knowledge and its contribution to the establishment of an Aboriginal cultural identity. The fourth theme concerned the perception of Anishnawbe Health as a bounded Aboriginal community and its significance to the clientele. Through analysis of these four themes, it appeared that the establishment of an Aboriginal cultural identity had a positive effect on the overall health and well-being of urban Aboriginal people (Skye 2006).

Conclusion

Current health disparities began with European contact and exposure to unfamiliar infectious diseases for which North Americans had no immunity. The ensuing invasion disrupted food supplies and access to nutrition, which further weakened immunity. Subsequent poverty, captivity, and the destruction of culture and meaning, fed growing health disparities.

Effective health services function within the culture and beliefs of the population served. Native American ideas of health and disease are different from those of the dominant culture and are worthy of further exploration. Among non-Indigenous traditions, narrative medicine and psychology offer the closest parallels to Native American thought. Within these perspectives it is important to attend to the story and to work within the story to produce change. Politics and power imbalances are acknowledged. Elders are respected as partners in delivering health care.

Those services that have worked within Native American culture and beliefs, such as Anishnawbe Health Centre in Toronto, are effective in improving health and reducing disparities. Elders, communities, and Native scholars have generated guidelines for working within Native communities and with Native American people, which produce more effective health care. Communities need to be active in influencing and directing their own health care to match their culture and needs. Culture is medicine that works.

References

Aboriginal Affairs and Northern Development Canada 2013. *Federal Programs and Services for Registered Indians*. [Online]. Available at: http://www.aadnc-aandc.gc.ca/eng/1100100028564/1100100028566 [Accessed 15 March 2013].

Action and Research Centre 2012. *RSA – Social Brain*. [Online]. Available at: http://www.thersa.org/action-research-centre/social-brain [Accessed 16 January 2012].

Alcántara, C. and Gone, J.P. 2007. Reviewing suicide in Native American communities: Situating risk and protective factors within a transactional-ecological framework. *Death Studies*, 31, 457–77.

Anderson, L. 1995. *Bedtime Stories for Tired Therapists*. Adelaide (South Australia): Dulwich Centre Publications.

Anishnawbe Health Centre 2012. *Anishnawbe Health Centre*. [Online] Available at: http://www.aht.ca/about [Accessed 17 January 2012].

Arnault-Pelletier, V. 2008. *Defining and Approaching Elders in Traditional Communities*. Saskatoon, s.n.

Baranowsky, A.B. et al. 1998. PTSD transmission: A review of secondary traumatization in Holocaust survivor families. *Canadian Psychology*, 39, 247–56.

Beals, J. et al. 2005. Prevalence of DSM-IV disorders and attendant help-seeking in two American Indian reservation populations. *Archives of General Psychiatry*, 62, 99–108.

Benson, J. 2006. A culturally sensitive consultation model. Advances in Mental Health. *Multicultural Mental Health*, 5, 97–104.

Bourdieu, P. 1972. *Outline of a Theory of Practice*. Cambridge: Cambridge University Press.

Bourguignon, E. 1973. *Religion, Altered States of Consciousness, and Social Change*. Columbus: The Ohio State University Press.

Brave Heart, M.Y.H. 2003. The historical trauma response among Natives and its relationship with substance abuse: A Lakota illustration. *Journal of Psychoactive Drugs*, 35(1), 7–13.

Centers for Disease Control 2011. *Summary Health Statistics for U.S. Adults: 2010*. [Online]. Available at: http://www.cdc.gov/nchs/data/series/sr_10/sr10_252.pdf [Accessed 23 January 2013].

Centers for Disease Control 2012. *Health United States, 2011*. [Online]. Available at: http://www.cdc.gov/nchs/data/hus/hus11.pdf [Accessed 23 January 2013].

Dell, C. and Lyons, T. 2007. *Harm Reduction and Persons of Aboriginal Descent*. Ottawa: Canadian Centre on Substance Abuse.

Dell, C.A. et al. 2011. From Benzos to Berries: Treatment offered at an Aboriginal youth solvent abuse treatment centre relays the importance of culture. *Canadian Journal of Psychiatry*, 56(2), 75–83.

Department of Health and Human Services 2001. *Mental health: Culture, Race, and Ethnicity—A Supplement to Mental Health: A Report of the Surgeon General*. Rockville, MD: US Department of Health and Human Services, Substance Abuse and Mental Health Services Administration.

Department of Health and Human Services 2011. *2010 National Healthcare Disparities Report*. [Online]. Available at: http://www.ahrq.gov/research/findings/nhqrdr/nhdr10/ [Accessed 14 September 2013].

Department of Health and Human Services 2012a. *Office of Minority Health*. [Online]. Available at: http://minorityhealth.hhs.gov/templates/browse.aspx?lvl=2&lvlid=52 [Accessed 31 March 2013].

Department of Health and Human Services 2012b. *Office of Minority Health*. [Online]. Available at: http://minorityhealth.hhs.gov/templates/browse.aspx?lvl=3&lvlid=532 [Accessed 31 March 2013].

Department of Health and Human Services 2012c. *Office of Minority Health*. [Online]. Available at: http://minorityhealth.hhs.gov/templates/browse.aspx?lvl=3&lvlid=5 [Accessed 31 March 2013].

Dickason, O. 2006. *A Concise History of Canada's First Nations*. Toronto: Oxford University Press.

Dudgeon, P. and Pickett, H. 2000. Psychology and reconciliation: Australia perspectives. *Australian Psychology*, 35(2), 82–7.

Dufrene, P.M. and Coleman, V.D. 1992. Counseling Native Americans: Guidelines for group process. *The Journal for Specialists in Group Work*, 17, 229–35.

Dufrene, P.M. and Coleman, V.D. 1994. Art and Healing for Native American Indians. *Journal of Multicultural Counseling & Development*, 22(3), 145–52.

Duran, E. 2006. *Healing the Soul Wound: Counselling with American Indians and other Native Peoples*. New York: Teachers College Press.

Duran, E. and Duran, B. 1995. *Native American Postcolonial Psychology*. Albany, NY: State University of New York Press.

Evans-Campbell, T. 2008. Historical trauma in American Indian/Native Alaska communities: A multilevel framework for exploring impacts on individuals, families, communities. *Journal of Interpersonal Violence*, 23, 316–38.

French, L.A. 2004. Alcohol and other drug addictions among Native Americans: The movement toward tribal-centric treatment programs. *Alcoholism Treatment Quarterly*, 22(1), 81–91.

Frideres, J. 2002. Overcoming hurdles: Health care and Aboriginal people. In: *Health, Illness and Health Care in Canada*, B. Singh Bolaria and H.D. Dickinson. Scarborough, ON: Thomson Learning, 144–66.

Gone, J.P. 1999. "We were through as Keepers of it": The "Missing Pipe Narrative" and Gros Ventre cultural identity. *Ethos*, 27(4), 415–40.

Gone, J.P. 2003. American Indian mental health service delivery: Persistent challenges and future prospects. In *Culturally Diverse Mental Health: The Challenges of Research and Resistance*, J.S. Mio and G.Y. Iwamasa (eds). New York, NY: Brunner-Routledge, 211–29.

Gone, J.P. 2007. "We never was happy living like a Whiteman": Mental health disparities and the post-colonial predicament in American Indian communities. *American Journal of Community Psychology*, 40, 290–300.

Gone, J.P. 2009. *A Community-Based Treatment for Native American Historical Trauma: Prospects for Evidence-Based Practice*. [Online]. Available at: http://saokioheritage.com/AcrobatFiles/JPGHistTraumaTx.pdf [Accessed January 2013].

Hay, D. and Morisy, A. 1978. Reports of ecstatic, paranormal, or religious experience for Great Britain and the United States – A comparison of trends. *Journal for the Scientific Study of Religion*, 17, 255–68.

Jones, D. 2006. The persistence of American Indian health disparities. *American Journal of Public Health*, 96, 2122–34.

Jones, D. 2003. Virgin soils revisited. *The William and Mary Quarterly*, 60(4), 703–42. [Online]. Available at: http://www.jstor.org/stable/3491697 [Accessed October 10, 2013].

Katz, R. 1982. *Boiling Energy: Community Healing among the Kalihari !Kung*. Cambridge, MA: Harvard University Press.

King, T. 2012. *From Benzos to Berries*. [Online]. Available at: http://www.ihe.ca/documents/Hopkins_v1.ppt [Accessed March 15, 2013].

Kirmayer, L.J., Brass, G.M., and Tait, C.L. 2000. The mental health of Aboriginal Peoples: Transformations of identity and community. *Canadian Journal of Psychiatry*, 45, 607–16.

Kunitz, S.J. 1994. *Disease and Social Diversity: The European Impact on the Health of Non-Europeans*. New York, NY: Oxford University Press.

Lambert, C. 2008. Trails of tears and hope. *Harvard Magazine*, 110(4), 39–43; 85–7.

Lavallee, L.F. 2008. *Balancing the Medicine Wheel through Physical Activity*. [Online]. Available at: http://digitalcommons.ryerson.ca/socialwork/1 [Accessed 17 January 2012].

Manson, S.M. and Altschul, D.B. 2004. *Cultural Diversity Series: Meeting the Mental Health Needs of American Indians and Alaska Natives*. Washington, DC: National Technical Assistance Center for State Mental Health Planning and National Association of State Mental Health Program Directors.

Marbella, A., Harris, M., and Diehr, S. 1998. Use of Native American healers among Native American patients in an urban Native American health centre. *Archives of Family Medicine*, 7, 182–5.

McCaa, R. 1995. Spanish and Nahuatl Views on smallpox and demographic catastrophe in Mexico. *Journal of Interdisciplinary History*, 25, 429.

Mehl-Madrona, L.E. 2007. *Narrative Medicine: The History and Power of Story in the Healing Process*. Rochester, VT: Bear and Company.

Mehl-Madrona, L. 2008. *Coyote Wisdom: The Power of Story in Healing*. Rochester, VT: Bear and Company.

Mehl-Madrona, L. 2009. What traditional Indigenous Elders say about cross-cultural mental health training. *Explore: The Journal of Science and Healing*, 5(1), 20–29.

Mehl-Madrona, L. 2010. *Healing the Mind through the Power of Story: The Promise of Narrative Psychiatry*. Rochester, VT: Bear and Company.

Mehl-Madrona, L. and Pennycook, G. 2009. Construction of an Aboriginal theory of mind and mental health. *Anthropology of Consciousness*, 20(2), 85–100.

Morrison, R. and Wilson, C. 2004. *Native Peoples: The Canadian Experience*. Toronto: Oxford University Press.

Morrisseau, C. 1998. *Into the Daylight: A Wholistic Approach to Healing*. Toronto: University of Toronto Press.

Myers, W.D. 1987. Cross-cultural medicine. *Behavioral Sciences Exchange*, 8, 113–19.

Newson, L.A. 1993. The demographic collapse of Native Peoples of the Americas, 1492–1650. *Proceedings of the British Academy*, 81, 247–88.

Puchala, C., Paul, S., Kennedy, C., and Mehl-Madrona, L. 2010. Using traditional spirituality to reduce domestic violence within Aboriginal communities. *Journal of Alterernative and Complementary Medicine*, 16(1), 89–96.

Russell, S. and Carey, M. 2003. Feminism, therapy and narrative ideas: Exploring some not so commonly asked questions. *The International Journal of Narrative Therapy and Community Work*, 2, 1–41.

Skye, J.S. 2006. *An Orchid in the Swamp: Traditional Medicine, Healing, and Identity at an Urban Aboriginal Community Health Center*. [Online]. Available at: http://digitalcommons.mcmaster.ca/opendissertations/6677/ [Accessed January 17, 2012].

Turner, R. and Whitehead, C. 2008. How collective representations can change the structure of the brain. *Journal of Consciousness Studies*, 15(10–11), 43–57.

US Commission on Civil Rights. 2004. *Broken Promises: Evaluating the Native American Health Care System*. Washington, DC: US Commission on Civil Rights.

Voss, R.W., Douville, V., Little Soldier, A., and Twiss, G. 1999. Tribal and shamanic-based social work practice: A Lakota perspective. *Social Work*, 44(3), 228–41.

Waldram, J. 1997. *The Way of the Pipe: Aboriginal Spirituality and Symbolic Healing in Canadian Prisons*. Peterborough, ON: Broadview Press.

Waldram, J.B. 2004. *Revenge of the Windigo: The Construction of the Mind and Mental Health of North American Aboriginal Peoples*. Toronto: University of Toronto.

Walji, R., Weeks, L., Cooley, K., and Seeley, D. 2010. Naturopathic Medicine and Aboriginal health: An exploratory study at Anishnawbe Health Toronto. *Canadian Journal of Public Health*, 101(5), 475–80.

Weaver, I.C. et al. 2004. Epigenetic programming by maternal behavior. *Nature Neuroscience*, 7 (27 June), 847–54.

Whitbeck, L.B., Adams, G.W., Hoyt, D.R., and Chen, X. 2004. Conceptualizing and measuring historical trauma among American Indian people. *American Journal of Community Psychology*, 33(3–4), 119–30.

White, C. and Hales, J. 1997. *The Personal is the Professional: Therapists Reflect on their Families, Lives, and Work*. Adelaide, South Australia: Dulwich Centre Publications.

Zahran, H.S., Kobau, R., Moriarty, D.G., et al. 2004. Self-reported frequent mental distress among adults – United States, 1993–2001. *Morbidity and Mortality Weekly Report*, 53, 963–6.

Chapter 13

Building Assets in Tribal Communities

Amy Locklear Hertel, Kristen Wagner, and Jessica Black

This chapter discusses the use of asset-building policies to address economic and social challenges in tribal communities. Appropriately, this chapter defines the terms asset and asset-building policy. It reviews the impact federal Indian policy has had on tribal assets and how tribes are now using asset building to rebuild Native economies, communities, and people. Further, this chapter examines models and frameworks that support the use of asset-building policies to move low-income families out of poverty and situate asset building in an American Indian context. Examples of various asset-building policies are offered and specific case studies of tribal communities implementing successful asset-building policies are provided.

Before discussing assets and asset building in tribal communities, we must first define what we mean by "tribal communities." For the purposes of this discussion, the term tribal communities refers to those communities consisting of a group of people belonging to one or more tribal nations that share in a larger identification as being either American Indian or Alaskan Native. Tribal communities may be located in reservation, rural, or urban areas.

What are Assets?

Assets are defined as something we accumulate, invest, maintain, or build upon for future use. They can be: 1) physical things like money, a car, a business, or a home; 2) things that create rights of ownership like a bank account, stocks and bonds, retirement accounts, and natural resources; or 3) intangible things that can be mobilized to create access to additional resources like education, social networks, and access to financial institutions (Adamson et al. 2004, Sherraden 1991). Most of the time when the term *asset building* is used, it refers to the building of physical financial assets. This is especially true of mainstream asset-building policies. Therefore, for the purposes of this chapter, we will limit our discussion to financial assets and programs and policies that promote primarily the development of financial well-being.

From an economic perspective, assets help individuals, families, and communities achieve economic security and expand economic opportunity (Nam et al. 2008). Assets are not the same as income. Income allows resources to flow in and out of a household for immediate consumption. In contrast, assets serve as a storehouse of wealth for future consumption.

The benefits to accumulating assets are many. Assets help protect individuals and families from being vulnerable in times of emergencies and hardships. Assets provide a financial cushion during times of seasonal work, job loss, or illness. When assets are leveraged as an investment, they have the ability to create positive returns that can result in improved well-being over time. Enhanced long-term well-being is the desired outcome of asset building policy (Sherraden 1991). There are also non-financial benefits that can result from the building of financial assets (i.e., increased human and social capital).

Asset Building and Public Policy

Asset building refers to ways in which individuals, families, or communities acquire assets. Other terms that refer to asset building include economic or community development. Regardless of the terminology, policies that aid in the acquisition, accumulation, control, or leveraging of financial assets are asset-building policies. Asset-building policies exist at the local, state, tribal, and federal level. Examples of asset-building policies in tribal communities are discussed later in this chapter and include Native Community Development Financial Institutions, the Earned Income Tax Credit, Individual Development Accounts and Child Development Accounts or Trust Accounts, and financial education programs.

Michael Sherraden, a social science researcher, was the first to advocate for social policies that promote saving and building assets as a wealth-building policy for low-income populations, as opposed to policies that provide only income support. In his book *Assets and the Poor*, Sherraden argues that accumulation of tangible financial assets should be the goal of any social welfare policy because of the potential financial assets have to lead to long-term well-being (Sherraden 1991). The presumption supporting asset-based policies is that "Asset accumulation and investment, rather than income and consumption, are the keys to exiting poverty" (Sherraden 1991, 294).

To date, policy makers have been slow to adopt asset-building policies as a welfare strategy for the poor, even though the United States has a long history of engaging in asset-building policies for the majority and the wealthy. The tax code is an example of a set of policies that has historically provided tax incentives to the upper and middle class who acquire and own assets (e.g., home ownership and business owner tax breaks). In contrast, the asset limits set by current social welfare policies have effectively prevented the poor from acquiring assets that could ultimately lead them out of poverty.

The definitions and frameworks related to assets and asset building have been largely based on Western models of asset development, like the ones mentioned above. However, they do not necessarily take into account the different priorities or values of tribal communities. Tribal perspectives on asset building and the historical, cultural, and political contexts of tribal communities are important to consider.

Federal Indian Policy and its Impact on Tribal Assets

While American Indian tribes are collectively the largest private land holders in the United States, they are some of the most economically disadvantaged. According to the 2010 US Census, the median household income for American Indians and Alaska Natives was $34,821, compared to $54,168 for White Non-Hispanic households (The Census Channel 2012). However, if one were to aggregate the reservation land of tribes in the lower 48 with Native lands in Alaska, the land mass would be so large that it would be the fourth largest state in the United States. Add to this land holding the presence and abundance of natural resources like timber, crop and grazing lands, gas, coal, and others and tribes should possess a great amount of power, wealth, and assets. However, given the history of federal Indian policy and the legal status of tribes as domestic dependent nations, this is not the case. Despite the fact that tribes own so many of these natural assets, they are still among the poorest communities in this country. This is due in great part to their limited control over these assets (Adamson et al. 2004, Hicks et al. 2005). In the United States, tribes have gone from periods of asset abundance (prior to colonization), to periods of asset stripping (Removal, Reservation, Assimilation, Relocation, and Termination Eras), to the current period of asset building (the Self-Determination Era). The tumultuous history of federal Indian policy has made it possible for an asset-rich population to be financially poor.

A Native Worldview of Assets and Asset Building

Saving money is not a new concept in American Indian communities. Historically, American Indian people worked, saved, and traded to meet their personal, family, and communal needs. Remnants of this practice exist today as American Indian cultures view budgeting, saving, and credit as each relates to the preservation and sustainability of communal and natural resources. Conversely, American cultures view budgeting, saving, and credit as each relates to acquiring material possessions and amassing individual wealth. One noteworthy distinction rooted in these perspectives is the difference between individual and communal assets. Research has shown that American Indian Peoples are not opposed to "individually" acquired assets (Hicks et al. 2005, Hertel et al. 2008, Finsel and Russ 2005, Lewis 2005). Yet anecdotally, American Indian community representatives have expressed concern about the potential loss of culture and communal spirit that could result from the development of, and tribal members' participation in, asset-building initiatives that are focused on the individual accumulation of wealth (CDFI Fund, 2001). This is a valid consideration when designing asset-building policies that will resonate in an American Indian context or tribal community.

In 1980, the First Nations Development Institute (FNDI) was founded to assist Native Peoples in the control and development of assets (First Nations Development Institute 2004). The principal belief behind the creation of FNDI was

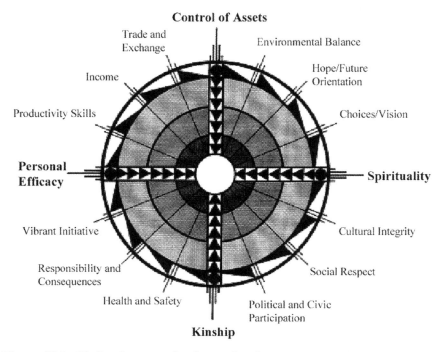

Control of Assets

Trade and Exchange

Environmental Balance

Income

Hope/Future Orientation

Productivity Skills

Choices/Vision

Personal Efficacy

Spirituality

Vibrant Initiative

Cultural Integrity

Responsibility and Consequences

Social Respect

Health and Safety

Political and Civic Participation

Kinship

Figure 13.1   Native framework of asset development
Note: Copyright 2004 by First Nations Development Institute.

that through the control and development of assets, tribes and Native communities would be able to better determine their economic futures in a way that best suited their priorities and cultures. Since that time, FNDI has been working closely and in partnership with Native communities and with regional Native coalitions to implement and enhance a range of asset-building programs and policies. The FNDI also serves as a grant maker to tribes and Native-based organizations, making funds available to Native communities interested in building their capacity for asset development.

Through these efforts, FNDI and their partner communities developed an asset-building framework that integrates the strengths of Native communities, traditional ways of knowing, and asset-building concepts that include both tangible and intangible assets as defined by Native people (see Figure 13.1).

According to this framework, the development of assets does matter, but only if linked to four key elements believed to be necessary to the process. These key elements are: 1) control of the assets at the individual, family, community, or tribal level in order to create wealth and foster communal well-being; 2) a responsibility to kinship connections with the belief that development in Native communities must be first and foremost about relationships and responsibility; 3) the development of personal efficacy which is the belief that one's skills and knowledge are valuable; and 4) a reverence to spirituality or the underlying value system of the culture. The elements included in this framework serve as a guide for policy and program development, but are neither prescriptive nor representative of all possible considerations for tribes trying to build assets in their own communities. In addition to these four key elements, the framework suggests 12 additional elements believed to be important outcomes associated with the asset-development process. For additional information on this model, see First Nations Development Institute (2004).

This framework was designed to encourage asset development by integrating elements that resonate with Native people. As a result, the framework not only focuses on building a sustainable economic future, but also strengthens the social and cultural values inherent in tribal communities. While the elements in the framework are not necessarily new or novel to tribal communities, their formal application through policy to development and control are relatively innovative. It is important to consider this framework as a model for asset-building policy, practices, and services in tribal communities.

Traditionally, tribal communities accumulated and shared assets collectively, either as families, clans, or tribes. However, many mainstream policies focus on the individual accumulation and consumption of assets for the benefit of an individual or household. Often, the well-being of the community is overlooked. In Native communities, this creates tension between the values of community and individuality. This tension has surfaced in discussions regarding asset-building initiatives taking place in Indian Country. At a 2004 convening to discuss culturally appropriate asset-building strategies for Indian Country at the George Warren Brown School of Social Work at Washington University in St Louis, Missouri, attendees felt strongly that outsiders should not make assumptions regarding how asset-building programs and demonstration projects should be designed in Indian Country, their intended effects, or how the study of the overall effectiveness should be undertaken.

Later, in 2005, a policy report titled *Asset Building in Tribal Communities: Generating Native Discussion and Practical Approaches* was released that examined six case studies of asset-building initiatives in Indian Country to identify common themes (see Hicks et al. 2005). Based on commonalities found across the case studies, the authors observed that successful asset-building initiatives take into consideration: 1) both the short-term and long-term accumulation of assets; 2) the sharing of accumulated assets in accordance with values of reciprocity; 3) a communal accumulation and sharing of assets; and 4) a broader definition of assets to include both tangible and intangible assets. The recommendation is a flexible approach to building assets that allows for not only individual asset building, but community asset building as well (Hicks et al. 2005). This dual focus appears throughout the literature regarding asset-building initiatives in Indian Country (Adamson 2003, Lewis 2005, Hicks et al. 2005) and is likely due to the communal structure, which still exists within tribal communities (First Nations Development Institute 2007, Hicks et al. 2005).

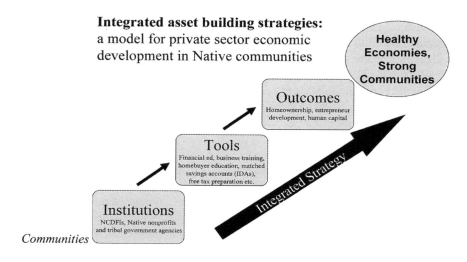

Figure 13.2   Model for integrated asset-building strategies for reservation-based communities
Note: Copyright 2006 by First Nations Development Institute.

In 2007, FNDI introduced a framework for building assets in tribal communities called the Integrated Asset Building Strategies Framework for reservation-based communities. The framework describes the long-term approach to asset building observed in Native communities that includes both tangible and intangible assets and addresses the challenges discussed above. For both tangible and intangible types of asset development, strategies that improve tribal communities' ability to control, retain, increase, utilize, leverage, and create desired assets are recommended (Adamson et al. 2004).

The Integrated Asset-Building Strategies Model may be found in Figure 13.2 (First Nations Development Institute 2007). According to the model, the foundation of all culturally appropriate asset-development initiatives in Indian Country is strong institutions. Institutions are the anchors that provide asset-related services to Native people. These institutions may include banks, credit unions, community development financial institutions (described later in the chapter), non-profit organizations, and tribal government entities. The next step in the model is tools. Tools are the services provided by the institutions and include a range of services such as education programs (e.g. first-time homebuyer education, financial education, business training) and financial products (e.g. IDAs, micro loans, savings accounts). These tools are used by tribal members to achieve certain desirable outcomes such as home ownership, business development, or increased human capital through post-secondary education attainment. Finally, the top right of the model illustrates that all of these components are necessary to build healthy tribal economies and stronger tribal communities (First Nations Development Institute 2007).

The model underscores the holistic approach to asset building which has been observed in tribal communities. Many Native institutions view their role as not only providing individual assistance to households and families, but contributing to a healthier, stronger, more stable tribal community (First Nations Development Institute 2007). Also apparent from the model is the notion that financially stable and well-informed Native individuals and families will contribute to the larger tribal community (First Nations Development Institute 2007). This model suggests asset-building strategies for tribal communities that are simply designed, with merely a product offering, will not work. Instead, the product may be more successful if imbedded within a trusted Native institution that understands its role in the provision of services to benefit individuals, families, and promote strong communities (First Nations Development Institute 2007).

Asset-Building Initiatives Taking Place in Indian Country

There are a number of tribally driven asset-building initiatives taking place in tribal communities. The following is a discussion of some successful asset-building policies.

Earned Income Tax Credit

The earned income tax credit (EITC), an income tax refund targeted to low-income households, may provide opportunities to build assets. The EITC is usually received in a lump sum and there are no restrictions on how it may be used. Although not originally designed as asset building, numerous studies indicate that EITC recipients are aware of and interested in building assets through the investment of EITC dollars (Johnson et al. 2004, Rhine et al. 2005, Romich and Weisner 2000, Smeeding et al. 2000). For this reason, an increasing number of tribes and reservation-based institutions are providing assistance to eligible families to claim their EITC.

Studies on how individuals utilize the EITC find that recipients invest in home ownership, automobile purchases or repairs, higher education, and small business development (Robles 2007, Smeeding et al. 2000). In a large study of Native EITC recipients ($N = 9,482$), just over a third of the households planned to use their EITC dollars for asset building, including education, home ownership, or to start/build a business (Wagner 2011). Smeeding et al. (2000) found that the majority of EITC recipients would not be able to fulfill these investment goals without the EITC. Linking tax refunds with savings mechanisms such as an Individual Development Account (IDA) is one possible vehicle that families may use (Beverly and Dailey 2003).

Case Study #1: Earned Income Tax Credit and Tax Preparation
The Alaska Business Development Center provides individual consulting to small business owners and commercial fishermen, including a volunteer Tax and Loan Program to help business owners comply with local, state, and federal taxes. Volunteer tax advisors travel from urban centers across the US to rural Alaskan communities where services are limited, to provide assistance at no charge. Another important service is the Personal Asset Growth Partnership, a matched savings program that provides an opportunity for participants to save their money for a home or small business. In addition to providing individual business owners and fishermen these much needed services, volunteers have an opportunity to learn about the people of rural Alaska, expanding their worldview, and participants are able to build and secure assets that match the cultural context in which they live. For more information about this program, visit www.abdc.org.

Native Community Development Financial Institutions

As noted earlier, institutions are critical to the success of asset building in tribal communities. Community development financial institutions (CDFIs), alternative financial institutions with community development as their primary mission, have led the way in this effort.

There are currently 71 certified Native CDFIs providing financial services in Indian Country (CDFI Fund 2009). Many of them are the sole financial institutions in the area, expanding access to credit and other financial products and services for Native community members. Typically, services offered through CDFIs have lower fees, and consumer qualifications are more lenient than banks, finance companies, or payday lenders. Native CDFIs also offer information and training on personal financial management, business development, and opportunities to build assets. Additionally, Native CDFIs are most often run by local people and services are based on culturally relevant principles that reflect the community they serve.

Case Study #2: Native Community Development Financial Institutions
Four Bands Community Fund, a certified Native CDFI, has grown to be the leading asset-building organization in Indian Country. Their mission is to help community members increase their financial capability through small business training and capital lending, along with entrepreneurship and financial education to both youth and adults. Four Bands' services have reached over 1,800 adults and 500 youth on the reservation. Programs and services "translate the tribe's traditional values of self-sufficiency, wise resource management, and a spirit of entrepreneurship" into practical applications that meet the needs of the tribal community today. For more information about Four Bands' efforts and success stories of their customers, visit www.fourbands.org.

Child Development Accounts

Child Development Accounts (CDAs), as originally envisioned by Sherraden in 1991, are a type of matched savings account given to children at birth that allow them to save for education, business development, or home ownership. It is believed that CDAs may have long-lasting economic, psychological, and social benefits affecting individuals, families, and communities (Sherraden and Stevens 2010). It is hypothesized that saving for education at a young age will change the way parents and caregivers think about education and the way they engage their child in learning (Zhan and Schreiner 2005). It may also change the expectation that children have for their own educational possibilities (Elliot 2007). Demonstration projects of CDAs include the I Can Save (ICS) program and the SEED for Oklahoma Kids (SEED OK) project (Gray et al. 2012). The SEED OK project includes a sample of American Indian study participants from across the state. Both projects explore aspirations and expectations for academic achievement associated with the presence of a college savings account.

Minors' accounts (or trust accounts) are a form of CDAs that are naturally occurring in Indian Country. For example, minors' accounts are savings accounts typically held by a tribe in trust for a tribal citizen, in this case a minor (Jorgensen and Morris 2010). Over half of federally recognized tribes have some form of minors' account. However, given the highly sensitive nature of minors' accounts and politically charged debates that surround tribal revenue redistribution policies, outcomes and lessons that may be applied to other tribal communities efforts to develop or sustain these types of accounts have not been fully examined (Jorgensen and Morris 2010).

Approximately 70 of the 225 tribes with gaming establishments make revenue distribution payments to minor citizens on a per capita basis (Jorgensen and Morris 2010). This represents only a minority of tribes. According to Jorgenson and Morris (2010), these accounts are similar to CDAs in the following ways:

- Accounts are established at birth for tribal citizens.
- Tribal government controls the accounts by making deposits directly into the accounts.
- Accounts are often held in trust for minor citizens.
- Account statements are sent regularly to parents or guardians of account holders.
- Access to accounts is limited for minor account holders, parents, or guardians until adulthood (18 years of age).
- Funds are paid directly to account holders at maturity (or when certain benchmarks are achieved).

While these accounts have a number of design features in common with CDAs, they differ in two distinct ways: universality and unrestricted use (Jorgensen and Morris 2010). Universality means that for tribes that include minors' accounts as part of a revenue distribution policy, accounts are available to all tribal citizens at birth (Jorgensen and Morris 2010). This practice underscores the commonly held belief that minors' accounts are not only a benefit for individual tribal citizens, but are also intended as a community-level benefit. These trust accounts are essentially asset-building policies that are culturally relevant and appropriate in tribal communities (Jorgenson and Morris 2010).

Unrestricted use supports the idea that individuals know how to best utilize their resources to improve their well-being. Currently, asset policy restricts use of accounts to education, entrepreneurship, and home ownership. However, the very idea of prescribed or restricted uses on these accounts has remnants of paternalism, which runs counter to tribal values of self-determination. There are compelling reasons to question the use of restricted accounts in Indian Country. Without a clear understanding of the values in tribal communities, it cannot be assumed that investments in education, entrepreneurship, and home ownership are the optimal assets for investment in Native individuals, families, and communities (Jorgenson and Morris 2010).

Table 13.1   Examples of minors' accounts in Indian country

Features	Tribal nation	Explanation of account
Minors' account established at birth	Tunica-Biloxi Tribe	Once a child born to a tribal member is enrolled as a tribal citizen, a trust account for the child is established following completion of a Trust Adoption Agreement.
Tribal government makes payments into the accounts	Eastern Band of Cherokee Indians	Revenue redistribution payments (also referred to as per capita payments) are made twice a year to minors. These funds are set aside in the Minors' Trust Fund until the minors become eligible to access the funds.
Funds held in trust	Confederated Tribes of Siletz Indians	Payments made to minor enrolled members are held in trust for the benefit of the minor until such time as he or she reaches the majority age.
Regular reports to account holders	Prairie Island Mdewakanton Dakota Community	Bank statements of funds in trust accounts for minors are made available monthly to the minor's legal guardian.
Limited or no access during accumulation period	Tulalip Tribes	Early withdrawal of funds is not permitted except if the minor has a terminal illness or can document a serious medical condition that will require long-term care.
Receipt of funds upon maturity or achievement of benchmark	Confederated Tribes of the Grand Ronde Community	The tribe holds funds in trust for each member until age 21; however, members who are 18 and have completed high school or received a GED may petition for an early withdrawal of their funds for purposes of education or a down payment on a home.

Note: This table was adapted from Jorgensen and Morris (2010).

Financial Education

Most of the asset-based policies presented in this chapter focus specifically on building tangible financial assets. As discussed earlier, intangible assets such as financial knowledge are also important to consider when developing asset-building policy and programs structures (Johnson and Sherraden 2007, Nyce 2005, Tennyson and Nguyen 2001, Sherraden 2008). Considering the increasingly challenging economic times and the complexity of financial service markets, consumers need to be knowledgeable so they can manage their finances effectively. Financial education has the potential to not only increase access to financial services and products but to empower individuals to better understand the risks and benefits of financial products and services, enabling them to make better decisions about their financial future.

Since the late 1990s, a growing interest in improving financial knowledge prompted at least half of the states in the US to adopt financial education policies that mandate personal finance instruction in high schools (Alexander 1989, NCEE 2011). In 2003, approximately 98 percent of US banks sponsored financial education programs, of which 72 percent targeted youth (Ginovsky 2003). Private sector organizations such as the National Council on Economic Education (NCEE), the Jump$tart Coalition, and the National Endowment for Financial Education (NEFE) have led development in this area (NCEE 2011, Jump$tart Coalition 2008). Investment in financial education is not exclusive to the US but has occurred across the world, including the United Kingdom, Canada, and Australia (Burgess 2003, Roy Morgan Research 2003, US Senate 2002). Research finds positive effects including increased knowledge and changes in financial behaviors in which individuals are more likely to plan for their financial future, engage in higher savings rates, and meet their financial goals (Bernheim et al. 2001, Hilgert et al. 2003).

The need for financial education is also evident in tribal communities where financial services are sparse, prior experiences with financial institutions have been negative or limited, and mainstream financial information is virtually non-existent. In recognition of these needs, the National Congress of Native Americans and the Department of Interior called for the development of financial education curricula for Native youth and adults to build personal financial skills among tribal members and develop future economic development leaders (NCAI and DOI 2007). Given this recommendation, financial education programs that serve children, youth, adults, and families are emerging in Indian Country (Malkin 2003). The types of programs that offer financial education vary and include primary schools, tribal colleges, housing offices, economic development programs, banks, mini-banks, credit unions, and community development organizations and financial institutions (Malkin 2003).

Proponents of increasing financial capability seek to provide individuals with both information and access to opportunities to increase their functioning in the economic world (Hilgert et al. 2003). People may obtain a basic level of understanding about financial concepts through parents, friends, school, or other more formal sources. However, experts now assert that if information and experience with financial institutions are linked, knowledge of available services and products will grow and a deeper understanding of financial choices will positively affect well-being (Zhan et al. 2006). Improved institutional structures that support financial planning and decision-making for Native American households are needed to ensure that these individuals are aware of financial opportunities, they know where to go for help, and have the information they need to make informed choices that may improve financial well-being (Lim et al. 2009, Sherraden 2008).

Case Study #3: Financial Education and Financial Capability
The Blackfeet Mini Bank, located in Browning, MT, was designed to introduce students in schools to the banking experience and to encourage students to save and effectively manage their money. Students can open a savings account with a deposit of $3.00. The actual account is a savings account at Native American Bank, the partner bank. There is also a student board responsible for operations of the school mini bank. This scaled-down bank within the school offers students financial education as well as a physical location where they can open savings accounts with an actual banking institution. Mini banks can serve as the "institution" necessary for building financial capability in tribal communities. For more information, see www.nacdc.org/minibank.html.

Conclusion

Asset building has the potential to balance economic, social, environmental, and cultural imperatives if tribes are provided with the necessary tools and resources. Given the values and priorities of tribal communities, the definition of assets should include both tangible and intangible assets. Approaches to asset building should be holistic, with an appreciation of the relationships between social, economic, political, and natural systems. The tribal community should provide the context that determines what types of assets should be developed and the best strategies for implementation. Strategies should be built on local, existing institutions and benefit the larger community, not just individuals. Furthermore, outcomes of these efforts should be clearly communicated to the individual, community, and tribal government levels.

Asset building is a long-term process that requires tangible and intangible investments by tribal members. First, tribes must evaluate asset needs in their community. Then, with community input, develop culturally relevant strategies to best meet the needs of Native families and communities. For example, current asset-building programs do not address traditional beliefs about the importance of reciprocity among tribal members or the importance of communal assets. In time, and with the right policy and program framework, asset-building efforts have the potential to help tribes reclaim assets previously stripped from their control, maintain such assets, and build a stronger foundation for the social and economic well-being of their community.

References

Adamson, R. 2003. Land rich, dirt poor: The story of Indian assets. *Native Americas*, Summer, 26–37.

Adamson, R., Black, S., and Dewees, S. 2004. *Asset Building in Native Communities: An Asset Building Framework.* Fredricksburg, VA: First Nations Development Institute.

Alexander, R.J. 1989. *State Consumer Education Manual.* Denver, CO: Education Commission of the States.

Bernheim, B., Garrett, D., and Maki, D. 2001. Education and saving: The long-term effects of high school financial curriculum mandates. *Journal of Public Economics*, 80, 435–65.

Beverly, S. and Dailey, C. 2003. *Using Tax Refunds to Promote Asset Building in Low-income Households: Program and Policy Options.* Policy Report. St Louis, MO: Center for Social Development at Washington University in St Louis.

Burgess, K. 2003. FSA to tackle financial literacy. *FT Money*, 30, 26.

CDFI Fund 2009. Financing Native leaders for tomorrow: Native initiatives strategic plan 2009–2014. Washington, DC: The Department of the Treasury. Retrieved September 14, 2013 from http://www.cdfifund.gov/docs/2009/naca/ Native%20American%20Strategic%20Plan.pdf.

Community Development Financial Institutions (CDFI) Fund 2001. *The Report of the Native American Lending Study.* Retrieved September 14, 2013 from http://www.cdfifund.gov/docs/2001_nacta_lending_study.pdf.

Elliott, W. 2007. *Specifying Children's Educational Expectations: The Potential Impact of Institutions.* CSD Working Paper 07-17. St Louis, MO: Washington University, Center for Social Development.

Finsel, C. and Russ, J. 2005. *Exploration and Use of Individual Development Accounts by Three American Indian Tribes in Oregon.* Policy Report. St Louis, MO: Center for Social Development at Washington University in St Louis.

First Nations Development Institute 2004. *Asset Building in Native Communities: An Asset Building Framework.* Fredricksburg, VA: First Nations Development Institute.

First Nations Development Institute 2007. *Integrated Asset Building Strategies for Reservation-Based Communities: A 27 Year Retrospective of First Nations Development Institute.* Fredricksburg, VA: First Nations Development Institute.

Ginovsky, J. 2003. Financial literacy: The case for banker involvement. *ABA Bankers News*, 11(14), 1–2.

Gray, K., Clancy, M., Sherraden, M.S., et al. 2012. *Interviews with mothers of young children in the SEED for Oklahoma Kids college savings experiment* (CSD Research Report No. 12-53). St Louis, MO: Washington University, Center for Social Development.

Hertel, A.L., Wagner, K., Phillips, J., et al. 2008. *Dialogues on Assets in Native Communities: Recording a Native Perspective on the Definition and Benefits of Retaining and Rebuilding Assets.* CSD-Buder Report 08-19. St Louis, MO: Washington University, Center for Social Development.

Hicks, S., Edwards, K., Dennis, M.K., and Finsel, C. 2005. *Asset Building in Tribal Communities: Generating Native Discussion and Practical Approaches.* Policy Report. St Louis, MO: Center for Social Development.

Hilgert, M., Hogarth, J., and Beverly, S. 2003. Household financial management: The connection between knowledge and behavior. *Federal Reserve Bulletin*, July 2003.

Johnson, D., Parker, J., and Souleles, N. 2004. *Household Expenditure and the Income Tax Rebates of 2001.* Discussion Paper #231. Woodrow Wilson School of Public and International Affairs, Princeton University.

Johnson, E. and Sherraden, M.S. 2007. From financial literacy to financial capability among youth. *Journal of Sociology and Social Welfare*, 34, 119–45.

Jorgensen, M. and Morris, P. 2010. Tribal experience with children's accounts. *Children and Youth Services Review*, 32, 1528–37.

Jump$tart Coalition 2008. *The Financial Literacy of Young American Adults: Results of the 2008 National Jump$tart Coalition Survey of High School Seniors.* Retrieved April 5, 2009, from http://www.jumpstartcoalition.org/assets/files/2008SurveyBook.pdf.

Lewis, J. 2005. *Building Tribal Economies: Linking Asset-building Strategies.* Report 05-23. St Louis, MO: Center for Social Development.

Lim, Y., Livermore, M., and Davis, B.C. 2009. Knowledge of the earned income tax credit and financial behaviors among low- and moderate-income consumers. *Journal of Consumer Education*, 26, 58–69.

Malkin, J. 2003. *Financial Education in Native Communities: A Briefing Paper.* June. Native American Financial Literacy Coalition.

Nam, Y., Huang, J., and Sherraden, M. 2008. *Assets, Poverty, and Public Policy: Challenges in Definitions and Measurement.* Urban Institute Poor Finances Series. Washington, DC: Urban Institute.

National Congress of Native Americans (NCAI) and the Department of Interior (DOI) 2007. *Developing Tribal Economies to Create Healthy, Sustainable, and Culturally Vibrant Communities.* Native American Economic Policy Report produced by NCAI and DOI. Retrieved from http://www.ncai.org/resources/ncai-publications/native-american-economic-policy-report.pdf.

National Council on Economic Education (NCEE) 2011. *Survey of the States: Economic and Personal Finance Education in our Nation's Schools in 2011.* Retrieved from http://www.councilforeconed.org/wp/wp-content/uploads/2011/11/2011-Survey-ofthe-States.pdf.

Nyce, S. 2005. *The Importance of Financial Communication for Participation Rates and Contribution Levels in 401(k) Plans*. Philadelphia, PA: University of Pennsylvania, Wharton School, Pension Research Council.

Rhine, S., Su, S., Osaki, Y., and Lee, S. 2005. *Householder Response to the Earned Income Tax Credit: A Path of Sustenance or Road to Asset Building*. Report of the Federal Reserve Bank of New York.

Robles, B. 2007. Tax refunds and micro-businesses: Expanding family and community wealth building in the Borderlands. *The ANNALS of the American Academy of Political and Social Science*, 613(1), 178–91.

Romich, J. and Weisner, T. 2000. How families view and use the EITC: Advance payment versus lump sum delivery. *National Tax Journal*, 4(2), 1245–65.

Sherraden, M. 1991. *Assets and the Poor: A New American Welfare Policy*. Armonk, NY: M.E. Sharpe.

Sherraden, M. 2008. *IDAs and Asset Building Policy: Lessons and Directions*. CSD Working Paper 08-12. St Louis, MO: Washington University, Center for Social Development.

Sherraden, M. and Stevens, J. (eds). 2010. *Lessons from SEED: A National Demonstration of Child Development Accounts*. St Louis, MO: Washington University, Center for Social Development.

Smeeding, T., Ross, K., and O'Connor, M. 2000. The EITC: Expectation, knowledge, use, and economic and social mobility. *National Tax Journal*, 53(4), 1187–92.

Tennyson, S. and Nguyen, C. 2001. State curriculum mandates and student knowledge of personal finance. *Journal of Consumer Affairs*, 35(2), 241–62.

The Census Channel 2012. Median household and individual income – Asian Americans top the list. Retrieved June 15, 2012, from http://censuschannel. net/cc/news/2010-median-household-individual-income-asian-americans-top-the-list-1330.

US Senate 2002. *Hearings on the State of Financial Literacy and Education in America*. Committee on Banking, Housing, and Urban Affairs, http://www. senate.gov.

Wagner, K. 2011. The Earned Income Tax Credit (EITC) and financial capability in Native households. Dissertation research.

Zhan, M., Anderson, S.G., and Scott, J. 2006. Financial knowledge of the low-income population: Effects of a financial education program. *Journal of Sociology and Social Welfare*, 33(1), 53–74.

Zhan, M. and Schreiner, M. 2005. Saving for post-secondary education in Individual Development Accounts. *Journal of Sociology & Social Welfare*, 32(3), 139–63.

Chapter 14

Mosquito Advocacy: Change Promotion Strategies for Small Groups with Big Ideas

Cindy Blackstock

First Nations children are dramatically over-represented in the Canadian child welfare system, and there is significant documentation that inequities in child welfare funding on reserves are a contributing factor. Traditional public policy change strategies were tried for over a decade, but Canada failed to implement solutions jointly developed with First Nations (McDonald and Ladd 2000, Loxley et al. 2005), or to fully implement recommendations made by the Auditor General of Canada (2008). First Nations children and their families continued to suffer, and there was little hope that continued discussions with Canada would yield substantive progress. In 2007, the First Nations Child and Family Caring Society of Canada (the Caring Society, a small four-person organization working for First Nations children) and the Assembly of First Nations filed a human rights case against the Canadian Government alleging that long-standing funding inequities in child welfare amounted to racial discrimination against First Nations children (Blackstock 2011). When the case was filed, about 20 supporters attended a news conference. Five years later, court rooms were overrun with people coming to watch the case, over 10,000 people and organizations from across the world were following the case online, and thousands of Canadian children were marching on Canadian legislatures and parliament demanding equity. The success was achieved through the development, implementation, and refinement of mosquito advocacy. Mosquito advocacy was developed at the Caring Society because of the urgent need for holistic peaceful public policy tools that equip small groups to effectively take on the big guys (in this case government) to advocate for evidence-based policy in change-resistant environments. Although existing literature provided some guidance on individual strategies and considerations, there was no comprehensive road map for advancing public policy with resistant colonial-based governments.

Amongst First Nations, the tiny mosquito has a legendary ability to tackle larger animals and people (Simpson 2010, *Manitoba Pageant* 1962). The mosquito advocacy approach leverages evidence-based solutions grounded in peaceful First Nations values, and is inspired by the following mosquito-like characteristics: 1) small and agile; 2) goal oriented; 3) infectious; 4) buzzing; 5) swarming; and 6) biting (using peaceful non-voluntary change techniques). This chapter begins by describing the need for peaceful alternatives to the "talking with government" approach to public policy, before describing how long-standing inequities in First

Nations child welfare led to the development of the mosquito advocacy approach. The next section addresses how peaceful values, proper risk assessment, and evidence-based public policy solutions shape mosquito advocacy strategies and implementation. Finally, implications for mosquito advocacy in other sectors and movements are discussed.

The Emergence of Mosquito Advocacy

Flawed and inequitable federal government policies are at the headwaters of systemic poverty, poor housing, and inequitable service access on First Nations reserves, undermining the safety and well-being of children. While other groups are also influenced by government agendas, First Nations are more deeply pressured because of the Canadian government's central role in colonialism (Royal Commission on Aboriginal Peoples 1996), the Indian Act, funding and regulation of First Nations communities (Auditor General of Canada 2008, 2011), and troubled treaty and self-government relationships (Royal Commission on Aboriginal Peoples 1996).

Restrictions placed on First Nations child and family service agencies by the Federal Government contribute to how these multiple pressures affect First Nations citizens. First Nations child and family service agencies provide child welfare services to children, young people, and families residing on First Nations reserves. The federal government exercises control over the agencies by, amongst other requirements, obliging the agencies to follow provincial/territorial child welfare laws in lieu of traditional forms of governance. The federal government provides funding to First Nations child and family service agencies while provincial/ territorial governments fund the same services off reserves.

Research indicates that First Nations child and family service agencies serve a higher-needs population (Sinha et al. 2011) with inequitable funding from the federal government. The Auditor General of Canada (2008) estimates that First Nations children are six to eight times more likely to be placed in child welfare care than other children. The factors contributing to the dramatic over-representation are poverty, poor housing, and substance misuse (Blackstock 2003, Trocmé et al. 2004). There are promising culturally based solutions available to mediate these factors, but First Nations child and family service agencies are constrained by provincial/territorial laws (Harris-Short 2012) and inequitable and flawed federal government funding regimes (McDonald and Ladd 2000, Loxley et al. 2005, Auditor General of Canada 2008, 2011, Standing Committee on Public Accounts 2009).

For over 10 years, the Assembly of First Nations (AFN), the national political organization representing First Nations in Canada, worked with the federal government to document inequities in child and family services funding on reserves and to propose solutions (Loxley et al. 2005), but the federal government failed to implement the needed changes. As talks continued between AFN and the federal government, Canada's own data showed that the numbers of First Nations children going into care between 1995 and 2001 rose a shocking 71.5 percent (McKenzie 2002). By 2006, it was clear to First Nations that talking with the government in the absence of meaningful, measurable progress at the community level had devastating implications for children (Blackstock 2011). In response, change strategies were developed that go beyond relying on the federal government's voluntary change motivation. I term these peaceful strategies "non-voluntary advocacy." A new era of First Nations child rights activism was about to emerge; this activism moved from the negotiating table with the government to public education, public engagement, and the Courts. The consequences for the Assembly of First Nations and the Caring Society would be vast. A key question facing both organizations was how they could effectively explore non-voluntary advocacy options with Canada's federal government and still operate. Most First Nations and national First Nations organizations are small scale, and many receive the majority of their funding from the federal government. At the time, this was certainly the case for the Assembly of First Nations. The Caring Society had a more diversified funding base, but still received federal funding. Implementing non-voluntary advocacy would test the limits of what both organizations were prepared to risk for the people they served, and the willingness of a democratically elected government to fund evidence-based dissent.

As a political organization, the Assembly of First Nations utilized political and legal processes to advance the complaint. As a non-political co-complainant, the Caring Society needed effective and peaceful non-voluntary advocacy options suited for this particular change context: 1) a small organization tackling a large and powerful one; 2) a largely misinformed public and Parliament whose views of First Nations are influenced by colonialism; and 3) probable funding cuts from governments who disagreed with our approaches could mean resource constraints or even closure of the Caring Society. A review of the literature on social movements, public policy, and activism revealed inspirational ideas (Bryce 1922, Lakoff 2004, Needleman 2007, Kidder 2003), but no road map. Innovation was required. The mosquito emerged as a premium example of where something very small, but enthusiastic, effectively challenges large and resistant entities. Mosquitoes are goal orientated, infectious, and persistent. They swarm and come from all directions, and some will bite, leaving a welt that itches for days as a lasting reminder of its presence. Experimentation with these strategies, and consultation with leading First Nations and non-Aboriginal advocates, emboldened the Caring Society to apply mosquito advocacy, and led to its application across disciplines to address inequities in education and health. The following section describes mosquito advocacy in action, using the funding inequities in First Nations child and family services as a case study.

The Advantage of being Small

Large organizations, particularly governments, often organize themselves into bureaucracies. Policies are often decided by those at the top of the organization, and the role of the other members is to implement the goals and protect those at the top from risks, such as financial losses, or losses in public confidence. They leverage their significant public influence and human and financial resources to set and implement public policy.

The mosquito's traits are instructive for small organizations or groups taking on large organizations. The mosquito is extremely small, and yet it regularly takes on much larger species and wins. The mosquito's small size means it is much more agile and quicker than its larger opponent. It can innovate and adapt to new environments much faster than a larger species that requires more resources to survive. There is no way for small groups to match the characteristics of large organizations in public policy advocacy. The real opportunity is to leverage the characteristic of being small. What small organizations lack in financial and human resources, they often make up for in their grassroots appeal, creativity, and enthusiasm. Being small means that when new situations arise, the organization can make decisions and act quickly, outpacing the lumbering bureaucratic processes of government. Additionally, small groups have less to lose than their larger opponents, and small groups acting in moral and ethical ways against a large opponent tend to evoke more public sympathy.

A case known as the "McLibel" case is instructive for small groups challenging the policies and practices of large organizations (Vidal 1997). In England, Dave Morris, a postal worker, and Helen Steel, a gardener, started handing out pamphlets arguing, among other things, that McDonald's Corporation had unfair labor practices and was contributing to environmental degradation (BBC 2005). McDonald's filed a legal action, claiming damages for libel, and thereby initiating the longest legal case in British history (Vidal 1997). Public sympathy and attention quickly mounted in Dave and Helen's favor, as images of these grassroots citizens defending themselves in court with their home-made signs against a plethora of well-paid corporate lawyers and executives filled newspapers and television screens. McDonald's mounted legal and public relations strategies to thwart the case and deplete the defendants' resources. The strategies backfired. As McDonald's was spending millions of pounds on its legal costs and generating a public relations fiasco, Dave and Helen were defending themselves, so had no legal costs, and were enjoying growing public support (Vidal 1997). Although McDonald's won the legal case, the David and Goliath nature of the battle created a public relations nightmare for them. The public was so enraged that when the Court found against Dave and Helen (in some, but not all respects), and ordered them to pay financial damages, McDonald's quickly announced they would not collect (Vidal 1997).

Dave and Helen were successful precisely because of their small grassroots approach. From the outset, they understood that the public was in the best position to motivate McDonald's to change its policies, since McDonald's depended on consumers to buy its products and keep it in business. They framed their message in ways the public could relate to, and then skillfully positioned their lack of resources against the much bigger McDonald's, securing public support and putting enormous pressure on the corporation. Additionally, even though McDonald's had a lot more to spend, Dave and Helen understood that they also had a lot more to lose. Large organizations like corporations or governments rely on the public to buy products/services or vote for them. Their large size means that they get noticed in the press for things they do right and things they do wrong. The last thing they want is to be held accountable by a couple of people who have nothing to lose, and whose arguments and character have a lot of public appeal.

Likewise, the Caring Society is a four-person organization operating on an annual budget of less than $400,000, whereas Canada has over a quarter of a million employees and a budget in the trillions. We leverage our small size in public relations and in our ability to respond quickly and creatively to new situations. For example, when each court date occurs, we invite hundreds of people, particularly children, to watch Canada making its arguments against the equitable treatment of children. As in the "McLibel" case, public sympathy has overwhelmingly favored the cause represented by the small, grassroots organization: in our case, overwhelmingly in favor of equity for First Nations.

In my view, small, persistent groups bound by peaceful values and evidence-based ideas are the most potent proponents of public policy change with large organizations. The best thing for small groups to do in a policy conflict with larger organizations is to act like a mosquito: embrace being small by leveraging creativity, grassroots appeal, lower risk exposure, and an ability to make decisions quickly.

Peaceful Values Matter

Successful policy-change movements create broad-based appeal by embedding policy change objectives and strategies in deeply held human values such as fairness, justice, democracy, and honesty, and by expressing these values in peaceful ways. The public credibility of the movement will depend on the coherence between the movement's values, and the actions of everyone acting in the name of the movement.

In an ideal world, all public policy players would play fair, but the reality is quite different. It is not unusual for governments to use unfair and aggressive tactics to derail policy change advocates who get in their way. The best response to these tactics is to make them public and respond with grace and respect. Appealing to the public when a change movement comes under attack will only work if the movement itself is working in accordance with public values. The old saying "people in glass houses should not throw stones" applies in public policy change, just as it does in life.

Those committed to changing public policy in the face of strong resistance by powerful and well-funded organizations must be willing to take personal and professional risks. They must honestly assess risks for themselves and, more importantly, for the movement. They must also assess the risks to the government or corporation that has the power to change the policy. Kidder (2003) sets out two forms of courage that help inform personal and organizational risk analysis: physical courage and moral courage. Whereas physical courage is typically rewarded in society, moral courage is often punished and framed as insubordination, unpatriotic, blowing the whistle, or rocking the boat. Moral courage is the act of standing up for your values in risky situations. Kidder (2003) argues that people are more likely to be morally courageous when there is a direct benefit for themselves or others close to them. Evaluating the moral courage of the movement and the organizations/individuals associated with it informs what change strategies can be implemented. Thinking back on "McLibel," it is clear that Helen and Dave were not only morally courageous, but also had the endurance to put up with the long-term nature of the resistance. While McDonald's also presented long-term resistance, most would agree that the values they were upholding had more to do with managing their corporate image than upholding moral courage or the public good (Vidal 1997).

The Caring Society has also had to be morally coherent and courageous in the face of significant pushback from the Canadian Government in the child welfare human rights case. The Caring Society survived the loss of federal funding and other pushback strategies by the federal government, such as their intense monitoring of my (the Director's) public and personal life in an effort to find "other motives" for the child welfare case (Aboriginal Affairs and Northern Development Canada 2011). Our strict adherence to our strong values, and our willingness to publicize the government's tactics, and to not reciprocate in kind, were major factors in our survival.

Conflict of interest guidelines are an important part of organizational value coherence. While organizations, like people, tend to take active roles in public policy change because the issue appeals to them, it is important to avoid making self-interest a leading motivation for public policy change. For example, if the Caring Society is successful in the child welfare human rights case, other than the repayment of legal fees, there will be no financial benefits to the organization—all the funds will go to help address the inequity for the children. The Caring Society is an important policy advocate, but we are not the beneficiaries; this avoids problems with conflict of interest.

While not all policy change movements will encounter the significant resistance experienced in the "McLibel" or Caring Society cases, the success of all movements is dependent on value coherence, a conscious assessment of risk, and the moral courage to endure pushback with grace and respect.

The First Domino Solution

Mosquito-based advocacy is anchored in evidence-based solutions termed "first domino" solutions. First domino solutions are not intended to solve all the problems, but rather to make solving the problems possible. For example, First Nations children face many risk factors, and a small organization like the Caring Society could spend time trying to develop evidence-based solutions to each. However, this approach would dramatically exceed our capacity and resources. Instead, we define the first domino solutions as making equitable, evidence-based and culturally based resources available to First Nations communities to implement their own best solutions for children. In the child welfare case, the appeal for culturally based and equitable funding is grounded in good research (Trocmé et al. 2004), joint reports with government (McDonald and Ladd 2000, Loxley et al. 2005), and ongoing consultations with First Nations.

Before initiating a change action, responsible advocates must conduct a thorough review of the literature, consult with experts and intended movement beneficiaries, and thoughtfully consider contrary positions to better understand the problem and best determine the specific courses of action. If research is not available, competent researchers should be engaged. It is also highly valuable to have the research peer-reviewed, and to have it independently assessed by watchdogs like the Auditor General, legislative committees, and leading experts and organizations in the field.

Notice that this section focuses on *the* first domino solution and not *a* first domino problem. The reason for this is that it is essential that policy advocates share in the responsibility to credibly document policy problems, create solutions, and to try to work with governments and others to address the issue. Moreover, the public engagement is much easier when you are asking people to stand *for* something versus *against* something. Having identified the first domino solution, the next step is to make it understandable to the wide variety of partners you will need to engage in your mosquito advocacy swarm.

Infectious Message: Framing the Problem and Solution

A movement "going viral" in mosquito advocacy involves framing the first domino solution in a way that is easy for both experts in your field and the public to understand and relate to. A basic understanding of linguistics is useful in this regard. Lakoff (2004) argues that people organize language based on deep cognitive frames grounded in fundamental national values and social structures. Social movement leaders such as Gandhi, King, and Mandela embedded their messages in concepts of freedom, fairness, and justice. The fact that these values were already widely shared amongst the populations in each country gave their messages an infectious quality, and made it difficult for opponents to argue against.

Lakoff (2004) also suggests staying away from using the language of the opposing side, as you can actually reinforce their message by arguing against it. The title of Lakoff's (2004) book, *Don't Think of an Elephant*, takes its name from the idiom "name an animal, but don't think of an elephant." By mentioning the elephant, the speaker makes thinking of other options very difficult. In the social justice field, groups often make the mistake of centering their communications materials on the language of incoming governments to make their proposals more appealing. Progressive social movements should develop their own messaging framed by deeply held national values.

Jordan's Principle is an example of how the Caring Society put Lakoff's work into action. First Nations children are often denied, or delayed receipt of, services available to other children because the federal and provincial/territorial governments constantly battle over who is responsible for paying for services on reserves. Government documents frame this as a jurisdictional issue rooted in confusion about the division of powers between Federal and Provincial governments regarding service delivery. Successive governments have avoided addressing the problem by framing it in ways that make the issue difficult to understand, and by disregarding the impacts on children. The Caring Society reframed this issue to demonstrate the impacts on children by showing how the Government's jurisdictional squabbles affected the life of one child in particular.

Jordan River Anderson, namesake of Jordan's Principle, was from Norway House Cree Nation, and he spent over two years unnecessarily in a hospital waiting for the Province of Manitoba and the federal government to resolve a payment dispute relating to his at-home care. Tragically, Jordan died before the dispute was resolved. By simplifying and personalizing the problem, and by proposing a solution, Jordan's Principle created a message that centers on social justice, and provides a clear framework for resolving the issue. Jordan's Principle says that when a government service is available to all other children and a jurisdictional dispute arises, the government of first contact pays for the service and then argues about payment as a secondary concern (Blackstock 2011).

This principle was unanimously supported in Canada's House of Commons on December 12, 2007 (Aboriginal Affairs and Northern Development Canada 2007). Canadian values of fairness and equality, and a general disdain for government red tape, underlie the framing of Jordan's Principle. It is also important to note that Jordan's Principle proposes a simple solution that resolves the problem for the child. Jordan's Principle is easy to understand and for Canadians to embrace. We provide an opportunity for people of all ages and organizations to learn more and express support for Jordan's Principle in an online statement of support at www.jordansprinciple.ca. We have found it important to not only heighten awareness of the problems, but also to actively engage Canadians in cost-free ways to advance the solutions. The online statement is a public display of the breadth and depth of support for Jordan's Principle, making it difficult for the government to sideline the issue as a special-interest concern.

The Buzz: Make Beautiful Noise and Choose an Effective Spokesperson

One of the most effective strategies mosquitoes use is making that irritating sound. Social activists need to do the same thing, and make sure it is as constant as possible; but the sound must be credible, evidence-based, and grounded in peaceful values and actions. Storytelling is an excellent way to deliver messages, but the stories must be relevant and fact-based. If using multiple stories, they must build on one another to contribute to the main argument. In other work, I have argued that less is more when it comes to public speaking (Blackstock 2009), and it is important to pay attention to the audience and speaking forum. It is also crucial to map out key dates and current events that coincide with the goal of the movement; this helps to create an environment favorable to the advocacy message. A favorable environment is also nurtured by working collaboratively with partners to stage communications strategies that keep the message in the public eye as much as possible.

Identifying a skilled spokesperson for the movement is essential. It is hard to imagine the African-American civil rights movement without Dr Martin Luther King Jr.'s eloquence and leadership at the center. It is the same with the anti-apartheid movement in South Africa led by Mandela, and Gandhi's emancipation movement in India. In my view, long-term effective social movements need at least one spokesperson and leader who is an eloquent and credible public figure. Choosing this person or persons carefully is essential. The person should have a natural passion for the issue, provide excellent leadership, be analytical, possess great communication skills, live their life by the values of the movement, be seen as credible, have humility, and be courageous. This person will likely become the lightning rod for any resistance, and it is essential, therefore, that they be above reproach and be willing to accept risks. This may sound like a difficult task, but in most small groups there are usually one or more people who can speak clearly, credibly, and passionately about the policy issue.

Great orators help instruct the rest of us about how to think carefully about the key message we want an audience to walk away with. They research the issue, giving due consideration to possible rebuttals from opposing sides. This promotes accountability and credibility. Orators should not avoid confronting legitimate issues contrary to their message (Cuomo 1993). The message and research are then put into a speaker's equivalent of a storyboard: an introduction to the key message; evidence framed in deep national values that builds the argument; consideration/ rebuttal to contrary opinion; and a summary of the key message and what audience members can do to help (Blackstock 2009). This type of thinking is also helpful for preparing small groups to engage others to promote the first domino solution in what is termed "swarming" in the mosquito advocacy approach.

Swarming: A Role for Peoples of Every Age and Income Level

Many non-governmental organizations (NGOs) target the wealthy for fund-raising and influence purposes. The Caring Society does the opposite. All of our campaigns are geared so that persons of low income are respected, and engaged as valued actors in building a better Canada by addressing the inequities faced by First Nations children. In our early history, the Caring Society made the mistake of doing public addresses to raise awareness of the problems facing First Nations children, and we failed to give people something specific, cost free, and meaningful they could do to help. At the time, our suggestions were broad (build relationships with local First Nations), time consuming (learn more about Aboriginal Peoples), age limiting (official petitions), and cost-ridden (donations). These created barriers for participation, and also did little to improve the situation of First Nations children. Today, we have seven free ways for caring people of all ages and organizations to make a difference in less than two minutes. Signing on to Jordan's Principle is one example. Coupling our public education with these seven easy and cost-free ways to engage all peoples has substantially improved the level of impact of our efforts. Public support for the campaigns has increased significantly. Additionally, we found that these simple, cost-free entry points make it easier for non-Aboriginal Canadians to break through the widely held stereotype that engaging with Aboriginal Peoples is complex and time consuming.

Mechanisms for encouraging engagement can also be inexpensive. For example, the Caring Society has set up a number of websites to provide information and opportunities to express support, and costs are minimal for the organization. Ongoing redesign and printing of public materials is avoided by keeping websites up to date, and by limiting public relations printed materials to the campaign name and URL.

Act Like Mosquitoes: Come from All Directions

Too often, social activists pursue only one strategy, making it easier for the opposition to quash the movement. The mosquito shows us that engaging multiple partners and multiple approaches creates a more effective social change climate. In order for partner engagement to be successful, sustainable, and growing, it is vital that partners are provided with the full evidence base so they can independently evaluate it and make an informed decision to engage in the change movement. Another vital component to respectful partner engagement is to make it easy and affordable for partners to integrate the movement goals into their core activities. The Caring Society leverages the significant evidence of the inequities for First Nations children by engaging other NGOs, professional organizations, and the media to write about the issues and promote awareness and engagement of their networks. In order to facilitate this, the Caring Society has a resource-rich website and provides partners with free printed and electronic materials with the campaign names and URLs. For example, our partners often include campaign bookmarks in conference delegate bags or distribute campaign information on their websites, social networking sites, newsletters, or e-broadcasts.

Identifying key organizations to strategically engage in the change effort is an important consideration. The Caring Society has an ethical screen for partners and donors, and we vet for complementary value sets and aims. Whilst the Caring Society welcomes all ethically aligned organizations to join the movement, the practical reality is that some organizations and people have more influence than others. Strategic identification of powerful people and organizations to invite into the movement is an important element of any social change movement. Unexpected allies are particularly useful. In any field, there are a series of predictable actors who are usually engaged in change. The engagement of unexpected allies surprises the opposing side, and broadens the base of the movement. For example, the Caring Society is honored to have a number of non-child-focused NGOs and labor movement activists supporting its campaign, as well as influential businesses across sectors.

To Bite or Not to Bite:
The Role of Peaceful Non-Voluntary Advocacy Strategies

Voluntary evidence-based solution implementation, in cooperation with the institutions or actors holding the power to create positive change, such as governments, is ideal, but not always possible. After voluntary change actions have been exhausted, peaceful, non-voluntary change strategies (the bite) come into play. It is important to note that voluntary and non-voluntary change actions are not necessarily mutually exclusive. In fact, some change actions begin as voluntary (e.g., meeting with government to develop solutions to the problem) whilst laying track for non-voluntary strategies (e.g., legal action) if needed. For example, engaging in joint solution building with the government demonstrates good will and, if progress is not made, it can also demonstrate to the Courts that the government clearly knew about the problem and its associated public harms, collaborated in solution development, and did little or nothing to rectify the problem. The decision of whether to bite (engage in advocacy that does not rely on the voluntary action of the opposing side) should be informed by the harms related to inaction, the exhaustion of voluntary efforts, and the respective risk thresholds of the activist and the opposing side. Threatening non-voluntary strategies and not following through diminishes credibility, as does anything associated with violence or the degradation of other people or groups. Effective non-voluntary change strategies simultaneously uplift movement beneficiaries and society as a whole. For example, Martin Luther King's civil rights movement clearly advanced the freedom and equality rights of African American peoples, but it also breathed life into fundamental American values, enriching the country as a whole.

The Caring Society and Assembly of First Nations' child welfare human rights case against the Government of Canada is an example of a "biting" strategy nested in other components of mosquito advocacy. The complaint alleged that the government racially discriminates against First Nations children by providing less funding, and therefore less child welfare benefits, to children on reserves. The legal action was, and continues to be, complemented by a public education and engagement campaign called "I am a witness." This campaign involved creating a website (www.fnwitness.ca) where the legal documents of all parties are posted along with relevant reports and news articles. The website is augmented with social media, such as an "I am a witness" Facebook page and a Twitter feed, which share breaking news and developments on the case. Individuals of all ages and organizations are then invited to commit to follow (witness) the case online and attend the legal proceedings in person, before making up their own minds as to whether Canada is treating First Nations children fairly.

The "I am a witness" campaign integrates all of the key elements of mosquito advocacy. As noted earlier, there is substantial evidence of the inequality, and several evidence-based solutions exist to address the problem. The first domino solution is to ensure the Government of Canada provides First Nations children and families culturally based resource equity to care for their children. The infectious framing of the message is based on "giving First Nations children the same chance to grow up safely at home as other Canadians." We invite individuals and organizations into the swarm by providing free mechanisms for learning and engagement such as the "I am a witness" campaign and legal case hearings. As noted earlier, when the case was filed in 2007 a handful of supporters attended the news conference; but now, with the aid of mosquito advocacy, there are now over 10,500 individuals and organizations witnessing the child welfare case, making it the most formally followed legal action in Canadian history. Given the growing number of people (particularly children and youth) and media attending the ongoing hearings, the hearings have to be held in larger and larger courtrooms. Also, the case has garnered the attention of an internationally known Indigenous filmmaker who is currently preparing a documentary on the case, which will provide further opportunities for public awareness.

The case is complemented by enhanced public education and learning events such as "Have a Heart" day, which was carried out on Valentine's Day in 2012. As the Federal Court of Canada was holding a hearing on the First Nations child welfare case, over 500 First Nations and non-Aboriginal children gathered outside of the Canadian House of Parliament with Valentine's messages for Members of Parliament and the Prime Minister asking that the Canadian Government "have a heart" and ensure equity for First Nations children. Four months later, the children who attended the "Have a Heart" rally helped invite over 5,500 other children to participate in over 50 walks across Canada for First Nations children's equity.

The growing awareness of the case has also reached international human rights bodies at the United Nations who are looking at the case in light of Canada's human rights obligations. The growing international discourse on the case creates another influential avenue of public accountability for the Canadian Government.

While the long-term impacts of mosquito advocacy in addressing the inequities First Nations children face is not known, early results are very encouraging. Research is being initiated to document the mosquito advocacy process, including the specific impacts of child engagement.

The Impacts of Mosquito Advocacy: A Work in Progress

Small groups of people throughout the world have created, and continue to create, social, economic, and political change in the face of strong resistance. Mosquito advocacy is a work in progress. This chapter suggests that proper solution definition, framing, and creative strategies inspired by the mosquito are useful considerations in change, and that we are alive to innovation and adaptation learned from others, and from our own experience. This discussion is not intended to be exhaustive, but rather to highlight key considerations for those tackling systemic problems in change-resistant environments.

The most important message is one that has been shared by many before. One person, or a group of people, *can* change the world. Just ask a mosquito.

References

Aboriginal Affairs and Northern Development Canada 2007. Jordan's Principle. Retrieved August 20, 2012, from the Government of Canada website: http://www.aadnc-aandc.gc.ca/eng/1334329827982/1334329861879.

Aboriginal Affairs and Northern Development Canada 2011. *Re: ATI release packages*. Email document obtained under the Access to Information Act. Access to Information document number 002562.

Auditor General of Canada 2008. *2008 May: Report of the Auditor General of Canada*. Chapter 4—First Nations child and family services program—Indian and Northern Affairs Canada. Retrieved from http://www.oag-bvg.gc.ca/internet/English/parl_oag_200805_e_30714.html.

Auditor General of Canada 2011. *2011 June: Status report of the Auditor General of Canada*. Chapter 4—Programs for First Nations on reserve. Ottawa: Auditor General of Canada.

BBC 2005. *McLibel: Longest case in British history*. Retrieved September 14, 2013, from http://news.bbc.co.uk/2/hi/uk_news/4266741.stm.

Blackstock, C. 2003. First Nations child and family services: Restoring peace and harmony in First Nations communities. In *Child Welfare: Connecting Research Policy and Practice*, K. Kufeldt and B. McKenzie (eds). Waterloo, Canada: Wilfred Laurier University Press, 331–42.

Blackstock, C. 2009. *Public Speaking Tips from a Graduate of the Scared School of Public Speaking*. Retrieved April 9, 2012, from http://fncaringsociety.com/sites/default/files/docs/PublicSpeakingTips_CB.pdf.

Blackstock, C. 2011. The Canadian Human Rights Tribunal on First Nations child welfare: Why if Canada wins, equality and justice lose. *Children and Youth Services Review*, 33(1), 187–94.

Bryce, P.H. 1922. *The Story of a National Crime: An Appeal for Justice to the Indians of Canada*. Ottawa: James, Hope and Sons.

Cuomo, M. 1993. *More Than Words: The Speeches of Mario Cuomo*. New York: St Martin's Press.

Harris-Short, S. 2012. *Aboriginal Child Welfare, Self-government and the Rights of Indigenous Children*. Burlington: Ashgate.

Kidder, R. 2003. *Moral Courage: Taking Action when your Values are Put to the Test*. New York: HarperCollins.

Lakoff, G. 2004. *Don't Think of an Elephant: Know your Values and Frame the Debate*. White River Junction: Chelsea Green Publishing.

Loxley, J., De Riviere, L., Prakash, T., et al. 2005. *Wen:de: The Journey Continues*. Ottawa, Canada: First Nations Child and Family Caring Society of Canada.

Manitoba Pageant. 1962. The origin of mosquitos: A Red River legend. *Manitoba Pageant*, 7(2). Retrieved September 14, 2013, from http://www.mhs.mb.ca/docs/pageant/07/originofmosquitoes.shtml.

McDonald, R. and Ladd, P. 2000. *First Nations Child and Family Services: Joint National Policy Review, Final Report*. Ottawa, Canada: Assembly of First Nations.

McKenzie, B. 2002. *Block Funding Child Maintenance in First Nations Child and Family Services: A Policy Review*. Unpublished paper prepared for Montreal: Kahnawake Shakotiia'takenhas Community Services.

Needleman, J. 2007. *Why Can't We Be Good?* New York: Putnam.

Royal Commission on Aboriginal Peoples. 1996. *Report of the Royal Commission on Aboriginal Peoples*. Ottawa, Canada: Indian and Northern Affairs Canada.

Simpson, C. 2010. *The First Mosquito*. Vancouver, Canada: Heritage.

Sinha, V., Trocmé, N., Fallon, B., et al. 2011. *Kiskisik Awasisak: Remember the Children. Understanding the Overrepresentation of First Nations Children in the Child Welfare System*. Ottawa, Canada: Assembly of First Nations.

Standing Committee on Public Accounts. 2009. *Chapter 4: First Nations Child and Family Services Program – Indian and Northern Affairs Canada of the May 2008 Report of the Auditor General: Report of the Standing Committee on Public Accounts*. Retrieved August 24, 2012, from http://www.fncaringsociety.com/sites/default/files/docs/402_PACP_Rpt07-e.pdf.

Trocmé, N., Knoke, D., and Blackstock, C. 2004. Pathways to the overrepresentation of Aboriginal children in Canada's Child Welfare System. *Social Service Review* (December 2004), 577–600.

Vidal, J. 1997. *McLibel: Burger Culture on Trial*. London: Macmillan.

Conclusion

The descendants of Sky Woman continue to occupy small pieces of Turtle Island after more than five centuries of colonization. While in many ways they struggle, their very survival in the face of adversity is a testament to their resilience. The authors of the preceding chapters speak to both the challenges and the strengths of contemporary Indigenous life.

Contemporary realities are grounded in history and policy, thus an examination of the past is helpful in understanding the present and looking toward the future. To set the stage for understanding contemporary social issues, Weaver and Hart and Rowe provided an overview of US and Canadian social policies related to Indigenous Peoples within these territories.

From the earliest days of the social work profession there have been interactions between social workers and Native Americans. The social work profession is built on a foundation of social justice and has always distinguished itself as a profession focused on assisting vulnerable and marginalized populations. While Indigenous Peoples have typically existed within the peripheral vision or out of sight of most social workers, the social work profession has had a major impact on Native people. Proto-social workers such as John Collier, a former settlement house worker, went on to initiate major policy reforms as the head of the Bureau of Indian Affairs in the 1930s and 1940s. Social workers also played a major role in the child removals that devastated Native families throughout much of the twentieth century. In spite of its value stance, the social work profession has a mixed history with Indigenous Peoples. Tamburro and Tamburro and Prue examine how this profession, so well positioned to challenge oppression, advocate for social justice, and support the empowerment of Indigenous Peoples, has historically interacted with Native Americans.

The chapter authors provide insight into many of the challenges faced by contemporary Native Americans. The discussion of disparities and challenges is balanced with models of best practices for moving toward solutions; both innovative models and those grounded in traditional practices. While not obscuring or denying the social, health, and economic disparities that exist in many Indigenous communities, the authors highlight hope and point toward potential solutions.

A theme running implicitly and at times explicitly throughout the chapters is the need for macro-level change in order to support wellness on an individual level. As Weaver points out, societal tolerance for violence and structurally supported inequities must change before these can consistently be reduced in individual households and communities. Bubar reminds us that we must be attentive to the intersectionality of marginalized identities. For Indigenous Peoples, the needed macro-level changes are intertwined with decolonization. Vestiges of colonization perpetuate power imbalances, oppression, and racism. These must be challenged in order to bring about meaningful change.

While long-standing inequities may seem virtually intractable, this need not be the case. Indeed, within these chapters are roadmaps to change. McEachern illustrates how academia, an institutionalized structure often notoriously resistant to change, can indeed be reformed in ways that are inclusive, accessible, and meaningful for Indigenous Peoples. It is possible to make inroads into institutions that are bastions of structural oppression. Likewise, poverty often seems intractable and serves as the foundation for a variety of social and health issues. Hertel, Wagner, and Black show us culturally relevant ways to enhance Indigenous assets.

Lucero and Bussey challenge us to rethink how we see disparities. They speak of "community challenges rather than individual deficiencies." A shift in mindset helps us to see how change is possible. Day reminds us how change can also be intertwined with tradition. Health and wellness for Indigenous Peoples is often grounded in the traditions and beliefs that have supported our survival and resilience since time immemorial. As Mehl-Madrona and Mainguy state, "culture is medicine that works."

Indigenous social workers, activists, community members, and our non-Indigenous allies continue to work for the restoration of well-being and balance in the lives of Native people. Often these efforts are conducted on a grassroots level beyond the notice of outside observers. Blackstock shows us that even though Indigenous Peoples may be small in number and limited in power, we can use the persistence of a mosquito to be recognized and have our concerns addressed. González and González-Santin remind us how we can draw on the power of a federal law to support the well-being of Native youth and communities. These are mechanisms that can be used to help mend the sacred hoop and restore our communities to wellness.

As Indigenous Peoples, people of the land, we have existed on Turtle Island from the beginning. Seven generations ago, our ancestors planned for us and made decisions to the best of their ability to insure our well-being, balance, and continued existence as distinct, Indigenous Peoples. Now it is our turn to do the same for those who will come after us. This book gives a glimpse into some of those efforts.

Index